BOWERS MANSION

Wilbur S. Shepperson Series in Nevada History

Michael Green, University of Nevada, Las Vegas, *Series Editor*

Nevada is known politically as a swing state and culturally as a swinging state. Politically, its electoral votes have gone to the winning presidential candidate in all but two elections since 1912 (it missed in 1976 and 2016). Its geographic location in the Sun Belt; an ethnically diverse, heavily urban, and fast-growing population; and an economy based on tourism and mining make it a laboratory for understanding the growth and development of postwar America and post-industrial society. Culturally, Nevada has been associated with legal gambling, easy divorce, and social permissiveness. Yet the state also exemplifies conflicts between image and reality: It is also a conservative state yet depends heavily on the federal government. Its gaming regulatory system is the envy of the world but resulted from long and difficult experience with organized crime. And its bright lights often obscure the role of organized religion in Nevada affairs. To some who have emphasized the impact of globalization and celebrated or deplored changing moral standards, Nevada reflects America and the world; to others, it affects them.

This series is named in honor of one of the state's most distinguished historians, author of numerous books on the state's immigrants and cultural development, a longtime educator, and an advocate for history and the humanities. The series welcomes manuscripts on any and all aspects of Nevada that offer insight into how the state has developed and how its development has been connected to the region, the nation, and the world.

Charcoal and Blood: Italian Immigrants in Eureka, Nevada and the Fish Creek Massacre
Silvio Manno

A Great Basin Mosaic: The Cultures of Rural Nevada
James W. Hulse

The Westside Slugger: Joe Neal's Lifelong Fight for Social Justice
John L. Smith

Gambling With Lives: A History of Occupational Health in Greater Las Vegas
Michelle Follette Turk

Monumental Lies: Early Nevada Folklore of the Wild West
Ronald M. James

World War II and Nevada: The Silver State's Contribution to Victory
Charles Weller

Profiles in Judicial Excellence: Territorial and Supreme Court Justices of Nevada
David A. Hardy

The Sagebrush State: Nevada's History, Government, and Politics, Seventh Edition
Michael W. Bowers and David F. Damore

Bowers Mansion: The Legacy of a Comstock Family
Tamera J. Buzick, with Ronald M. James and Michael A. "Bert" Bedeau

Like Friends, Like Foes: Japanese Americans and Nevada through World War II
Andrew B. Russell

Bowers Mansion

The Legacy of a Comstock Family

Tamera J. Buzick

With Ronald M. James and
Michael A. "Bert" Bedeau

University of Nevada Press | *Reno & Las Vegas*

University of Nevada Press | Reno, Nevada 89557 USA
www.unpress.nevada.edu

Manufactured in the United States of America

FIRST PRINTING

Cover design by Louise OFarrell

Cover: Photograph courtesy of Bowers Mansion photo collection, donated by Ed Parsons; map: from Wells Drury, *An Editor on the Comstock Lode* (1948), courtesy of Ronald M. James, private collection

Library of Congress Cataloging-in-Publication Data

Names: Buzick, Tamera J., 1963– author. | James, Ronald M. (Ronald Michael), 1955– author. | Bedeau, Michael, author.

Title: Bowers Mansion: the legacy of a Comstock family / Tamera J. Buzick with Ronald M. James and Michael A. "Bert" Bedeau.

Other titles: Wilbur S. Shepperson series in Nevada history.

Description: Reno: University of Nevada Press, [2026] | Series: Wilbur S. Shepperson series in Nevada history | Includes bibliographical references and index. |

Summary: "*Bowers Mansion*, one of the grandest estates to survive from the great gold and silver mines of the Comstock Lode, has remained a cherished icon since its construction in 1863. This compelling account is a tale of wealth and poverty, of decay and revival, offering up a powerful story from Nevada's history." —Provided by publisher

Identifiers: LCCN 2025029924 | ISBN 9781647792237 (paper) | ISBN 9781647792244 (ebook)

Subjects: LCSH: Bowers, Allison, 1824–1903. | Bowers, L. S. (Lemuel Sanford), 1833–1868. | Bowers Mansion (Nev.) | Comstock Lode Mining District (Nev.) | Washoe County (Nev.)—History. | Nevada—History.

Classification: LCC F847.W3 B89 2026

LC record available at https://lccn.loc.gov/2025029924

The paper used in this book meets the requirements of American National Standard for Information Sciences—Permanence of Paper for Printed Library Materials, ANSI/NISO Z39.48–1992 (R2002).

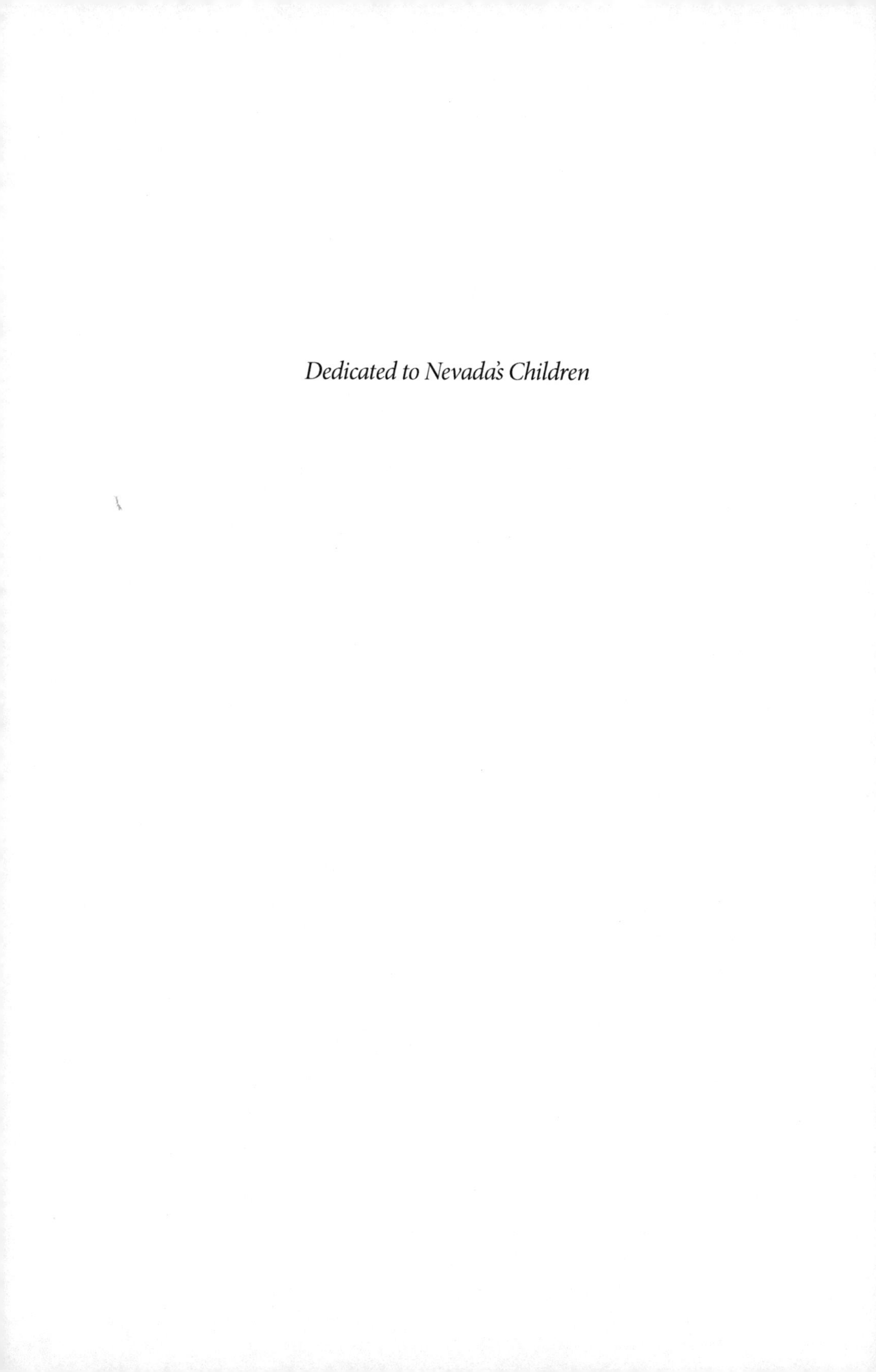

Dedicated to Nevada's Children

Contents

List of Illustrations ix

Foreword by Ronald M. James xi

Preface and Acknowledgments xiii

Chapter 1. Emigrating to America 1

Chapter 2. Carson County 9

Chapter 3. Life in a Mining Camp 21

Chapter 4. The Comstock Lode 33

Chapter 5. Comstock Millionaires 45

Chapter 6. Bowers Mansion Resort 59

Chapter 7. Seeress of Washoe 71

Chapter 8. The Final Years 89

Chapter 9. A Resort for a New Century 103

Chapter 10. Restoration 121

An Architectural History
Michael A. "Bert" Bedeau 135

A National Context
Ronald M. James 141

Notes 151

Selected Bibliography 173

Index 177

About the Authors 191

Illustrations

Fig. 1. Forfar, Scotland 2
Fig. 2. Map of the Mormon Trail 6
Fig. 3. Early sketch of Salt Lake City 8
Fig. 4. Map of Utah and New Mexico Territories 11
Fig. 5. Map of the California Trail 12
Fig. 6. Captain Simpson's expedition in 1859 14
Fig. 7. Washoe Valley in the 1920s 17
Fig. 8. Gold Canyon in the 1940s 22
Fig. 9. Survey of Comstock mines in 1864 27
Fig. 10. Sandy and Eilley Bowers 31
Fig. 11. Bird's-eye view of Gold Hill mines 34
Fig. 12. Lithograph of Virginia City in 1861 37
Fig. 13. Gold Hill in 1865 41
Fig. 14. Eilley and Persia Bowers 49
Fig. 15. Bowers Mansion in the 1860s 51
Fig. 16. Mill in Washoe Valley in 1864 52
Fig. 17. Sandy Bowers 58
Fig. 18. Virginia & Truckee Railroad route 63
Fig. 19. Bowers raffle ticket 67
Fig. 20. The playroom of Persia Bowers 69
Fig. 21. Persia Bowers and Ella Worth 70

Fig. 22. Eilley's sitting room 72
Fig. 23. Bowers Mansion in 1880 75
Fig. 24. Comstock Lode cross section 80
Fig. 25. Crown Point Trestle 83
Fig. 26. Behringer painting of Bowers Mansion 94
Fig. 27. Bowers Mansion kitchen 96
Fig. 28. San Francisco Exposition 1894 97
Fig. 29. Bowers Mansion in 1902 101
Fig. 30. Bowers hunting party in 1912 109
Fig. 31. Henry and Edna Riter in 1943 114
Fig. 32. Reno Women's Civic Club 116
Fig. 33. Bowers bedroom set 117
Fig. 34. Washoe County flag 122
Fig. 35. Bowers Mansion third-story demolition 128
Fig. 36. Bowers Mansion in the 1860s 129
Fig. 37. Bowers Mansion in 1968 130
Fig. 38. Martin Clayton at Bowers Mansion in 1946 132
Fig. 39. John Riddell Design #22, 1861 139

Foreword

THE STORY OF SANDY AND Eilley Bowers has long enthralled Nevadans. The couple was fortunate to have struck a bonanza of gold and silver just as the identity of the Comstock Mining District and the western Great Basin was taking shape. Fate embedded their story into the history of the region.

To this day, the Bowers legacy lingers. For more than one and a half centuries, their estate, including their famed mansion, has served as a place of escape, entertainment, and relaxation. Many have attempted to write about these early millionaires and the grand home they built. Most efforts have been plagued by profound shortcomings. Nevertheless, there clearly was—and is—an important story to be told.

In 2012, I invited representatives of the National Park System to visit Bowers Mansion. Although their observations were tentative, there was a consensus that the site had significance that ranked it among those few resources eligible for the coveted designation of National Historic Landmark. If achieved, this would lift Bowers Mansion above its previous listing in the National Register of Historic Places. One of the things that was lacking was a comprehensive, reputable documentation of the building and of Sandy and Eilley Bowers.

Tamera Buzick provides just that sort of history. She conducted research for decades to address the inadequacies of earlier publications. Her meticulous work and gifted ability to tell this tale have yielded an important benchmark in the writing of Western history. What has emerged will certainly stand for many years as the definitive treatment of Bowers Mansion and the people who made it what it is today.

RONALD M. JAMES

Preface and Acknowledgments

It was the fall of 1982. I had finally made it to the University of Nevada, Reno, and was eager to learn everything there was to know about American history. In a classroom in the Effie Mona Mack building, I listened to professor John Folkes describe the syllabus for US History 101, which included a research project. I was excited by the prospect of writing a paper on any topic I chose, but there were just too many possibilities. He made several suggestions, including a few about Nevada history. When he mentioned Eilley Bowers, memories of trips to Bowers Mansion flooded my mind. I had spent many days there as a child playing on the grounds and in the pool. I remembered taking swimming lessons in the new pool when I was just four years old. It had not been particularly fun because the pool was too cold for a skinny little kid, something that I recalled vividly. There were also my dad's stories from the Great Depression. His uncle Pat would put all the cousins in the back of the truck and drive them to Bowers for a full day of family fun. Within all the memories, I realized I had never been in the mansion. That was about to change.

That weekend I gathered together some of my dorm mates, and we headed to Bowers Mansion for a tour. Our guide was Betty Hood, the mansion curator. She asked us what brought us out there, so I told her about my plans to write a research paper on the Bowers family and their mansion. She was very encouraging and told me to bring it out for her to read when I was finished.

The mansion was amazing. It felt like I was taking a trip back in time. The furniture was from the Victorian era and was arranged in such a way that looked like Eilley could walk in the door and feel at home. Betty shared pieces of the Bowers story. How the twice-divorced immigrant and boardinghouse keeper became a millionaire with her third husband

and built a mansion in Washoe Valley. How she traveled through Europe and adopted a little girl. How she transformed her home into a resort and after a twist of fate, ended up telling fortunes in San Francisco. It was like something out of a movie.

As soon as I got back to the university, I headed to Getchell Library and began reading everything I could find on Eilley. Most Nevada history books mentioned her, but they did not include many details, often giving varied versions of her life. I kept searching until I had enough for a college-worthy research paper. I turned it in and received an A-. The minus was not for my research but for my poor grammar. English 101 was still a work in progress.

With what I felt was a beautifully written paper in hand, I headed back to Bowers to show Betty. She began reading, and every paragraph was filled with comments like "That is wrong" or "That never happened." It was very discouraging. I had earned an A. I obtained all my information from books. How could everything be wrong? I became determined to uncover the real story behind Bowers Mansion. I spent the next four years using Eilley Bowers as the topic of every research paper I was assigned. I soon discovered Getchell Library's Special Collections Department, and I went to Carson City to explore the Nevada State Library, Archives and Public Records. I began looking through primary sources. In the 1870 census manuscript, I discovered that their adopted daughter Persia's place of birth was listed as New York and not on a ship heading toward Liverpool, like many sources had described. I took my findings to Betty to see what she thought. She told me she had never seen that before. This was new information. With that, I was hooked. The Bowers story was still evolving. There was new information to be discovered, and I was determined to find it.

After graduating, I became a math teacher at Reno's Proctor R. Hug High School. There was no longer a need to write research papers, but the story still intrigued me. I spent the next twenty years traveling the world in search of information—including Virginia City, the Bay Area, Salt Lake City, New York, and even Scotland, where I had the good fortune of traveling the countryside with Eilley's great-great-grandnephew. I sipped tea in a Scottish church in Clackmannan, where Eilley was first married to Stephen Hunter. I walked the grounds in Oakland, California, where she lived her final days. I spent many spring and winter breaks in Salt Lake City exploring in the Family History Library. Countless hours were consumed scrolling through microfilm trying to find any new information about her life.

The most exciting discovery came after taking several trips to Salt Lake City trying to solve the mystery of when Eilley came to the United States. After one long week of finding nothing, I was ready to give up and go home, but I decided to try one last time. I was at the library when it opened, hoping to search in *Zetland* ship's log one more time. *Zetland* was the most logical ship for her journey. With weary eyes, I finally saw it. The name Ellison was written below a fold on the original document that ran through her husband's name. As I looked through the fold, it appeared to read Stephen Hunter. That could not be right. I must be seeing what I wanted to see. I made a copy and began running through the library asking anyone I could find what they thought the name was. Time after time, strangers said, "It looks like Stephen Hunter." The library staff connected me with a researcher who was creating an immigration index for the Church of Jesus Christ of Latter-day Saints. He cross-referenced the ship log with a New Orleans customs report. It was, in fact, Stephen and Ellison (Eilley) Hunter. The connection between Scotland and America was complete. Eilley had emigrated to America and crossed the plains in 1849 at the brink of the California Gold Rush.

With that, it was time to put all my research into writing. While studying her life, I inadvertently learned a lot about Nevada history. The stories were intertwined. Eilley's life was constantly changing, as were the times, from the 1850s when pioneers settled western Utah Territory, to the 1859 discovery of the Comstock Lode, and Nevada statehood in 1864. Eilley's biography was more than just her story. It was a narrative of how the region changed and shaped her life. It was a complete biography, but that was not enough. This was just a story of a woman who once lived in the West with the mansion at its center, the grand house that provided the anchor for all that unfolded. Despite all the research, the saga was not ready to be published. I placed it in my closet where it rested for another twenty years. In the meantime, I continued doing research for Betty whenever she needed it. Every so often, I would come across some new information, but the biography remained on the closet shelf.

In October 2008, the county announced that the mansion and pool would be closed for the 2009 season. With this announcement, Betty Hood retired as curator after forty seasons of faithful service. Only one ranger was left to oversee the park. I spent the next two summers driving out there whenever possible to help care for the grounds. In 2011, with my retirement as a public school teacher only a few years away, the county hired me as the new curator. My first task was to update the mansion inventory.

In 1946, a group of women from the Reno Women's Civic Club ran a campaign to save the mansion from being sold and to preserve it as a park for Nevada's children. After it became a Washoe County park, they asked locals to donate Victorian-era furniture and trinkets that would transform Bowers Mansion back to the days of the Comstock Lode. Under the guidance of Superintendent Alice Addenbrooke, they logged every donated item. Their carefully typed inventory cards included the date and family name of every donation. It was an extensive list of local families who cared enough about the mansion to give away their precious antiques. I began to realize that I was not the only person who had a connection to the mansion.

With the inventory updated, the rooms cleaned, and a new concept of tours prepared, the mansion was ready to reopen to the public on Memorial Day weekend 2012. I was still unsure about our new process, so we had a soft opening a week earlier to give a few tours to anyone who happened to be walking through the park. As I stood on the porch awaiting visitors, I thought of Eilley standing on that same porch hoping for customers when she first opened the mansion as a resort in 1870. Neither of us knew what the day would hold. Her guests were coming to the mansion for the first time. They had no expectations or previous experiences. Everything was new and exciting. At the end of May 2012, I was greeting people who came with a different perspective. They were returning to the mansion filled with childhood memories.

My first tour consisted of two people. The next tour had almost a dozen, and each tour throughout the weekend seemed larger. The press had mentioned the opening, and countless inspired locals were arriving early to have a look. They were so excited that the mansion was again open to the public. Many eagerly shared their own stories. A Reno High School alumnus talked of hiding beer in the ditch that runs past the Bowers Cemetery the day before the school picnic only to have it float away before it could be retrieved. A gentleman recalled finding peace beneath the shade trees when his wife lay in a bed at the Carson City Hospital. Two women recalled the 1946 campaign to save the mansion from being sold. One told of playing on her grandmother's porch the day one of the twelve women from the Reno Women's Civic Club came to pick up her grandmother. They were hoping to persuade Henry Riter, the owner of Bowers Mansion, to delay the sale until they could raise $25,000. The other lady proudly told the crowd that she gave a quarter to the campaign. The furniture also conjured memories. One woman pointed to the apron draped over the kitchen rocking chair. Her grandmother had embroidered the ducks and kitten that lined the apron's hem. The harp, a statue, a small table, an old book, and even a stained backsplash embroidered with dark red thread brought pride to family members who had been told their ancestors had donated the items.

I quickly realized that Eilley was only one part of the mansion's alure. This beautiful setting at the foothills of the Sierra Nevada held thousands of stories of its own. While the mansion is valued by all who are interested in Nevada history, this treasure truly belongs to Nevada's children. After ten years of hearing visitors' memories, I realized it was time to take Eilley's biography off the closet shelf and dust it off. With the help of Ron James, we cleaned it up, added missing information, and wrote additional chapters to add the twentieth century to the portrait, including, an architectural history by Michael "Bert" Bedeau. This is not merely the tale of one of Nevada's first pioneer women. It is about a community's loving embrace of a magical place. Comstock historian Grant Smith captured it best in 1943 when he ended his reminiscence of childhood visits to Bowers Mansion by concluding, simply, "It was a trip to Paradise" (Smith 1998, 233–34).

The narrative of Bowers Mansion is not just one story, and it was completed by more than just one person. Hundreds of people have contributed, beginning with Eilley Bowers herself, who first opened her beloved home to children in 1870. Those early days of the resort began childhood tales that would be passed down through the generations. Numerous unknown newspaper reporters wrote about Eilley's life from the days before she struck it rich, through the good years, and even after she had lost everything worldly. Early publishers recording Nevada's history recognized the significance of the Bowers and their mansion by recording their story in Bancroft's *History of Nevada, 1540–1888* and Myron Angel's *History of Nevada, 1881*. Henry and Edna Riter kept the mansion alive during their years as owners. Riter researched the family history and retold it to newspaper reporters and visitors.

The members of the Reno Women's Civic Club had childhood memories of playing at Bowers Mansion and wished it to become a park for Nevada's children, but they also sought the truth behind the Bowers' story. Alice Addenbrooke shared her research with local newspapers and wrote *Mistress of the Mansion*. She then donated all her research to the Nevada Historical Society, making it available for future researchers. Gloria Mapes, Maude Taylor, Ella Gottschalck, and Harriet Spann followed Addenbrook's lead and published an account simply titled *Bowers Mansion*. Myra Sauer Ratay, who grew up next to the mansion, extensively researched the Bowers and Washoe Valley before publishing *Pioneers of the Ponderosa*. She then donated her research to the Special Collections and University Archives Department, University of Nevada, Reno, Libraries. During the 1960s, Thomas Cooke, Leonard Smith, Paul Luksza, and others worked closely with architect Ed Parsons on researching the mansion while restoring and preserving it for future generations. They then donated their research, notes, and photos to that same university repository, also making their findings available to the public.

All this research would never have been compiled into one manuscript if it was not for my own childhood memories of swimming and playing at Bowers Mansion. From my father's stories of going to Bowers Mansion as a child to my own time spent there with my sister and friends as my mother waited patiently for us to become exhausted and ready to return home, each adventure added to my connection to the park. As curator of Bowers Mansion, I had the privilege of hearing hundreds of personal stories of people who have a link to the mansion. Each person who shared a story added to my love of this project.

When I began my research in the 1980s, I was always greeted by friendly and helpful staffers at every institution I visited. Among those who helped me find information to uncover the true story of Bowers Mansion: researchers and librarians at the Nevada Historical Society; the University of Nevada, Reno, Special Collections Department; the Nevada State Library, Archives and Public Records and its Oral History Program; numerous Washoe County departments and offices, including county recorders, the county courthouse, county commissioners, and regional parks and open spaces; the Storey County Courthouse, and the Family History Library in Salt Lake City. Eilley's great-great grandnephew Andrew Crawford shared his research and family stories. Relatives of Alexander

Cowan and Stephen Hunter also shared oral histories about Eilley during her years before Nevada statehood.

In 1976, staff from the Nevada State Parks, which implemented the federal mandate for a historic preservation program at the time, saw the significance of the mansion and worked to preserve it by having it listed in the National Register of Historic Places. In 2012, Ronald M. James, the state's historic preservation officer, helped amend that National Register nomination noting that it is more than just a resort: "The structure is also an excellent expression of the socio-economic implications of an important phase of mining development in the United States that brought the industry, in the form of underground hard rock excavations, east from California into the Intermountain West beginning in the late 1850s" (James and Buzick 2012, 4).

After Bert Bedeau and James spent many hours helping me complete a written version of the compiled research from the previously mentioned sources, Margaret Dalrymple, Curtis Vickers, JoAnne Banducci, Caddie Dufurrena, Ryan Masteller, Paul Szydelko, and others at the University of Nevada Press, recognized the need for a complete narrative of the Bowers' story and their mansion for future generations.

Like the mansion itself, this history would not exist without the help of hundreds of contributors.

BOWERS MANSION

CHAPTER 1

Emigrating to America

THE MORNING OF AUGUST 19, 1901, marked an end of an era as an older woman stood on the Reno Depot platform. Before she boarded the westbound flyer, she turned, and with a husky Scottish brogue that faltered from a saddened, lonely heart, she softly uttered, "Farewell Nevada! Farewell!" A reporter, sent to document the event, wrote, "But fare you well, Mrs. Bowers, and our blessings (if nothing else) be with you."[1]

Fortunes made and fortunes lost. Everything she had worked for and everything she had achieved were gone. Even her husband and children were gone. All that remained was her beloved mansion, which she had constructed with her husband during Nevada's heyday. Given how difficult it had been to make a success of the huge structure when she converted it into a resort, the idea that this would be her enduring legacy would have seemed improbable.

It had been fifty-two years since the same woman, then a young Scottish lass, had stood on the docks in Liverpool, England, ready to board a sailing ship bound for America and the adventure of a lifetime. Alison (Eilley) Oram's life began on September 6, 1826.[2] The Orams lived in Forfar, in the Scottish central lowlands, fewer than thirty miles from the North Sea, amid low green hills covered with patches of trees and vast fertile fields ideal for agriculture. Old castles and other stone structures together with glacial lochs still add to the region's beauty and romanticism. Forfar was an administrative center at the easternmost end of Loch Forfar in the beautiful Strathmore Valley.

Eilley grew up in a troubled world. After the final defeat of Napoleon in 1815, Britain faced disruptive change. Fluctuations in the cost of food in particular affected many. Like the rest of Britain as well as North

FIG. 1. The town of Forfar, Scotland, is depicted here in an engraving by Robert Havell from the 1820s (after an image by J. H. Clark). This was home to Eilley Oram and her family during the first years of her life. She grew up in the lush central lowlands not far from the North Sea. Courtesy Angus Council Collections cared for by ANGUSAlive Museums, Galleries and Archives.

America, Scotland was at the center of the industrial revolution, transforming an agricultural society into one dominated by cities.

We know little of Eilley's childhood except that her only brother, John, was born in 1821 in Dunfermline, not far from Edinburgh. It appears that their father's employment demanded frequent moves. Sometime between the birth of John and Eilley, the family established a new home on the eastern coast of Scotland at Forfar. Then at some point the Orams relocated again, this time eighty miles southwest of Forfar to Clackmannan in the interior of Scotland.[3]

It was here where Eilley Oram met her future husband, Stephen Hunter, a Clackmannan native. This eldest son of a coal miner was born in 1822.[4] It is not clear whether Stephen followed his father into the coal mines. If he did, it would have made for a difficult life, given the danger and low pay.

No matter his occupation, nineteen-year-old Stephen sought to share his life on April 11, 1842, when he married Eilley, four years his junior.

Eilley's first marriage took place in a beautiful twelfth-century stone building of the Church of Scotland, but that did not promise a commitment to the religious conventions of previous generations.[5] Changing times included new influences and choices. Among these, the Presbyterians were facing divisions between moderates and emerging evangelicals.

In addition, American missionaries from the Church of Jesus Christ of Latter-day Saints were traveling throughout Europe, seeking converts, a call that included free passage to America. Stephen found himself attracted to the message of these "Mormons," as they had become known. On April 10, 1848, Stephen left the divided Church of Scotland and became a baptized member of this new faith.[6] For unknown reasons, Eilley, six years into her marriage, did not convert even though she agreed to travel with him across the Atlantic.

Part of the allure of the Mormon religion was the promise of American prosperity. Brigham Young, the church president in Salt Lake City, Utah Territory, offered a better life in his new world. He had built a grand city in the isolated desert of the Great Salt Lake Valley for his followers. Any man could own a farm and live off the land. Education was available to all, and there was solidarity behind a single religion. The Great Salt Lake sounded like paradise to a Scotsman confronted with constant change and conflict and an oppressive economy. With this new American church's promise, Stephen agreed to leave the only home he had ever known.

While many endured hardship and great cost to cross the Atlantic, the church chartered ships from European countries to help bring a significant number of new members to their new home. Although Eilley had not converted, she traveled with her husband and the primarily Mormon company at the beginning of 1849. Like most immigrants, they said goodbye to friends and family assuming they would not return to their homeland.

The Hunters' journey began in Liverpool, where they joined 355 other church members, and Elder Orson Spencer, president of the British mission.[7] The Mormons set sail on January 29, 1849, aboard *Zetland*.[8] The Hunters had left behind the beautiful green country of Scotland for the great desert of the Salt Lake Valley. Once on board, Spencer broke the company into wards and organized the immigrants. They came from various parts of Britain in small parties, each foreign to the others. Yet they had not been a couple of hours on board when they established their own police, made their own regulations, and set their own watches at all the hatchways. Charles Dickens once wrote of a Mormon ship, "Before nine o'clock, the ship was as orderly and as quiet as a man-of-war."[9]

The Spencer Company generally experienced good weather and pleasant sailing for the next two months.[10] A typical day began with a bugle call at about six o'clock, notifying the passengers that it was time to rise and dress behind a small curtain in front of their berth. A little after seven, the bugle again sounded so that the wards could begin their morning prayer meetings. Afterward, they made their beds, arranged their belongings, and prepared breakfast.[11] Included in each passenger's fare were flour, oatmeal, rice, potatoes, tea, sugar, molasses, and one gill of vinegar, to be poured into stale drinking water.[12] Like everyone, the Hunters were responsible for cooking their food with supplies they had brought aboard.

Small facilities made preparing a meal a tedious ordeal.[13] After breakfast, Eilley spent the remainder of the day at her leisure. According to accounts of the journey, passengers walked the deck, visited with one another, and sang and danced. Meals broke the monotony of long, uneventful days. Supper consisted solely of a biscuit accompanied by rice one day, followed by oatmeal the next, and potatoes the day after that. Typically, passengers gathered for evening prayer and then retired by nine or ten o'clock.[14] Stephen and Eilley then went below deck, where they shared a wooden berth. These six-by-three-foot bunk-bed type compartments lined both sides of the ship with an additional row filling the center aisle making for snug sleeping accommodations. Each Sunday, Spencer preached to the company, and the gentiles (as Mormons called those not of their faith) who wrote of the journey recorded that there was some scoffing among the unbelievers.

On April 1, *Zetland* navigated through the Gulf of Mexico, where Eilley caught her first glimpse of America. A steamboat pilot came on board and instructed the crew on towing a ship up the Mississippi River to the Port of New Orleans.[15] As they began their journey up the magnificent river, Eilley saw rich fertile fields, splendid mansions among the rich, beautiful forests, and various trees, shrubs, and flowers lining the Louisiana riverbank. Nothing could be more beautiful after sixty-three days at sea. Late in the day, on April 2, 1849, the Hunters landed in New Orleans.[16]

The captain bid farewell to the Spencer Company, no doubt grateful for a voyage reported to have been pleasant for all.[17] Eilley and Stephen gathered their belongings from *Zetland* and loaded them aboard the

Mississippi River steamboat *Iowa*.[18] They remained in New Orleans only a few days before they began their Mississippi journey to St. Louis, Missouri.

By then the California Gold Rush of 1849 had begun, and thousands of Americans were leaving their homes in the East to follow dreams of instant wealth, and a better life. The Mormons were not the only group traveling the river before heading west. Many gentiles were also bound for California, and they joined the Spencer Company, making gold a lively conversation topic.[19]

After changing steamboats in St. Louis, they began their final water-bound journey aboard *Eliza Stuart* as she took them up the Missouri River. As they traveled upstream, signs of settlements on the shore became less frequent. On May 4, the Hunters arrived at Council Bluffs, Iowa. Here Eilley and Stephen took up residence with a Mormon family until the end of the month.[20] They rested and prepared for their cross-country journey by buying necessities such as a wagon, cooking utensils, firearms, livestock, and food.

The Hunters then joined a group consisting of one hundred wagons, including the Spencer Company from Britain, some American Mormons from Illinois and other states, and a few California gold seekers. The forty-niners agreed to follow the Mormon rules and regulations as a condition of traveling with the group.[21] Everyone was eager to begin this final part of the journey. Because wagons were used primarily for hauling goods, Eilley had more than one thousand miles to walk before reaching the valley of the Great Salt Lake.

The Spencer Company followed the north bank of the Platte River, wishing to stay apart from the thousands of California-bound forty-niners who traveled along the south side of the river. Nevertheless, their paths crossed in many places along the trail, allowing Eilley to hear rumors of California and its hidden treasures. Faced with dangerous river crossings, storms, heat exhaustion while crossing the Great Plains, and then with frigid mountain nights in the Rockies, the Mormons worked together and rested on the Sabbath whenever possible. On several occasions they had to bury family members who had succumbed to various maladies, including cholera. After crossing the Continental Divide on September 3, the Spencer Company met a few Salt Lake Mormons heading east with supplies to help another group, which had started west much later in the season. The encounter was auspicious. Eilley and her husband's destination was near.[22]

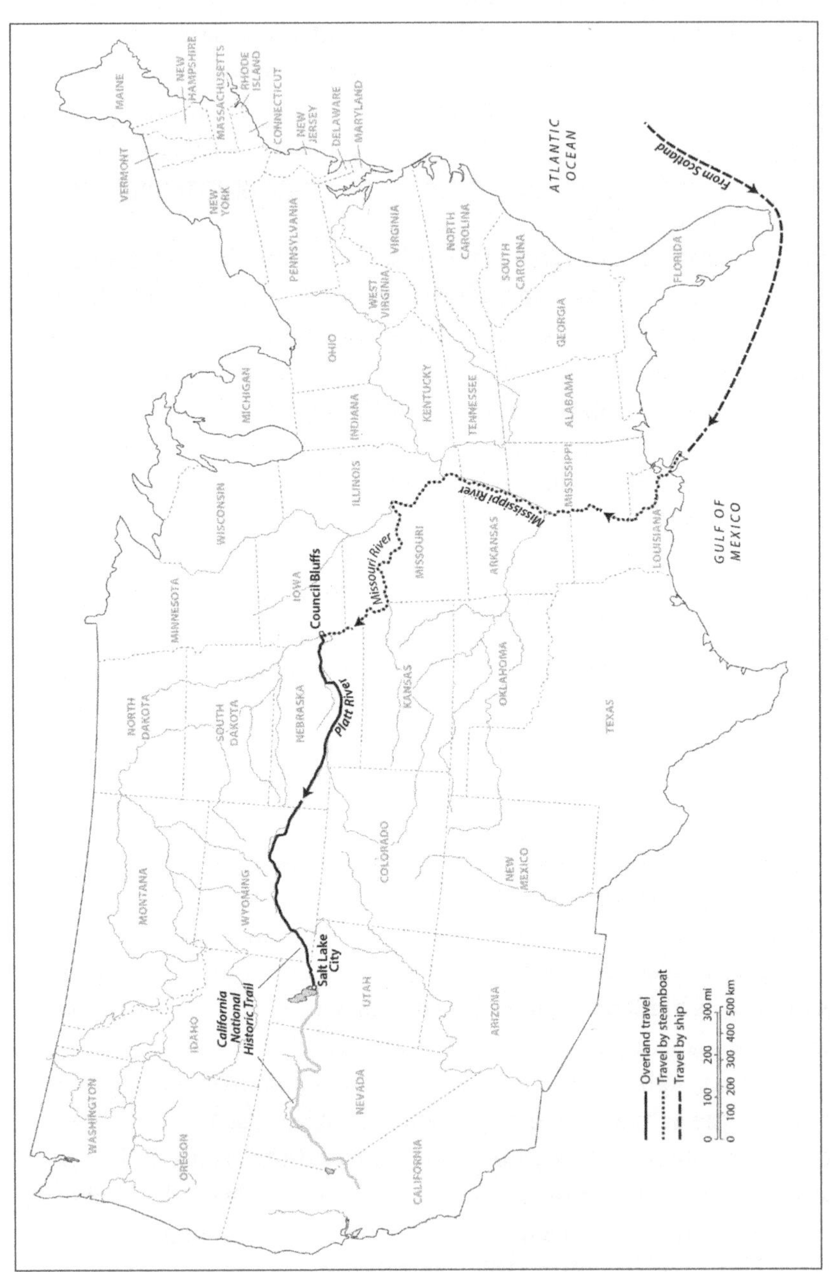

FIG. 2. Immigrants heading west in 1849 consisted primarily of two main groups. A diary preserved in Salt Lake City describes California gold seekers traveling along the south bank of the Platte River while Eilley, who was with the Church of Jesus Christ of Latter-day Saints, stayed primarily on the north bank. Cartography by Bill Nelson.

After four months of hard travel, the Spencer Company reached the summit overlooking the Great Salt Lake Valley.[23] From this ridge, Eilley saw the expanse of the place she would call home. Their group began its steep descent from Emigration Canyon.[24] On September 23, 1849, almost nine months after leaving Scotland, Eilley and Stephen arrived in Salt Lake City.

As they drove down Emigration Street, Eilley gazed upon a new community filled with wide avenues, buildings, stores, adobe houses, and flourishing gardens, all surrounded by land cultivated with crops and fruit-bearing trees.[25] She had not left civilization. Instead, she had found a new, burgeoning one. The Salt Lake Mormons welcomed the arrivals. Coming in so late in the season, the newcomers could not begin farms of their own, so settled Mormons invited them to stay in their homes. Each member of the company immediately began to work for themselves, the community, and the church's survival. In return, the faithful helped them start their new lives.

By the time the Hunters reached Utah, it appears that there had been a strain on their marriage. After eight years of being together followed by a long, arduous immigration, Eilley and Stephen separated in 1850.[26] Early Utah divorces were rarely documented with a new government and still-forming legal system. The act of moving out of a spouse's house could be sufficient to achieve a legal divorce.[27] Reasons for and the exact time of their separation were not recorded.

Stephen chose to remain in Salt Lake City and continued living as a faithful member of the Mormon church. About two years after Stephen and Eilley's separation, Stephen married Martha Clark, an English woman with whom he had five children. Only two of them, both girls, lived past childhood. At twenty-six, Martha gave birth to her fifth child on October 23, 1860. Seven days later, she died of complications from childbirth, her newborn son following her to the grave three days later. Stephen then married Fanny Teague on December 29, 1860.[28] Fanny had no children and helped raise Mary Ellen and Martha, Stephen's surviving daughters.

Stephen lived a long life as a dedicated member of Salt Lake City's Seventh Ward. According to family history, he spent his later years referring to Eilley as "the sweetheart of his youth." His daughters kept in touch with Eilley through letters up until the time of her death. Stephen Hunter

FIG. 3. As Stephen and Eilley Hunter neared the end of their nine-month journey that began in Scotland in January 1849, they saw Salt Lake City in the distance. This sketch by Frederick Hawkins Piercy from his book, *Route from Liverpool to Great Salt Lake Valley*, captures what they would have seen. Courtesy Brigham Young University; original held in L. Tom Perry Special Collections, Harold B. Lee Library, Brigham Young University.

died from old age and cystitis at the age of seventy-eight on August 20, 1900. His obituary described him as a faithful and giving man.[29]

Eilley, like Stephen, forged a new path for herself. Although she continued living in Salt Lake City for the next two years, little can be deduced about what she did during that time. What immediately followed shaped the rest of her life.

CHAPTER 2

Carson County

BY LATE 1853, EILLEY APPEARS in documents as being with a twenty-two-year-old Scottish native named Alexander Cowan. Born in December 1830, in Campsie near Stirling, Scotland, he was the youngest of John and Agnes Cowan's ten children. In the 1840s, his entire family joined the Church of Jesus Christ of Latter-day Saints and immigrated to America in separate companies in 1848 and 1849.[1]

Alexander and his older brother William were among those who sailed on the first of those voyages. The two boys wintered in St. Louis and saved money to help their parents cross the plains the following spring when they joined a Mormon party heading west. Their mother, Agnes, died en route to Utah, and was buried along the trail. Alexander and his family arrived in Salt Lake City in late summer 1849.[2] By 1850, the Cowans lived in several neighboring houses in the community's Fifth Ward. His sister Margaret and her family lived next door, while his father and two brothers had houses nearby.[3]

In the four years following Alexander's arrival, he helped develop a drainage system in the lowlands at the south end of the valley. He also brought granite from nearby mountains to construct the future temple and helped in the public works system. In 1852, Alexander started his own business when he and a partner contracted to make adobe bricks for the walls of the temple grounds. In July 1853, he volunteered to serve in a war against the Indigenous Shoshone people.[4]

On August 16, 1853, despite his father's objections, Alexander Cowan married Eilley Hunter in a civil ceremony.[5] Three months after their wedding, Alexander left Eilley at home while he followed the church's call. He went on a mission to Willow Creek, about twelve miles southwest of Fort Bridger, in what was eastern Utah Territory but is now within Wyoming.

With the increasing number of those arriving in Utah or going on to California, Brigham Young established many trading posts including Willow Creek along the Emigrant Trail. Because of his system of trading posts and forts along the route, companies traveled in safety without a shortage of supplies. These posts also allowed Mormons to control trade by selling goods to gentile travelers.

Elder Orson Hyde organized the mission to Willow Creek, which consisted of fifty-three young men, thirty-six wagons, fifty head of beef cattle, and almost as many cows kept for their milk. They also brought tools, clothing, blankets, leather, and nails. Alexander accompanied a second company, leaving for the cold mountainous valley on November 16, 1853.[6] While he stayed at Willow Creek, another small Mormon settlement, this one on the eastern slope of the Sierra, faced political problems. These concerns would soon take Alexander hundreds of miles to the far western border of the territory and cause irreconcilable differences in his marriage with Eilley.

Two years after the Mexican War (1846–1848), President Millard Fillmore had appointed Brigham Young, president of the Church of Jesus Christ of Latter-day Saints, to be governor of the new US territory known as Utah. In 1850, the territory included most of the land that would become the future states of Utah and Nevada. The westernmost region of Utah Territory included Carson Valley, flanked on the west by the Sierra, five hundred miles from Salt Lake City. Although the Washoe Indians had lived there for millennia, there were now a few Californians prospecting in Gold Canyon about thirty miles to the northeast of the Sierra foothills. This quiet region became a center of trade over the next few years. As California-bound immigrants reached the eastern base of the Sierra Nevada range, near the present town of Genoa, Nevada, they rested along the streams fed by runoff from the melting snow and relaxed in hot pools created by the abundance of geothermal springs. The land was fertile, the grass plentiful, and the temperatures moderate.

In April 1850, a small party of Mormon emigrants, under the leadership of Hampton Beatie, decided to build a trading post. The following year, another Salt Lake Mormon, John Reese, moved to Carson Valley to set up a more prominent settlement he named Mormon Station at the base of the Sierra. By 1853, this young community had grown into a significant town. Residents constructed frame houses, a blacksmith shop, and a grist and sawmill. They also had a post office. Farming and stock-raising had

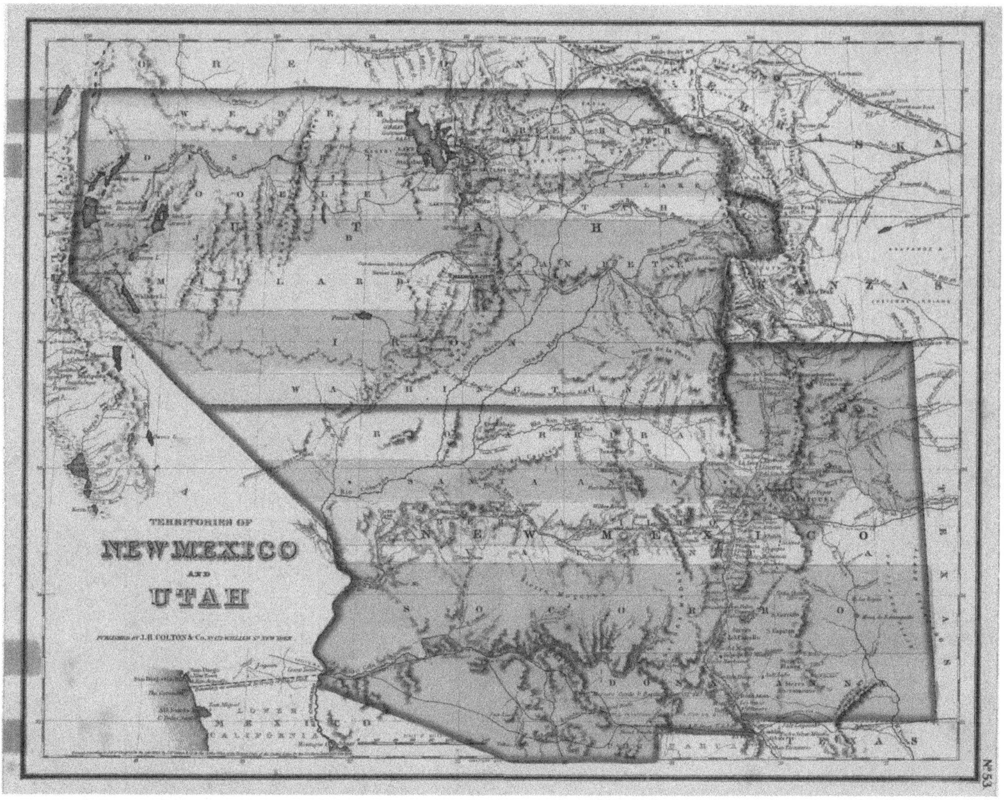

FIG. 4. This 1855 map of New Mexico and Utah depicts the enormity of Utah at the time when Eilley moved to the eastern foothills of the Sierra Nevada with her second husband, Alexander Cowan. Utah Territory and the Church of Jesus Christ of Latter-day Saints had directed him to help establish a government in the remote western edge of the Great Basin. Courtesy Ansari Map Collection, University of Nevada, Reno.

become their primary trade. A steady stream of immigration was good for business, and they had everything a frontier community needed to establish law and government.[7]

Soon, California traders, farmers, ranchers, and miners became neighbors of the Mormons, and several hundred settlers were living in Reese's valley and other parts of Western Utah Territory. With the rapid expansion of the region's population, managing a far-flung territory with an increasingly diverse population presented problems that Young could no longer ignore. Many resident gentiles disagreed with Mormon ideas

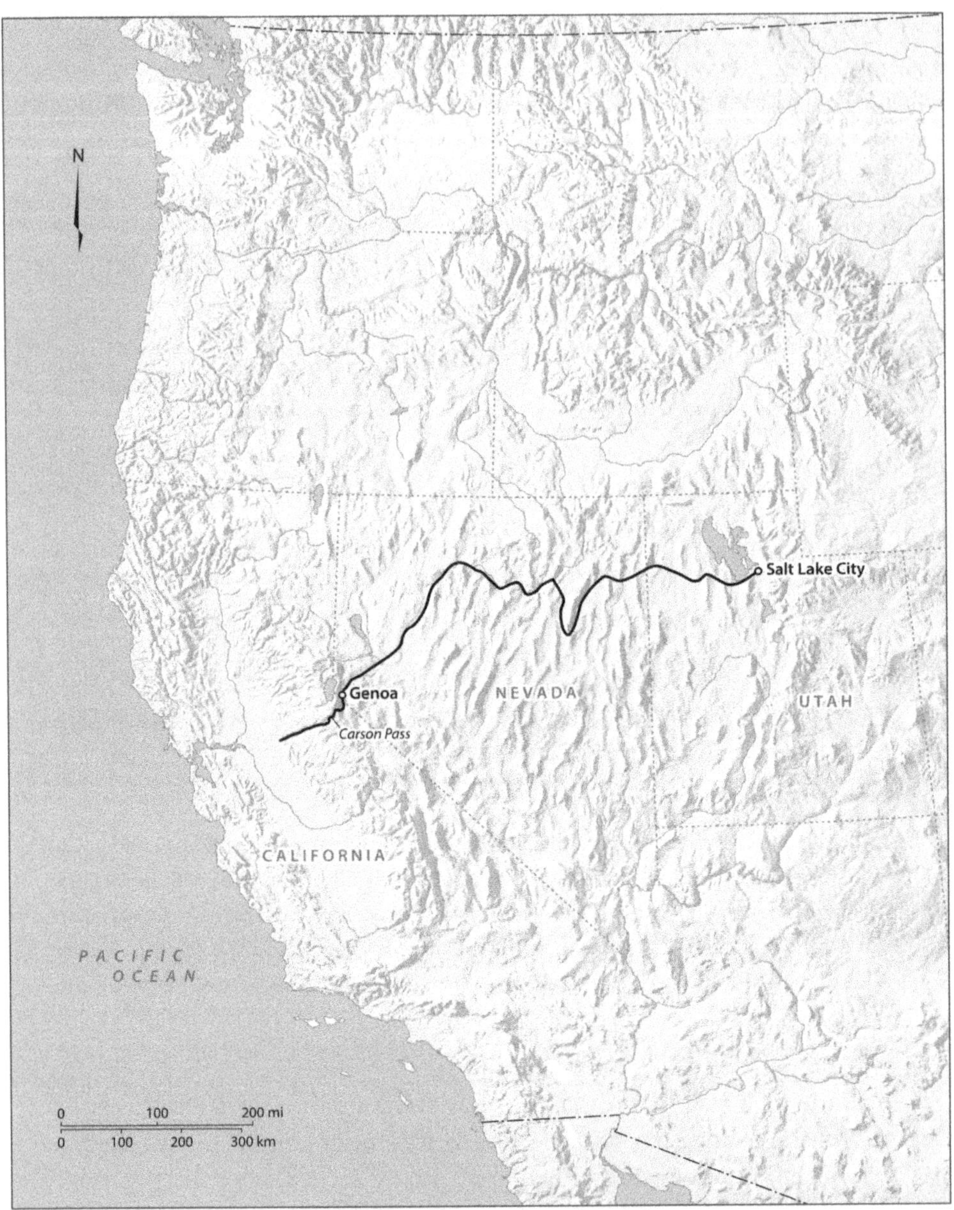

FIG. 5. The California Trail across the Great Basin presented many challenges for those who endured an inhospitable landscape. The Mormon companies traveling between Salt Lake City and Genoa used the Carson Pass route that opened in 1848. Cartography by Bill Nelson.

and leadership. They were concerned about land claims, timber, water rights, toll roads, bridges, and other necessary issues of territorial law. As a result, the Utah territorial government established Carson County as the Third United States Judicial District of Utah Territory on January 17, 1854. Carson County was now a legal entity that could elect its officials. Although this framework for local government was established, Young did nothing to organize it, so problems persisted.

In 1855, Brigham Young finally decided to exert his authority over western Utah by sending officials to live and work in Carson County. He appointed George P. Stiles as US justice, J. L. Haywood as US marshal, and Hyde as probate judge and as leader of an expedition from Salt Lake City. On May 16, 1855, Hyde and thirty-eight other men began their journey to Carson Valley.[8]

Over the next few months, Young sent other Mormons to western Utah to help in the organization of the county. Once again, the church and Hyde called on Alexander Cowan. This time, Eilley went with him, accompanied by her husband's twelve-year-old nephew, whom they had agreed to raise after the death of his mother. Young Robert Henderson was born in England in 1843 to Alexander's older sister, Margaret. Robert and his four brothers and sisters lost their father before emigrating to America. Margaret brought her children to Utah in 1851, in time, marrying William Tattersall. Sometime after their arrival, Margaret died, leaving her five orphaned children in need of homes, and Alexander and Eilley agreed to care for Robert.[9]

After only five years of living in the Mormon capital, Eilley was once again heading west by wagon train. The five-hundred-mile, six-week journey from Salt Lake to the base of the Sierra was the most challenging part of the Overland Trail. Nevertheless, the Cowans were rested and well prepared for their mission, unlike the exhausted fortune seekers who traveled this same route from farther east to California. Once the Cowans were ready, they met other Mormon missionaries at Bear River, outside Salt Lake City.

The travelers faced a succession of hills and playa flats on a trail winding past snow-capped mountains, and across an alkali desert.[10] The route along the Humboldt River at least provided water, but then they faced the arid expanse of the forty-mile desert, a remnant of a dried, prehistoric lake. After almost a month, they reached the cool and shady waters of the Carson River.

FIG. 6. This 1859 sketch showing Captain James Simpson's expedition arriving at the eastern base of the Sierra Nevada captures what Eilley likely saw when she first arrived at Mormon Station (now known as Genoa, Nevada) in the summer of 1855. Courtesy Nevada Historical Society.

As they traveled along the Carson River, they encountered placer miners, many from California, who were beginning to transform the western Great Basin into a place where Mormon dominion would become increasingly unwelcomed. Without knowing it, Eilley was meeting future friends. Local miners had established a prosperous settlement at the junction of Gold Canyon and the Carson River. Spafford Hall, from Indiana, kept a station and trading post, which employed James McMarlin and his wife for $60 a month. Across from the station, there was a blacksmith shop built from used wagon beds, and up the canyon, Walter Cosser had a mercantile line at a mining camp known as Johntown, which apparently was prone to move with the seasons.[11] For the most part, the area had attracted itinerant miners, so only a handful of women lived there. Besides Mrs. McMarlin, there was Mrs. Laura Ellis, a nurse who would eventually become close friends with Eilley.[12]

About twenty miles farther along the river, the company entered the lush western expanse of the Carson Valley, which was to become their new home. Some of the Mormons who made the journey later described it as a successful trip filled with good spirits, no profanity, only a few livestock deaths, and answered prayers. The travelers also documented times when local tribes attempted to take their cattle.[13]

On September 20, 1855, Hyde held the first territorial election in Carson County. With one exception, members of the Mormon church won all offices. Mormon Station became the county seat, and its name officially changed to Genoa. With the settlement established and the government formed, Hyde was systematizing the political fight to keep the bountiful location under Utah jurisdiction.[14]

Hyde continually sent letters requesting instructions from Young, who rarely replied. Without help from Salt Lake City, life was difficult for the Cowans and the other Mormon settlers. Church records describe high prices and a grasshopper plague, which destroyed most of the town's crops and placed the community in jeopardy as winter approached. Since there were few other ways to make money, mining seemed an easy source of income. Young discouraged such activity, but some Mormons felt a need to become prospectors to survive, and so a few moved east to Gold Canyon.[15]

Alexander was faithful to his church and found other ways to earn money. On October 10, 1855, he signed an agreement with John Reese to construct an irrigation ditch. Alexander agreed to dig an eighteen-inch deep and thirty-six-inch-wide ditch nearly two miles out from Reese's mill. For his efforts, Reese paid him seventy-five cents a rod (16.5 feet).[16]

As time passed, Hyde was pleased with his settlement, but he had become troubled with the actions of some of the Mormon settlers. The most prosperous store, owned by Reese, seemed to cater only to the needs of the miners, drinkers, and gamblers.[17] The questionable conduct of the gentiles influenced the church members more than the righteous actions of the church. On October 29, 1855, Hyde wrote to Young, "There are many Mormons here, but I fear no Saints."[18]

With no word from Young for more than five months, Hyde decided to send most of the missionaries back to Salt Lake with the intent of returning in the spring with their families and additional supplies, including oxen, cattle, tools, utensils, and seeds.[19] Alexander, Eilley, and Robert were among the few who chose to remain in Genoa that winter.

In January 1856, gentiles petitioned Congress to annex Carson County into California. Hyde was in the midst of the contentiousness. He knew the county was worth saving because it could financially help the government of Utah through the immigration trade. He believed that if the Mormons made up most of the population, he could suppress dissent and keep the region within Utah Territory.[20] Gentiles were an increasing presence, so Hyde searched for additional locations where the faithful could settle.

In March 1856, Hyde began surveying valleys to the north, hoping to create a new settlement entirely of church members.[21] Being in a position to decide how resources would be dispensed, he chose the best lands for himself and the faithful. He considered Steamboat Springs and Carson, Eagle, Truckee, Jacks, and Washoe Valleys to offer the greatest opportunities of the surrounding areas. Because of its fertile land, many streams, and a large lake, Washoe Valley was the most promising of these.

On April 2, California suggested moving its boundary line three longitudinal degrees to the east. Hyde feared that he must move quickly or lose the land. California's ploy would not likely have been successful, but Hyde and the faithful may have felt some urgency as they worked to retain Washoe Valley and the rest of the area as a place for the Latter-day Saints and as a part of Utah.[22]

One year after relocating to Mormon Station, the Cowans helped secure land for the faithful by relocating to Washoe Valley. On May 19, 1856, Alexander paid $100 for 320 acres in the northwestern part of that rich farmland known as ranch #2, stretching from the base of the hills, eastward across the valley toward Washoe Lake.[23] The land included a corral and a three-room log dwelling.[24] Both hot and cold springs provided freshwater, and massive pine trees offered plenty of afternoon shade. The Cowans moved into their new home and waited for the rush of Mormons already en route to the valley.

Six weeks later, on June 24, the first Mormon company arrived in Washoe Valley.[25] Here they found the beginnings of Hyde's grist and sawmill, the Cowan Ranch, a few homes, and acres of unoccupied, fertile land, ignoring, of course, the rights of the Indigenous Washoe Indians. Young had sent his missionaries to build a settlement out of nothing. After initial uncertainty, they realized the region's value. The valley had rich soil, heavy forests, brushwood, abundant grass, brilliant flowers, and sweet water. They surveyed, developed, farmed, and even mined the land.[26]

FIG. 7. This 1920s image depicts the west side of Washoe Valley. When the Mormons settled here, they built houses along the base of the Carson Range, allowing their farms to stretch eastward toward Washoe Lake. Eilley and Alexander lived on a farm at the north end of the new community of Franktown. Courtesy Nevada Historical Society.

Eilley watched as almost twenty-five families settled in Washoe Valley. Most of them took land south of her ranch, where most built log houses and barns near the mountains to the west, allowing them to plant their crops on the flatlands reaching toward the lake. Richard Bentley had a prime lot at the mouth of a creek, where he built a log house. Hyde's house was opposite the stream, William Jennings had the adjoining lot, and Christopher Layton had a farm on the east side of the valley. The Cowans' ranch ended up being just north of a new town that was taking shape.[27]

On August 14, 1856, Elizabeth Bentley gave birth to the first child born in the settlement. His parents named the baby, Frank Richard Bentley, inspiring the name of their emerging community, which they called Franktown.[28] Residents in the valley were pleased with their accomplishments and wished to stay. That fall, they sent a protest to Washington, DC, expressing their opposition to becoming part of California, angering many gentiles who still resisted the long arm of Salt Lake City over the region.[29]

Since Hyde's mission was temporary, Young permitted him to resign as probate judge. Hyde felt it was his duty to organize a church presence before leaving. On September 28, a group of Mormons met in Carson Valley with the intention of organizing the community according to church standards. By October 4, Hyde and his company prepared to leave the county even though his mill was not yet complete and the county's fate was still unsettled. He leased his mill to Jacob Rose for one team of mules, a worn-out harness, two yoke of oxen, and an old wagon. In November, Orson Hyde left Carson County, never to return.[30]

At the same time, Brigham Young was becoming increasingly concerned about a possible invasion of troops representing the national authority in Washington, DC. Widespread disapproval of the religion's practice of polygamy and what many saw as a theocratic government combined with Mormon militancy inspired suspicions in the East and calls to bring the perceived renegade territory back into line. In response to this perceived threat, Young began to consider summoning his far-flung followers for the defense of Salt Lake City.[31]

Despite the possibility of such an order from the Utah territorial government, many Franktown Mormons did not wish to leave. Instead, they continued to build their community. This included the construction of the Franktown School, which educated twenty-five children.[32] On February 14, 1857, the *Western Standard* newspaper quoted a letter from Richard Bentley stating, "We have built up quite a little town in Washau [*sic*]. This valley seems more like home in the Salt Lake Valleys than any other in this part of the country does. The brethren generally are alive to their duty. They manifest a spirit and disposition to live their religion and carry out the plans and designs of the First Presidency of the Church."[33]

As the town grew, both Mormon and gentile residents recognized the need for new roads. On February 22, Cowan and many other prominent Franktown residents signed a petition for the venture. Over the next few months, the community came together to work on their road project.[34] The inadvertent effect of these efforts was to make the eastern slope of the Sierra more accessible to gentile fortune seekers from California.

By May 1857, Chester Loveland, the new mission leader of western Utah, had not heard from Young regarding a summons back to Salt Lake City. The settlers remained in the dark about the church's wishes. Rather than await an answer, several Mormons had already chosen to return to families they left behind.[35] The Cowans and many others, continued to work and plan as if they were to stay for the following winter. One resident recorded in his diary, "We are also thinking of soon breaking up and leaving this country, but we have no word to leave yet, so we go ahead with all our might to fix our farm in good order and have everything in good rig for we are living on the best farm I ever owned in my life. . . ."[36]

On June 3, Young, in his role as president of the Mormon church, finally sent word about a possible recall of church members, but because of the distance between Salt Lake City and Washoe Valley, the residents did not receive their order until the end of July. Young assured those who had not already returned that they could stay: "You were not and are not recalled from your mission . . . (Those) who would rather not stay, let them return to this place."[37] Alexander's duty was to remain and develop his land.

By August 1857, Franktown residents heard false rumors from California newspapers that Utah was under military rule.[38] With more than five hundred miles between Washoe Valley and Salt Lake City, the brethren were unaware of what was really happening to their church and government.

In Salt Lake City, Young's problems were increasing. The US government openly challenged Utah's acceptance of polygamy, its organized militia, and its blending of church and state. President James Buchanan appointed a new territorial governor and other officials to replace Young and his followers. By midsummer 1857, US Army soldiers marched west toward Salt Lake City, escorting the new territorial appointees. Young, seeing this as a threat to religious freedom and his territory, began to arm the Mormons and prepared to fight.[39]

On September 5, the residents of Franktown received news: Riders were arriving at all Mormon missions with a message from Young, who finally made the call for all the faithful to return. They were to dispose of their property, secure ammunition, and return to Salt Lake as quickly as possible. Young's message told them to "make no noise about your business, but let all things be done quietly and in order."[40]

The message did not quell the chaos, and less than two years after arriving in Carson County, a life-altering decision confronted the Cowan family. Alexander, now a high priest, chose to remain faithful to his church and planned to return with most of the Mormons. Eilley and Robert, now a young adolescent, did not follow the order and chose, instead, to stay behind. After only four years of marriage, the Cowans separated on September 26, 1857. He would eventually return to western Utah and Eilley, but their lives had changed forever.

In a rush, some Mormons were able to sell their land while others just accepted their losses. A few, like Alexander, chose to leave the matter until financial matters could be addressed in an orderly manner. Besides, Eilley and Robert still needed a place to live. Those who left their land lost all they had, as gentiles quickly took control. After all the confusion and hasty decisions, nothing became of the expected Utah War. In anticipation of federal troops, Mormon militias had destroyed many resources along the trail leading to Salt Lake City and barricaded the passes to the Salt Lake Valley. Since the federal troops arrived too late in the season to launch a campaign into the Mormon capital before snows fell, they camped in what is today western Wyoming. New officials quietly took over Utah government offices the following spring, and Brigham Young stepped down as governor. Federal troops finally arrived, but they camped apart from most of the settlement, reducing potential conflict. Although Young remained the church's president until his death in 1877, he never held public office again.[41]

Five years after the Mormons' hasty retreat, Orson Hyde cursed Washoe Valley and its residents when Jacob Rose and his partner, Richard Sides, refused to pay him $20,000 for his grist and sawmill. Hyde claimed he had only leased the mill and therefore remained the rightful owner. Hyde declared that Washoe Valley would be ". . . visited of the Lord of Hosts and with thunder and with earthquake and with flood, with pestilence, and famine until your names are not known amongst men, for you have rejected the authority of God."[42] Hyde's curse was the final action of the Mormon church's earliest chapter in Carson County, Utah Territory.

With the Mormons gone, Eilley and Robert began their new lives. Alone and unemployed, they would soon find new ways to survive in this changing Western society.

CHAPTER 3

Life in a Mining Camp

SOMETIME AFTER ALEXANDER COWAN RETURNED to Utah, Eilley and Robert left a depopulated Franktown in Washoe Valley and headed for Johntown, a mining community to the east about seven miles above the base of Gold Canyon. By the winter of 1857, Johntown housed about 180 people, most of whom searched the eroded sands in the drainage systems for gold. The outpost consisted of about a dozen shanty structures. In the warmer months, they did not need buildings. Many of the miners slept on blankets among the sagebrush beneath the open sky.[1]

In the beginning of the 1850s, the newcomers to the western Great Basin fell into two groups. There were those who established trade centers and marketed fresh oxen and what could be grown in the narrow band of fertile, well-watered land at the base of the Sierra, and there were the itinerate placer miners working claims in the more arid mountains east of the Sierra. Over time, the situation grew complex as others engaged in a range of commercial enterprises to support the emerging communities. The recall of the Mormon mission and the extension of authority of the general government, as the federal authority in Washington, DC, was known at the time, signaled changes that would affect the far West, tying it more firmly with the rest of the nation. At thirty-one, Eilley's life was about to change dramatically as well.

The West was becoming a different place. In 1858, John Butterfield began carrying the US mail across the expanse of the West. He then established a stage line from Missouri to California, offering transportation as well as delivering correspondence, outpacing the plodding wagon trains and, importantly, traveling in both directions. The new service connected St. Louis, Santa Fe, Denver, and San Francisco, helping to bind together the far reaches of the nation even as it faced the threat of civil war. Although

FIG. 8. After Eilley's second husband returned to Salt Lake City, she moved to Johntown, a small mining camp in Gold Canyon just north of today's town of Dayton, Nevada. This photo, taken in the 1940s, shows the lower Gold Canyon area near where she lived with about two hundred prospectors searching for their fortunes. Courtesy Nevada Historical Society.

wagon trains still traveled the trails, immigrants now had a choice. They no longer had to leave friends and family behind and spend up to six miserable months traveling to the West. Now a traveler could purchase a ticket for $200 and be in San Francisco in only twenty-two bone-wrenching days. That same year, Colonel J. B. Crandall established a stage line from Placerville to Genoa, making triweekly trips allowing people, merchandise, mail, and news to travel back and forth between California and Western Utah Territory.[2] Eilley and the other residents of Carson County were no longer isolated from the affairs of the outside world.

In Johntown, Eilley found the beginnings of a town even if the community may have occasionally shifted its footing up and down the canyon.

Not everyone there spent their time searching for gold. Histories of the developing district mention several men who opened mercantile businesses and saloons. The largest of these did not carry more than two or three tons of groceries at a time. The most prominent stores included Major Orsmby's, operated by S. A. Swager,[3] Job's store kept by H. B. Camp, John Child's run by Mart M. Gage, and another maintained by Harris Jacobs and Lal Weil. Nicholas Ambrose "Dutch Nick" ran an often-mentioned establishment, a store that doubled as a saloon. Orin Gray and John McBride owned another place to buy a drink in the camp. As an example of the turmoil of the times, a few months after Eilley's arrival in Johntown, vigilantes arrested Gray and McBride before acquitting them of being part of an outlaw gang.[4]

A handful of women and children also lived in the small settlement. Of the families, there were Lyman Jones with his wife and baby girl; Will Dover, also with a wife and young boy; "Dutch Nick" and his wife; and of course, Eilley Cowan and her husband's nephew. Coming from an influential family of the local Northern Paiutes, Sarah Winnemucca, her sister Mary and their brother Natchez, later a leader in the tribe, also spent part of the winter there. It is not clear what Eilley did in Johntown, but the many ways she might have made money included laundry work, cooking, and mending clothes. It is doubtful that she mined, but that would not have been impossible for a woman at the time.

By January 1858, the threat of the so-called Utah War ended, and Alexander returned to Eilley and Robert.[5] As he passed through the canyon on his way to Johntown, he could not anticipate the dramatic upheaval that was about to occur. Warm spring weather melted the snow covering hills above, allowing miners to resume prospecting in Gold Canyon. Working "rockers," crude wooden boxes used to wash away worthless dirt, miners had been eking out a meager existence with local gold deposits throughout the 1850s. As the decade was concluding, however, rich deposits proved increasingly elusive. Many contemplated leaving even as several miners found larger diggings. Although hard work could yield these placer miners as much as five dollars a day, most had to be satisfied with far less.[6]

Prospectors had also found some deposits in Six Mile Canyon, which descended to the east from the mountain above. Dutch Nick subsequently moved his establishment to the neighboring ravine, where he set up his tent saloon, restaurant, and boarding house. Fourteen dollars a week bought meals, a blanket, and some soft ground among the sage-brush flats near the saloon.[7]

After a fair summer of mining surface gold, most miners from Gold and Six Mile canyons moved back to Johntown as winter neared. In August, Alexander decided it was time to move as well. He returned to Great Salt Lake City.[8] Once again, Eilley and Robert disregarded his wishes and chose to stay behind.

During the snowy months, the region returned to its isolation from the world. To help the nearby settlers, John A. "Snowshoe" Thompson repeatedly crossed the Sierra Nevada between Genoa and Placerville, carrying mail, news, and supplies to and from California. According to Thompson's later recollection, Eilley once gave him an unusual request when she asked if he would search Sacramento for a peepstone. She already had one with her, but it had grown old and cloudy. Eilley regarded herself as having second sight, as clairvoyance was termed in Scotland. She believed in her ability to see things others could not, and she relied on a crystal stone to focus her talent. Thompson combed the shops of Sacramento but was unable to satisfy the unusual request.[9]

Some miners believed in Eilley's spiritual powers and visited her for readings. Lyman Jones would later recall one tale that involved Joe Webb and a stolen sack of gold dust. Webb went to the seer to find the culprit. She consulted her ball and informed him of the name of the thief. Webb and his friends confronted the accused man, who denied having taken it. After a severe whipping, he admitted to the robbery and took the accusers to the hidden sack of gold dust.[10]

January 1859 brought spring-like weather, causing the light snowpack to melt, feeding local streams. As the water flowed toward the Carson River, it freed some gold held within the decomposing quartz ledges higher on the slope. Although most of the gold veins remained hidden deep beneath the hills, James "Old Virginny" Finney, John Bishop, and several other miners walked uphill and managed to discover some large gold flakes by using the simple process of panning. After ten years of finding only gold dust in the canyon below, miners were now able to pull fifteen cents per pan and earn up to $12 a day for their efforts.[11] Within a few months, six companies worked the new diggings, ranging from depths of three to twenty feet. The miners soon retrieved five to twenty-five cents per pan, increasing their earnings to as much as forty dollars a day.[12]

The discoverers named the rise where they were working "Gold Hill," and with that, a town that survives to this day was born. Although most residents lived in tents or crude huts, this simple settlement soon became the center of mining activity, enticing most of the residents of Johntown, including Eilley and Robert, to move there.

The high desert made for an unlikely location to build a town. The barren land lacked the many resources needed to live, let alone to mine gold.[13] Timber, streams, agricultural land, and pastures were abundant in nearby valleys, but roads capable of carrying wagons did not exist. Nevertheless, the discovery in early 1859 demonstrated that gold was plentiful on the mountain slope, and the new residents purchased or created whatever they needed to make the community survive.

Gold Hill quickly began to resemble an actual town. Buildings appeared along a main street, the first belonging to Dutch Nick, who moved his business yet again. Next came Eilley's boarding house and restaurant, built of logs cut from the surrounding hills. From this "rude and comfortless sort of abode," as journalist and miner Henry De Groot observed, she made a good business of washing clothes and caring for the miners. A sixteen-square-foot frame grocery store came next. These may have been humble, but more soon followed. Most of the former residents of Johntown now lived in Gold Hill, as did many new arrivals to the region.[14]

Once her business opened, Eilley found herself living among various colorful characters. History remembers some of these early residents, but others were soon forgotten. William Hickman Dolman later wrote about a few of the noteworthy miners, but perceptions were easily clouded as reputations were influenced by legend more than fact. While his observations can be called to question, Dolman's recollections are valuable in the way they portrayed many of the people Eilley Bowers knew. There was Henry P. Comstock, sometimes portrayed as an industrious visionary prospector, though more often remembered as slothful and little more than half-witted. "Old Virginny" Finney was a frontier hunter and miner, a man of more than ordinary ability in his class but also credited with being something of a buffoon and practical joker. He was a hard drinker when he could get liquor and he was an indifferent worker. Peter O'Riley was "half-cracked," lazy and stupid. Joseph Kirby was sober and honest but indolent. John Walker was a violinist, Mormon, and violent partisan. Joseph Webb was also a Mormon, a miner, and exceptionally well educated for his class. He also kept others informed as he penned a local handwritten newspaper called the *Gold Canyon Switch*.[15]

Lemuel Sanford (Sandy) Bowers was among those attracted to Gold Hill by the promise of wealth. He was an unassuming muleskinner, a period term for a teamster or wagon master who specialized in handling mules. He was born on February 24, 1833, in Madison County, Illinois, but little is known of his family. After coming west in 1856 and spending some time in Sacramento, he relocated to Gold Hill. Bowers quickly began investing in mining claims, recording new ones and buying, selling, and trading his investments. One transaction occurred on May 21, 1859, when Sandy Bowers, James Rogers, Joseph Webb, and J. A. Hammack located six hundred feet of mining land. Two months later, Bowers bought out Webb's share for $200. During the spring, he and several of his partners located more than eight such claims totaling nearly five thousand feet. On June 30, Bowers and Rogers saw the growing need for lumber and claimed two hundred acres of land and timber.[16]

Sandy's most famous holding involved others, including Henry Comstock, Joe Plato, William Knight, and Rogers. Together, they claimed fifty feet of mining land at the north end of Gold Hill, which was divided into ten-foot strips creating five small, separate mines. Combined with claims by Finney, John Bishop, Alec Henderson (no relation to Robert), and Jack Yount, these properties became the Little Gold Hill Mines.[17] The tangled assertions of ownership left plenty of room for litigation.

Modern readers can be confused about what these "feet" of claims represented. According to the conventions of the day in the American West, prospectors could lay claim to ownership of orebodies in lineal feet. They were often restricted as to how many feet they could claim, to prevent a single person from owning miles of a deposit that could not realistically be put into production, and which would prevent others from being able to prosper. Owning lineal feet of an orebody included all aspects of that part of the deposit as it drifted underground, with all the "spurs, dips, and angles," no matter in what direction or depth the ore followed within the claimed amount of lineal feet.[18]

On the Comstock, the "lode bearing" ore erupted at the surface in a general north-south direction. According to the rules of the day, a claimant was entitled to follow his ore thousands of feet below as well as however many feet the ore drifted to the west or east. "Ten feet" of a claim, then,

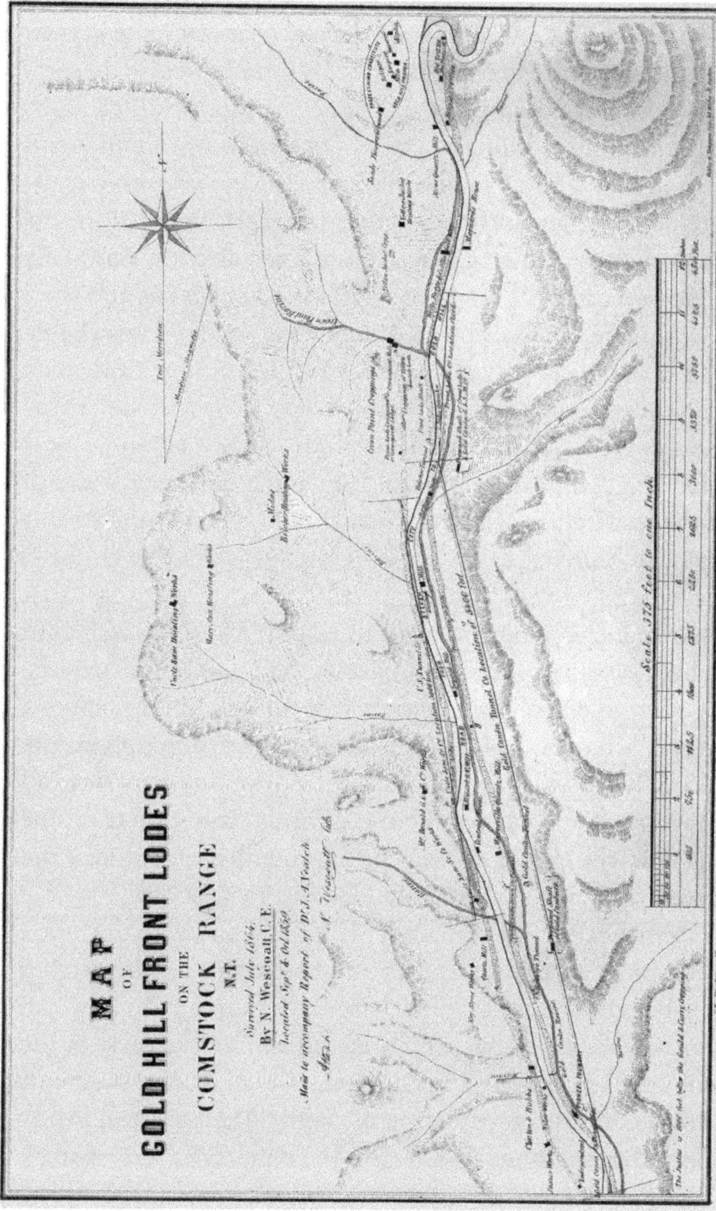

FIG. 9. The Gold Hill Front Lodes of the Comstock Range, Nevada Territory surveyed July 1864 by N. Wescoatt. The ellipse to the right shows the site of the Little Gold Hill Mines originally claimed by Sandy Bowers, Henry Comstock, Joe Plato, William Knight, and James Rogers. Eilley purchased Rogers's claim and combined it with Sandy Bowers when they married, forming the Bowers Mine. Courtesy Stanford Library.

might extend hundreds of feet or more underground. As it turned out, the Comstock Lode was eventually demonstrated to drift far to the east as it sunk to ever-lower depths, but none of this was apparent in 1859.[19]

Indeed, only a small extent of the vast deposit that would be known as the Comstock Lode had been found in the first months of 1859. In early June, two Irish immigrants named Peter O'Riley and Patrick McLaughlin began digging along Six Mile Canyon about a mile and a half north of Gold Hill. Snowshoe Thompson recalled that during a psychic reading, Eilley directed O'Riley and his partner to search for gold in this particular location up Six Mile Canyon, but this recollection was likely apocryphal.[20] According to the story, they followed her advice, and soon the two men discovered a concentrated deposit of gold. More reliable accounts of the day of discovery on June 8, 1859, tell of how Comstock was riding by in the evening and recognized that O'Riley and McLaughlin had made a significant find. With his well-known fast talking, Comstock persuaded the two miners to grant him and a partner a share of the new claim. Fortunately for all, it was valuable enough to support this growing company of miners.

An assay made a few weeks later revealed the astounding fact that the ore from what had become known as the Ophir Mine was rich with not only gold but also silver. The wealth in the mountain promised legendary proportions, and soon miners were recovering $1,000 or more a day.[21] News of the rich assay quickly spread excitement throughout the region, setting off the famed "Rush to Washoe." Fortune seekers from all the surrounding towns and valleys, from California, and soon from the East now flocked to the new, growing community that would take the name Virginia City, soon to exceed Gold Hill, just to its south.[22]

The new mining district was still under Utah rule, and with the influx of people to the Comstock Lode, disputes over land rights and ownership erupted. People bought and sold claims daily according to rules they had established on their own without territorial authority.[23] As early as the end of June, the miners organized a mining district to resolve problems associated with the title and recordation of claims. They selected Sandy Bowers and four other delegates to represent the miners of the Comstock Mining District in their local government. They also appointed a local blacksmith, V. A. Houseworth, to serve as recorder. He logged his notes in a book kept on a shelf behind the bar of a local saloon. The vague, inaccurate, and often altered entries caused as many disagreements as they likely settled. Controversies over landholdings showed the need for law and government, which Utah's Carson County had not enjoyed since the Mormons' hasty retreat in 1857.[24]

In anticipation of the wealth of the area, Wells Fargo & Company built the first bank in Virginia City on the corner of A and Sutton Streets.[25] The town soon became a lively place filled with shanties, canvas houses, and a restaurant that served up to six customers at a time, with meals costing seventy-five cents.[26] People around the world began to hear word that the Comstock Lode supported a fully established mining district with prospering communities. New arrivals attempted to stake their own rights to ore-bearing rock, but it was not long before the best properties were claimed. Some came with enough money to buy shares in established mines, but most found employment as wage-earning miners. Still others recognized that arriving with goods to sell could be a quick means to profit.

The Little Gold Hill Mines prospered. On July 9, 1859, the *Territorial Enterprise*, published at the time in Genoa, reported that "L. S. Bowers & Company" crushed selected ore from one pan, using an ordinary mortar and obtained $100. Of the nine original locators of the Little Gold Hill Mines, Bowers and Plato were the only two who retained and worked their claims by that summer. Comstock and Knight sold out to Frink, who created a company later incorporated into the Empire Mine. Rogers sold his ten-foot share to his landlady, Eilley Cowan. Rogers lived at Eilley's boarding house and needed to settle his boarding bill. He offered to sell Eilley his ten feet for $100 per foot.[27]

Eilley had been involved in other claims as well. At the end of June, she owned a strip three hundred feet wide and one thousand feet long. On July 13, she staked out another claim stating, "Notice that we the undersigned claim a ten feet wide and running up the Yellow Jacket Ravine for four hundred feet lying between J. Cary and J. B. Benny's claim on the south of Gold Hill, signed Elen [*sic*] Cowan." Then, Eilley and her nephew Robert entered three claims of two hundred feet each on the American Flat to the southwest of Gold Hill.[28]

Of all her mining properties, the most significant was the ten feet purchased from Rogers. Not only was this claim extraordinarily rich in ore, but it also adjoined ten feet belonging to Sandy Bowers, another of her boarders. Eilley Cowan had the entanglement of a previous marriage, but her separation from Alexander Cowan could be taken as the equivalent of a divorce, and legalities could be sorted out later. The door was open for her to become friends with Bowers and then to take it a step further. On August 9, 1859, they joined their claims and lives when the Reverend Jesse L. Bennett, a local Methodist pastor, married thirty-two-year-old Eilley to twenty-six-year-old Sandy in Gold Hill.[29]

The newlyweds established the Bowers Mining Company. After retrieving valuable ore near the surface, Sandy began a shaft, which was likely accessed with a simple winch. The couple constructed a two-story home nearby. As winter approached, the Bowers Mine was among the few with owners laboring themselves as Sandy continued his underground exploration.[30] At some point he would have likely begun excavating the shaft at an incline, following the slope of the vein of ore. As he explored the depths with horizontal "adits," Sandy would have laid tracks, allowing an ore car to move tools and ore in the deep excavation. Although these first approaches to Comstock mining were primitive, engineers in the district were soon inventing and installing many innovations that the industry would use worldwide for decades.[31]

As winter neared and temperatures dropped, some Californians chose to return to the warmth of the western slope of the Sierra Nevada. Many felt that the 1859 strikes were not as rich as people had claimed. Nevertheless, faithful miners prepared for their cold stay. By the fall of this first year on the mountainside, more than 130 miners had staked claims in the Comstock Mining District, and several hundred lived in Carson County. By this time, Gold Hill consisted of various wooden structures, a few buildings made of rough stone, many canvas huts, and other dwellings created by using old shirts, empty whiskey barrels, potato sacks, and anything else available.[32] With such a large population remaining in the area, many of those taking up residence were not even lucky enough to live in rudimentary structures.

Some miners dug holes in the ground and covered them with sagebrush to keep warm. Others excavated extra-wide tunnels where they made bedrooms and parlors to protect them from the cold.[33] As early Nevada historian Myron Angel noted, dugouts housed from six to twenty miners "as congeniality, interest or necessity assorted them." In this way, they "passed the most dreary, comfortless, severe cold winter ever known in Nevada, warmed by scant wood and cheered only by a golden hope of the future."[34]

On November 22, 1859, it began snowing, and it did not stop until it accumulated to a depth of almost six feet.[35] Sandy Bowers and other

FIG. 10. Only a few photos of Sandy and Eilley Bowers exist. These images became famous when they were later printed on postcards and sold throughout the region. Courtesy Bowers Mansion collection.

prominent mine owners with enclosed shafts continued digging. For most of the town, all activity stopped. Idle residents spent money in saloons eating, drinking, gambling, and wasting time. With few provisions because of their snowy surroundings, store owners raised prices on everyday items.

As the cold persisted and most residents suffered, the Bowers continued working their mine. On December 16, Sandy and partners Webb, Plato, and a man named F. D. Casteel made an agreement with J. H. Mills and Paul W. Coppers to run a tunnel until they struck the ledge. In payment, the owners relinquished their right to a percentage of the valuable ground, and on completion, they would all become partners.[36]

By the end of 1859, Sandy and his numerous partners controlled more than fourteen separate mining claims totaling almost ten thousand lineal feet. The long and eventful year had brought about many changes in the lives of Sandy and Eilley Bowers. Money was plentiful, and the new decade promised the hope of great things.

CHAPTER 4

The Comstock Lode

WITH THE MINE RUNNING SMOOTHLY, Sandy and Eilley Bowers emerged with extravagant wealth at the turn of the decade. Most people living in the western Great Basin were not as fortunate. The winter beginning in 1859 brought heavy snow. The severe storms caused widespread hardship and suffering. Miners dwelt in meager shelters with insufficient food and other essentials necessary to face the cold.[1]

By March 1860, with the opening of the passes across the Sierra, supplies began to arrive and warming weather allowed most residents to resume work.[2] At the same time, many more Californians traveled to the Comstock Mining District. Local crews cut roads and brought in lumber from sawmills in Washoe and Carson Valleys. They built houses and other permanent structures on the side of Mount Davidson even while miners engineered and timbered their excavations deep underground. J. Ross Browne, a contemporaneous traveling writer and illustrator, described the area's excitement in April 1860 when he recalled, "Men, on meeting, do not inquire after each other's health, but rather after their claims. . . . They do not extend their hands in token of friendship on approaching, but pluck from their well filled pockets a bit of rock, and, presenting it, mutually inquire what they think of its looks. . . . Little care they whom you choose President; . . . all [are] devoted to [the] single pursuit of finding, buying, selling, and trading in mines of silver and gold. Everybody makes haste to be rich."[3]

As spring warmed the Comstock, Sandy began obtaining returns from his initial claims.[4] To add to what must have been their sense that these were the best of times, Eilley, at age thirty-three, was pregnant with her first child.

FIG. 11. A bird's-eye view published in 1866 depicts mining facilities in Gold Hill, Nevada. The buildings in the center show the Imperial, Empire, and other mines that began as the Little Gold Hill Mines. The Bowers Mine was to the left of the Empire Mine structure. The main road connected Virginia City and Gold Hill. Courtesy of Special Collections and University Archives Department, University of Nevada, Reno, Libraries.

Despite all the excitement, Eilley still had to deal with the affairs of her second marriage. When Alexander left Eilley to return to Salt Lake City, they still lived under early Utah law, which stated that moving out of a spouse's house was considered a legal divorce. In 1860, with the issue of land in question, Sandy and Eilley brought in lawyers to legalize the divorce and settle the ownership of the Cowan Ranch in Washoe Valley. On February 2, 1860, Alexander Cowan gave a Washoe Valley neighbor power of attorney to handle the sale of half of the Cowan Ranch.[5] Six weeks later, Sandy Bowers had the other half surveyed.[6] He then published a notice in the *Territorial Enterprise* prohibiting anyone from making any improvements on or purchasing the ranch formerly known as the Cowan Ranch.[7]

On April 18, 1860, Eilley Bowers petitioned Alexander for a formal divorce. She stated that Alexander had "left her bed, board, and society without cause or provocation," and she felt that he left her in a helpless and destitute condition. Alexander did not dispute the contention. On June 4, Robert Henderson, Alexander's nephew living with the Bowers, witnessed their divorce. As for alimony, Eilley received 160 acres of the old Cowan Ranch.[8] Later that summer, the other half sold for $1,250.[9] As a result of Eilley remaining in Carson County and living on or near the Cowan Ranch, Alexander made more than a thousand dollars in profit on his initial investment. This was a reasonable sum since most Mormons took a loss on their property when they left western Utah Territory.

While working for the church to help Mormon emigrants cross the plains, Alexander met Elizabeth Ratz. Upon arriving in Salt Lake, the two married. Cowan family tradition holds that his other wife, Jane Mitchell, accompanied the couple to the church the day they were married.[10] In 1862, Alexander moved his family to Payson, Utah, where he purchased a peach orchard for the price of a team of oxen. He later took a homestead south of town and bought a 150-acre ranch north of town. Eventually, Jane lived on the farm while Elizabeth stayed at the homestead.

Alexander remained a high priest of the church where he served as a choir member for fifty years. Over the years, he fathered fifteen children. Jane gave him six boys and three girls, while Elizabeth contributed three boys and three girls to the growing family. Alexander Cowan lived well into the twentieth century, dying at eighty-eight on Christmas Day 1918. His family remembered him as a loving husband, devoted father, and dedicated church member.[11] Alexander did not claim Eilley as one of his wives after 1860.[12]

Meanwhile, Sandy tried to secure their investments in Gold Hill. With vague laws and uncertainty over land occupation, miners sometimes used force to protect their claimed property. Possession was only part of the law. When a dispute between the Bowers Company and the Savage Mine erupted over landholdings, Sandy built a crude stone fort near his mine, laid in provisions, ammunition, and a garrison that could accommodate thirty armed men. The courts ruled in favor of Bowers before any violence erupted.[13]

While Eilley settled her past and Sandy occupied himself with running the mine, larger issues were emerging that would affect the entire region. Thousands arrived with the opening of the passes in the spring of 1860. This caused enormous stress on the fragile environment of the western Great Basin. Merchants struggled to import sufficient goods for newcomers, but the promise of profit inspired the growth of a network of roads, teamsters, and entrepreneurs. For the Indigenous people, the destruction of crucial resources and the hostility of many of the emigrants were threatening their very existence.

In late April, local tribal leaders held a council at Pyramid Lake to consider their grievances against the settlers. The account of what happened there quickly became more a matter of legend rather than necessarily accurate history. Except for Chief Numaga, also known as Young Winnemucca, all favored war. As Numaga spoke of peace, word came of an incident at Williams Station, a stage stop on the Carson River, now on the bed of the Lahontan Reservoir. On May 6, several Northern Paiutes went to the station on word that the men there were keeping two girls from the tribe at Pyramid Lake captive for their amusement. Despite conflicting reports, the outcome was clear: The men at the stage stop were killed, and the warriors returned to the council gathering with news of the action. Chief Numaga responded that "there is no longer any use for counsel; we must prepare for war, for the soldiers will now come here to fight us."[14]

In the surrounding area, the reaction to the incident at Williams Station was swift as people demanded that the American Indians be taught a lesson. The call to action was met as untrained, undisciplined, and unorganized men gathered to join in the fight. Sandy Bowers chose to support the war effort with money rather than the force of his own arms. He and Eilley loaned the Utah territorial government $14,000 to help finance the protection of the settlers.[15] Authorities in Salt Lake City never repaid the debt. The resulting Pyramid Lake War of 1860 lasted less than a month and consisted primarily of two battles. During the first, on May 12, the Native Americans used superior strategies and their knowledge of the terrain to devastate those who came to assault their encampments. This left roughly seventy dead among the 105 volunteers, more white casualties than in any conflict with Native Americans in the United States and its territories for the previous seventy years.

White settlers were thrown into a panic. Some fled the western Great Basin, while others established crude forts in various communities. Telegrams to California pleading for assistance resulted in more than five

FIG. 12. African American artist Grafton T. Brown created this lithograph of Virginia City, Nevada Territory in 1861. The image, capturing the community from the south, shows the rapid growth of the mining district, which had been open space just a few years prior. Courtesy Library of Congress.

hundred regular troops and volunteers crossing the Sierra to renew the fight against the Paiutes and their allies from other tribes. The second battle, on June 2, 1860, resulted in the retreat of the Native Americans into the northern desert. They had avoided high losses, but it was impossible to survive there, and the Paiutes eventually sued for peace.

As Sandy and Eilley resumed their business and life, she gave birth to John Jasper Bowers on June 28, 1860.[16] Eilley could celebrate with a son, a home, and a gold and silver mine, all while living in a region that was booming beyond imagination. Graded streets and numerous buildings appeared up and down the slopes of Mount Davidson and other nearby hills. The new International Hotel had a barroom, dining hall, kitchen, and twelve sleeping rooms. Gold Hill, Silver City, and Virginia City housed miners, blacksmiths, tailors, saloonkeepers, merchants, barbers, carpenters, teamsters, bootmakers, jewelers, tinners, brewers, millers, gunsmiths, bankers, lawyers, doctors, and members of every other trade needed to sustain a growing town. The settlement and wealth of the district also attracted ministers of various denominations, establishing a presence for several faiths. In addition, gamblers, thieves, and vigilantes filled the streets, keeping things lively.[17]

A telegraph line had been built from Genoa over the Sierra to California in November 1858, but it did not extend to the Comstock. With the establishment of the Pony Express in April 1860, news flowed more rapidly in and out of Virginia City. The *Territorial Enterprise*, which was soon to move to the mining district, and other local newspapers recounted local stories and carried news from around the world. National and foreign newspapers began writing updates from the Comstock Mining District. Excitement grew daily, and it appeared that nothing could go wrong for the western Great Basin or the Bowers family. Their mine produced a steady supply of valuable ore, and Sandy and his partners sold off their unwanted mining claims at a considerable profit. During 1860, they traded almost 1,100 feet of land for almost $20,000.[18]

One problem for the Bowers Mine was processing ore to separate gold and silver from worthless rock, which demanded a concentrating facility or "mill." At the time, California housed the nearest stamp mills. Dr. E. B. Harris reported that Sandy and Eilley shipped two thousand pounds of ore to San Francisco at the cost of twenty-five cents per pound. Although this high-grade ore produced $2,200 in gold and silver, they lost $500 of their profit with freight charges alone.[19]

Harris was interested in the processing aspect of mining, so he decided to construct a mill in the new mining district. His method would break down large pieces of rock by using large, steam-driven pistons, known as "stamps," to crush the ore from the mine. He attempted to make a money-saving agreement with Sandy, Eilley, and J. H. Mills, their silent partner. While planning the construction of a stamp mill, Sandy's lawyer convinced him not to give their money to a "Yankee Doctor." Harris maintained that the lawyer was only interested in controlling the Bowers's mine and money.[20]

Even without the couple's support, Harris went on with his plans, and his "Old Pioneer Mill" was soon in operation. The mill received a percentage of the recovered bullion. While Sandy and Eilley did not invest in the mill, they used it to crush their ore, and most of its profit came from the Bowers Company and the other early-day preeminent moneymaker, the Gould and Curry Mine. The Bowers ore alone was now consistently yielding more than $400 per ton in gold and silver. Even though the early mills could only extract 70 percent of the precious metals, there was still enough wealth in the rock excavated from the couple's mine for the Pioneer Mill to pay for itself within the first month of operation.[21]

On August 27, Eilley and Sandy's luck turned against them when their two-month-old infant son died suddenly from unknown causes.[22] As they mourned the loss of their baby, national events were about to affect their lives. In November, voters elected Abraham Lincoln to become the sixteenth president of the United States. On December 20, South Carolina rebelled by seceding from the Union. Six other states quickly joined the revolt. Then on March 2, 1861, just two days before Lincoln's inauguration, a bill authorizing territorial status for Nevada, passed both houses of Congress, and President James Buchanan signed it into law. In fewer than twelve years, Carson County's population had grown from a dozen settlers in 1850 to just less than 7,000 in 1860 and was continuing to grow. Two years later, a territorial census recorded more than 15,000 residing in Nevada.[23]

On April 12, 1861, the South Carolina militia began shelling Fort Sumter, near Charleston. The Civil War had begun. Most Nevadans were fierce in their support of preserving the national union, but Southerners were also living in the territory. Although secessionist sentiments occasionally flared, incidents were quickly suppressed, and in general, Nevadans just wanted to keep working and acquire wealth.

Boosters of the Comstock Lode claimed this was the most productive mineral deposit in the world, and there was reason to believe that they might have been correct. Bullion-producing mines stretched three miles from Seven Mile Canyon north of Virginia City to below Gold Hill in the south. The mining district employed thousands. Estimates about how much its mines yielded suggest the bullion production was worth $1 million in 1860, $2.5 million in 1861, $6 million in 1862, and an incredible $12.4 million in 1863. The deeper miners probed, the more wealth the ore yielded as they followed the meandering vein, first west and then east in its descent.[24] The miners of the Comstock were among the best-paid industrial workers in the world, earning as much as $4 a day.[25]

The prosperity of the mining district meant that Eilley's Comstock rarely had a quiet moment. Mills continually dropped their stamps, loudly crushing ore. Black-power blasts echoed from far beneath the city as miners loosened rock in deep tunnels. The mines, mills, and surrounding towns operated twenty-four hours a day. As one shift worked, another slept, and another ate, gambled, played, and went about their daily business. Comstock citizens came from all over the country and the world, bringing many different cultures and traditions to early Nevada. Nevertheless, they shared one dream. A lucky mine owner could become a millionaire, a lowly miner or miller could maintain a good life, and eager entrepreneurs could make a fortune by providing services for everyone.

Sandy and Eilley Bowers lived the dream. Their mine became the richest of the Little Gold Hill Mines, producing astonishing amounts of gold and silver every week.[26] It had been almost a year since Sandy pulled out of the deal to build a mill with Dr. Harris, but the idea persisted and he eventually decided to add a stamp mill to the Bowers Mining Company. Having a mill near the mine meant he could more efficiently process his ore and reduce costs. He could also charge others for the same service. Sandy went to San Francisco to purchase the machinery for the Quartz Mill.[27] Newspapers recounted that upon returning, "Mr. Sandy Bowers had made his wife a present of one hundred tons of rock. Since then it has been crushed, and has yielded $7,000. That will furnish Madame with pin-money for some time."[28]

Named after the national emblem of Eilley's native Scotland and constructed near their home in Crown Point Ravine, the Thistle Mill soon began processing ore for the Bowers Mining Company and other nearby operations. The building was forty-four by sixty-five feet and housed a twenty-stamp mill. It took five and a half cords of wood a day to fire its sixty-five-horsepower steam engine, while its thirty Knox pans in the amalgamating department allowed it to process twenty-two tons with only fourteen employees.[29]

On June 16, even while the couple was expanding their Bowers Mining Company, they welcomed their second child, naming her Theresa Fortunatus, perhaps in recognition of their unfolding good fortune. Sadly, three months later, she went the way of her infant brother, dying from unknown causes.[30] Growing business matters forced the Bowers to move on with their lives, leaving little time to mourn.

As the war in the east grew more devastating, the mining district was completing its transition from remote outpost to an established part of the nation. News was carried more rapidly to the Comstock as Western

FIG. 13. This 1865 panoramic photograph of Gold Hill was taken from the east. The Bowers's Thistle Mill is near the top of the ravine. To the left of the mill is the Bowers home, where they lived before striking it rich. The couple continued using the house whenever they were in Gold Hill for business. Courtesy Special Collections and University Archives Department, University of Nevada, Reno, Libraries.

Union completed the transcontinental telegraph that fall. Nevadans were no longer isolated from the world and with the improvements in the community, they did not need to fear the worst as winter approached. In less than three years, the slopes of Mount Davidson transformed from barren hills to a place filled with permanent structures and thousands of residents. Besides the sprawling neighborhoods of houses, the larger mines and mills were enclosed and protected from the harsh environment, so they no longer slowed or stopped production because of weather.

Early in the history of the mining district, Comstock mining engineers faced a peculiar problem linked with the fabulous wealth of the orebody. By late 1860 as the shaft of the Ophir Mine reached a depth of 180 feet, miners exposed a rich deposit, wider than anything they could remember discovering elsewhere. They had been using long pine poles as pillars to secure the unstable soil of the underground chambers, but no tree was thick enough to support caverns excavated of this great width. This meant that the ore could not be removed safely.

The Ophir Mine superintendent, W. F. Babcock, hired Philip Deidesheimer, a California engineer originally from Germany, to solve the problem, inspiring a system called "square set" timbering. Deidesheimer used posts from five to six feet long to build square cribs to brace the mine. Deidesheimer refused to patent the innovation so all mines could be made safer. When finished working the orebodies, miners filled the supporting structure with waste rock, forming pillars of stone and creating a wall of rock to support the roof of excavated chambers. This also had the benefit of reducing the cost of hoisting worthless material to the surface.[31] Like most mine owners, Sandy began using this process.

With the implementation of square-set timbering, the Bowers Mine became even more extensive. Underground, the Comstock took on the appearance of large, subterranean buildings with many floors or levels. The excavation now consisted of stations, drifts, shafts, chutes, and winzes to facilitate a carefully planned operation where miners tunneled their way to large orebodies that lay beneath the surface of the earth.

The Bowers Mine employed a superintendent to watch over the entire operation, but it was the couple's responsibility to control the business financially. They used profits to pay for mining supplies, equipment, timber, repairs, and of course, salaries. They also supported a stamp mill, sawmill, and blacksmith shop. These extra operations constituted something of a vertical monopoly, allowing profits from various services to return to the Bowers company, but mining still proved to be costly.

The year 1861 had been financially good for the Bowers. Aside from their tremendous gold and silver production, they had earned a large sum of money from their investments. Bowers and Company made more than $23,000 by selling fewer than 220 feet of a claim. They also increased their holdings by buying 216 more feet of a claim for less than $5,000, including Eilley's investment of $100 for fifty feet in the Flowery Mining District, to the east of Virginia City. In addition, that year they borrowed $10,000 to support their operation, an indication that bullion was not always sufficient to meet expenses. Nevertheless, they repaid the debt on time and with interest.[32]

The winter of 1861–1862 was severe.[33] The Comstock survived heavy snowstorms, cold temperatures, and spring flooding, able now to keep supplies arriving on newly cut roads. By spring, Virginia City had grown tremendously. The community now boasted three large churches, a theater, a courthouse, several flourishing schools, the beginnings of the V. C. Water Company, a gas and coal company, and wagon roads in every direction, and there were plans for a railroad.[34]

At the time, Alexander Cowan's nephew, eighteen-year-old Robert Henderson, still lived with the Bowers while working in the Bowers Mine. Robert's older brother James had recently moved to Gold Hill and took a job with the Bowers company.[35] Robert increased his mining wealth when he purchased fifty-nine feet of the Bowers mining claim from Sandy for $2,000.[36]

With 1862 well underway, the Bowers celebrated Nevada's heyday. No records exist to calculate their actual wealth, but the Bowers were consistently being referred to as millionaires. Life was rich and the future hopeful.

CHAPTER 5

Comstock Millionaires

As the weather warmed and flowers bloomed, life returned to Gold Hill in the spring of 1862. Sandy and Eilley Bowers found new and lavish ways to spend their fortune. Chief among these was constructing a mansion grander than any other in the area. It would have handcrafted inserts, hinges, and doorknobs made of gold and silver from their mine and elegantly cut marble fireplaces and furnishings from Europe. The rowdy town of Gold Hill was unsuitable for a castle of such splendor. They needed to build it in a beautiful valley with snow-topped mountains to the west and a clear lake to the east. A place where hot springs flowed freely and the surrounding lands were open and fertile. Eilley and Sandy's mansion would be framed by the Sierra Nevada while overlooking Washoe Lake. They chose the land Eilley acquired from the divorce settlement with Alexander.

While Sandy planned for the construction of their mansion, he was sinking even more money into their mine. On March 28, 1862, Bowers and several other Little Gold Hill Mines contracted with Robert McLellan to dig a two-hundred-foot vertical shaft. Sandy paid $300 for the project if completed within twelve months. He also added a steam engine pump to help the mining operation. The pump removed the tremendous influx of water found belowground.[1]

With everything apparently under control, the newly minted millionaires planned a grand excursion to Europe. Eilley intended to buy lavish furnishings and exquisite works of art to adorn her new home. She also looked forward to purchasing elegant clothes and expensive jewelry. The couple hosted a farewell banquet at the extravagant International Hotel in Virginia City in honor of their journey. According to Myron Angel's 1881 history, "everyone was invited" and received champagne as freely as if it were water in a spring flood. The guests toasted their hosts, and everybody enjoyed the grand ball.[2] That night, Angel reported that Sandy gave a speech: "I've been in this yer country amongst the fust that come here. I've had powerful good luck, and I've got money to throw at the birds. Thar ain't no chance for a gentleman to spend his coin in this country, and thar ain't nothin' much to see, so me and Mrs. Bowers is agoin' to Yoorop to take in the sights. . . . I hope you'll all jine in and drink Mrs. Bowers' health. Thars plenty of champagne, and money ain't no object."[3] Their farewell party became the highlight of Virginia City's social scene.

Toward the end of April 1862, Sandy made two final sales of mining property totaling $1,000.[4] Then with business matters settled, Sandy and Eilley left the Comstock Mining District for the trip of a lifetime. Their journey began on the California Stage to San Francisco, where they stayed at the elegant Russ House Hotel.[5]

On May 1, the couple sailed from San Francisco aboard the steamship *Golden Gate*, which carried mail and two hundred and fifty passengers. There was plenty of room on board the large passenger ship. After customary calls in Mexico at Manzanillo and Acapulco for coal, Sandy and Eilley arrived in Panama two weeks later. They then crossed the isthmus on the Panama Railway, before setting sail aboard the steamer *North Star*. Designed as a yacht for Commodore Cornelius Vanderbilt in 1852, *North Star* became known as one of the most prestigious steamships of its time. Eight days later, on May 23, they arrived in New York City.[6]

Although the East was embroiled in the Civil War, New York City had not experienced the devastating battles waging elsewhere. On May 29, Sandy obtained his passport, allowing him to travel abroad.[7] After touring New York City, the couple, joined by Sandy's unmarried, eighteen-year-old sister, were ready to depart. They most likely boarded the *Persia* on the voyage to England, in which case, they would have left New York Harbor on June 18, 1862.[8]

While Sandy and Eilley Bowers were away, life on the Comstock continued as usual. Although Robert Henderson was now a man of eighteen years, the courts still viewed him as a minor. With his legal guardians away in Europe, he could only handle some family matters independently. In August, Robert wanted to sell his mining interest in the Bowers Mining Claim to pay for moving his sixteen-year-old orphaned sister from Salt Lake City to live with him and his older brother James.[9] Being too young to sell his claim, he petitioned the courts to have his brother James appointed as his guardian. With judicial approval and the help of his brother, he then sold his mining interest for $5,700. Elizabeth soon moved to Virginia City.

Before leaving on their trip, the Bowers couple gave former California governor, and now Carson City attorney, J. Neely Johnson, authority to act as their agent in charge of the construction of their mansion. By the beginning of August, Washoe Valley residents began seeing work on the stone structure that would be forever known as Bowers Mansion. Laborers D. D. Matson, J. J. Peck, George Talbot, and Charles Poffle prepared the ground for construction. Two months later, Francis Mackin and James Fitzgerald were cutting granite stone to decorate the front of the structure. In November, Samuel McFarlin and John Collins began preparing lumber for the project.[10]

Throughout this time, the Bowers party was consumed with their tour on the other side of the Atlantic. Unfortunately, aside from travel dates, a letter Sandy wrote to John Oram, Eilley's brother in Scotland, and some stories passed down by friends, few details remain of their European excursion. Many sources described it as elegant and lavish. One account passed down through the Oram family tells of Eilley riding in a carriage and throwing silver coins to the children standing along the streets of Scotland.[11]

Despite the fanciful notion that Eilley hoped to visit Queen Victoria, such a meeting did not take place and was probably never sought. Later folklore would assert that the queen refused to meet with a divorced woman, but a meeting with a traveling American couple without proper credentials would not likely have been granted. During their tour, Sandy and Eilley purchased furniture and decorations for their mansion. They spent a tremendous amount of money and made a lifetime of memories.

By October, Sandy and Eilley had grown weary of traveling. In Sandy's letter to John, he wrote that their health was good except that Eilley and his sister had both been feeling ill. He explained that they would be in Scotland in a few weeks but would only stay a day because they still wanted to visit Ireland, Paris, and Germany. They had recently toured London and had no desire to return anytime soon.[12]

After their nine-month adventure, they returned to the United States aboard the *City of Manchester*, arriving on February 10, 1863. The travelers docked in New York Harbor and then returned to Nevada.[13]

Over time, accounts amplified their European excursion into a great adventure, but stories also attempted to explain one of the strangest additions to their entourage. On returning to Nevada in March 1863, they not only had luxurious furniture, expensive clothes, and elegant jewelry, but they also possessed a mysterious baby girl named Margaret Persia Bowers. To this day, despite decades of endless speculation, no one knows when or how the couple became the parents of this beautiful child. Several stories tell about her birth. The most common account includes an unmarried woman named Margaret giving birth to the baby on June 3, 1862, while sailing aboard the *Persia*. According to this tale, the young mother died from complications from the birth, and Eilley and Sandy took the infant, naming her Margaret Persia after the mother and the ship. Myra Sauer Ratay, in her 1973 history, even claims that Eilley bribed the ship's captain to make no record of the birth, death, or transaction.[14]

Nevertheless, these are just stories without facts to support them. The most apparent discrepancy is that Sandy and Eilley were in New York City on June 3, the supposed date of the birth.[15] Based on newspaper articles of the time, the *Persia* was sailing from Liverpool to New York and did not arrive in New York until June 6.[16] Sandy spoke of an unknown baby in his letter to Eilley's brother when he wrote, "The baby is growing fine but do not think we will bring her with us but do not know yet."[17] They then returned to New York without any mention of a baby.[18] Whatever transpired, they had her with them when they returned to Nevada. Only Eilley and Sandy knew the precise nature of the enigmatic birth, and when they eventually died, they left an enduring mystery. Whatever the circumstance of her birth, Persia arrived in Nevada as the only living child of the Bowers family.

Soon after they returned to Nevada, Sandy was faced with a lawsuit regarding the mansion. Even though the estate was still under construction, two workers prepared to foreclose on a lien for what amounted to less than five hundred dollars.[19] The cause of this legal action went unreported. In any event, Sandy handled the situation, and construction continued.

Sandy and Eilley returned to their Gold Hill home. On arriving there, they found a larger, growing community. Nevada was in its glory, and it appeared that nothing could destroy it. Virginia City had become a significant city, and the Geiger Grade toll road was open, leading directly from the Comstock, north to the Truckee Meadows. Virginia City's gas plant was in operation, allowing gas lights to brighten dark city streets. Grand buildings, hotels, saloons, stores, and churches had been established in the shadow of Mount Davidson. Maguire's Opera House on D Street would soon open, hosting entertainers from around the world.[20]

FIG. 14. After striking it rich, Sandy and Eilley Bowers headed to Europe for a grand excursion. When they returned to Nevada in 1863, they were accompanied by a nine-month-old girl whom they had adopted. This photo of Eilley Bowers shows a superimposed image of Persia in the background. This is the only known image of their daughter as an infant. Courtesy Bowers Mansion photo collection; donated to Bowers Mansion by Crissie Caughlin.

By late summer 1863, Eilley lived the dream of Nevada. She now had everything a thirty-seven-year-old woman could want. Their mine was still producing gold and silver. Their nearly completed mansion was valued at more than $200,000. Together with her husband and daughter, now over a year old, they prepared to move into their new home.[21] The two-story dressed-granite mansion consisted of sixteen rooms finished with Jeffrey pine and Douglas fir. The main entrance hall allowed visitors to pass through the house and into the rear courtyard. To the right of the entry was a staircase with a mahogany handrail that curved as it neared the second floor. To each side of the entry were welcoming parlors. To the south a formal parlor for guests connected to a smaller smoking parlor or library separated by sliding doors. To the north lay a parlor and nursery for the family's private use. Four beautifully handcrafted Carrara marble fireplaces warmed the downstairs, while a plaster of paris frieze border decorated the ceilings, moldings, and medallions above the chandeliers.

To the rear of the main structure lay two ells surrounding a courtyard. The south ell housed a dining room and kitchen with all the most modern amenities, including piped-in hot- and cold-running spring water. The north ell was designed for a ballroom with a small bath and dressing room connected to what may have been intended as a nursery in the main building. Beneath the ballroom housed a stone line wine cellar with a stone floor to allow a cold spring to run beneath the wing keeping the north side of the house cool.

On the second floor, Sandy, Eilley, and Persia each had a suite of rooms, including a bedroom and sitting room. Expensive toys and beautiful dolls filled Persia's playroom. An additional upstairs room housed a luxurious hand-sculptured billiard table for the entertainment of guests. Ascending to the next level was an octagonal cupola, an observatory offering a 360-degree view of the valley and surrounding hills. Inside the glass room contained a center table, chairs, and a rocking chair which could be used by Eilley and little Persia.[22] Alcoves and china closets added to the mansion's elegance. Two to four large windows with French plate glass and built-in shutters lit each room. At night, kerosene lanterns and candles illuminated the beautiful mansion, which was grander than any other house in Nevada Territory at the time.

Washoe Valley had changed dramatically since the days when the Cowans farmed the land in the 1850s. The mining industry overtook the quiet Franktown community. A $250,000 stamp mill was now refining Comstock ores. At the same time, two large lumber mills operated just south of Washoe Lake and helped supply Virginia City with its increasing need for timber from the Sierra Nevada. About one mile northeast of the mansion, the new town of Ophir boasted an ore mill, costing $500,000 and featuring seventy-two stamps and 165 employees. More than 300 residents now lived and worked there, centering on the mill owned by the Ophir Mining Company of Virginia City. Saloons, stores, a post office, a blacksmith shop, law offices, and other businesses essential for a town now thrived near Eilley's home.[23]

FIG. 15. This photo of Bowers Mansion was taken soon after construction was complete in 1863. Only two early photos of the mansion exist, apparently captured on the same day. This depicts an unknown event held at the estate. Courtesy Bowers Mansion photo collection; donated to Bowers Mansion by Ben H. Farquar.

With the cutting of Ophir Grade and the Washoe and Virginia Road, it was possible to travel from Gold Hill to Washoe Valley in only a few hours. The new road passed right behind the Bowers Mine and mill above Gold Hill. It then took the Washoe and Virginia cutoff near the tollhouse, connecting with the route known today as Jumbo Grade, off East Lake Boulevard in Washoe Valley.[24] The $75,000, mile-long Dall's, or Ophir, Toll Bridge, or causeway, allowed people, wagons, timber, and ore to cross the marshy ground at the north end of Washoe Lake.[25] From the town of Ophir, travelers had a short jaunt to the mansion, and this meant that Sandy and Eilley could live comfortably in the valley while still attending to mining affairs in Gold Hill.

Soon after the couple moved into the mansion, Dr. Simeon Bishop and his family passed through the valley while immigrating to Nevada.

FIG. 16. Washoe Valley grew quickly after the birth of Virginia City in 1859. Towns such as Franktown and Ophir flourished during the boom years. This 1864 lithograph by Grafton Brown shows the mill of the Ophir Silver Mining Co., about one-half mile northeast of the mansion. Courtesy Special Collections and University Archives Department, University of Nevada, Reno.

The Bishops' daughter, Ella, was only three months old when they stopped at the mansion. Years later, Ella Bishop would recount to her husband, Nevada journalist Wells Drury, that her family received "a hearty welcome [from Eilley], who was ever a lover of children. When she heard me fretting, she gathered me up in her large, capable arms and directed, 'Sandy, you go right out and get milk from that Jersey cow of ours. This child must have rich milk.'"[26] The Bishop and Bowers families remained friends after that. Their children frequently played with Persia. In 1866, when Simeon's wife, Rowena Bishop, gave birth, she named her new baby girl Persia.[27]

With the Bowers family living in Washoe Valley, Robert and his brother James chose to remain in Gold Hill, where they continued working for the Bowers Mining Company.[28] Robert was now an adult and independent of the Bowers's parental responsibilities.

Over the year, Sandy slowed his buying and selling of mining interests. He only sold twenty-five feet of mining land for $800 and paid $15,000 for twenty-seven feet of mining claim and 160 acres of farm and timberland in Washoe Valley. Eilley, on the other hand, was busy as an investor. She made three separate transactions totaling thirty feet for $1,700.[29] Sandy and Eilley Bowers also helped the widow Plato gain control of her husband's mine after his death. The combined claims became known as the Bowers and Plato Company.[30]

By this time, their mine also appeared to be producing less silver. In November 1863, Sandy and Eilley borrowed $40,000 from Wells Fargo Bank at 3 percent interest. For collateral, they put up their twenty feet of mining ground, a steam quartz mill, machinery, two houses, a blacksmith shop, a barn, a retorting and smelting house, and other buildings and tenements near their mine. The bank only allowed six months to repay the money before borrowers would forfeit their property.[31] Later that month, the Bowers's property incorporated the Bowers Gold and Silver Mining Company. Beginning on November 14, anyone could buy stock in the Bowers Mine for only $500 a share. Sandy sold 1,600 shares for a total market value of $800,000.[32]

In these early prosperous days of Nevada Territory, not everyone searched for their fortunes below ground. Some just took it. Highway robbers worked the roads and trails leading to and from Virginia City. Stages were their primary targets, but robbers also watched for private wagons.[33] One cold December day, the Bowers' extraordinary luck changed when they were returning from Virginia City and encountered highway robbers. The bandits robbed them of $12.50, the equivalent of four days' work for an average salaried miner.[34] For the millionaires, it was an insignificant amount, but it seemed to anticipate a bleak future and the incident became a memory that Eilley kept with her.

Nevada had a fairytale beginning and a tremendous early heyday, but the Comstock's first phase of glory eventually ended. After the winter of 1863–1864, the Comstock boom began fading when it appeared the massive vein had played out. The following June, the couple's $40,000 loan from Wells Fargo came due, and they were on the verge of losing everything. Sandy borrowed another $40,000 from Nicholas Luning of San Francisco to pay the loan and save the mine. Sandy gave the same mine and property that he had already promised the Wells Fargo Bank for collateral. Two days later, he paid Wells Fargo in full.[35]

It seemed the Little Gold Hill Mines had reached the end of their rich ore body. Many owners used tunnels connected far beneath the ground to consolidate operations and reduce costs, but Sandy continued using his hoisting works as he tried to save the mine. Perhaps to fund the ongoing operation, on June 18 Sandy sold some of his lands to the neighboring Imperial Mining Company for $2,000.

By the fall of 1864, the toll of a lingering war was being felt in the East, and yet the conflict was going in favor of the North. Nevadans were able to read about Sheridan's recent victory in Virginia, Grant's power over Richmond, the large fleet off the coast of Charleston, and the Rebels' retreat from Georgia.[36] With the tide shifting to the Union, President Lincoln was sure to win the next election. He believed Nevada's support could help him with his plans for a second term, constitutional amendments, and rebuilding the country. To strengthen the Northern cause, he signed a proclamation recognizing Nevada's statehood on October 31, 1864.

At 1 o'clock that afternoon, Governor James W. Nye sent a telegram to various Nevada newspapers stating, "The pain is over, the child is born. Let us see that Nevada is not only in the Union but for the Union." The *Gold Hill Daily News* simply ran an article in bold-faced type, "NEVADA IS A STATE—Nine cheers for the silver state."[37]

Nevada supporters of Lincoln and of General George B. McClellan, his Democratic opponent, marched and held rallies to voice their opinions about the election, only a matter of days later. Sandy Bowers spoke, declaring that he did not support the present administration. He felt the rights of the Southern people ought to be "pertected" and as "a Northern man, with Northern man's rights," he thought he had the right to say so.[38]

Several McClellan supporters marched before the election, but on November 8, Nevada showed loyalty to the Union by giving the majority of its votes to Lincoln. Finally, on November 11, the long wait was over. The *Gold Hill News* reported, "Mr. Lincoln will, if he lives, be the President of the United States until March 4, 1869."[39]

With statehood achieved and the election over, mining again became the people's top priority. By the end of 1864, it seemed that the gold and silver ore was exhausted, causing the Comstock to enter its first depression.[40] By year's end, the new federal Internal Revenue Service tried to sell the Bowers Mine for taxes and penalties amounting to $3,600.78, but for the moment, the couple was successful in keeping their mine.[41]

Sandy soon gave up his right to operate his mine when Henry Donnelly and James Wright paid him $1 for the privilege of doing the work. They gave Sandy a third of the ore taken from the property while keeping the other two-thirds for their effort. This agreement lasted for six months.[42]

For the other Little Gold Hill Mines, 1865 did not start with the usual bang that they had come to expect. At 7 a.m., on March 5, 1865, the Imperial, Eclipse, and Empire, three of the neighbors of the Bowers property, experienced a devastating cave-in. It began at the line of the Imperial and extended as far south as the Challenge Mine. The ground above shook so hard that the engines of the Empire and Eclipse hoisting works broke, and rubble filled the upper levels of the three mines. The crash threw stones from three hundred feet below ground up to the roof of the Imperial building. Heavy timbers crushed like shattered eggshells. The six acres surrounding the engine houses and buildings sunk two or three feet on the surface. More than one hundred men were underground at the time, yet no one died.[43]

On Tuesday morning, April 11, residents received good news. Two days earlier, on Palm Sunday, General Robert E. Lee surrendered at Appomattox Court House. The war was ending. Comstock writer Dan De Quille recalled that all the bells and whistles in the city rang at noon. Local newspapers quickly printed an extra and agreed to issue no paper the following day. Within three hours, it seemed most of the residents were drunk and that they remained so throughout the night. Soldiers from nearby Fort Churchill came to the Comstock and fired two cannons in the streets, where flags flew everywhere. Anvils, pistols, and everything else that could make noise did so.[44] It was a celebration unlike any ever seen in the streets of Virginia City.

Four days later, a telegram came over the wires telling of Lincoln's assassination. Everything turned dark and gloomy as all the local shops and saloons closed. The same bells that rang in joy now tolled in mourning. Flags that flew in victory now hung at half-staff. Both the *Enterprise* and *Union* ran extras with the details of Lincoln's death. Journalist Alfred Doten recorded in his journal that "knots of people gathered everywhere—everybody seemed at a loss of what to do, or think, or say."[45]

While the country mourned, Nevadans began to accept the fact that the earth below the Comstock seemed to have given all it could. As Mark Twain discovered during his days as a Nevada miner, it may have been easy to get rich in this country, but it was not easy to remain so.[46]

The end of the Civil War brought about many changes in the West. The construction of railroads, the rise of the cattle industry, and the opening of far-flung mining districts brought even more people in search of opportunity. The new American West transformed in the years to follow while Eilley's Comstock seemed to be dying slowly.

During 1865, the depression of the mining district deepened. As Myron Angel's history would describe, "In the opinion of many, ruin and general desertion of the town was apparent. Residents moved entire houses to more promising communities. Some went to Meadow Lake and some even to Reese River."[47] Many mine and mill owners were unable to continue operations, forcing them to turn to banks for loans. William Sharon, manager of the Bank of California, was willing to risk loaning money to people who had no realistic means of paying him back. The once free-spending Sandy Bowers joined the ranks of risktakers when he, too, took a loan from the mighty Sharon.[48]

At the time of the loan, the Bowers Mine reached a depth of four hundred and fifty feet and produced eighteen tons of ore daily. The mine superintendent, William Bewick, oversaw thirteen employees. The Bowers's Thistle Mill also continued production. It had twenty stamps and thirty-five feet of amalgamating pans. A sixty-five-horsepower steam engine crushed twenty-two tons of ore per day. James Livingston supervised the mill and fourteen employees.[49]

By November, Sandy again contracted to have other people work his mine, allowing them to take some of the proceeds. This time he held an injunction to stop the work because his ground was again beginning to yield a more valuable ore than previously taken from the mine, and the arrangement to share profits now worked against Bowers. Unfortunately, miners quickly exhausted this ore pocket. Over the next year, gold and silver yields from the Bowers and other partners in the Little Gold Hill Mine declined while expenses continued to accrue. It seemed that the only solution was to excavate deeper into the earth to find more ore. In January 1866, the combined Imperial and Empire mine began building a hoist work large enough to accommodate several nearby mines. Before the year ended, the neighboring Eclipse mine also improved its investment by overhauling its hoisting works.[50]

In late December, Sandy paid off his loan to William Sharon.[51] Then on January 7, 1867, he borrowed $100,000 from George Waters. Sandy offered his twenty feet of mining and all his Gold Hill properties for collateral. He was to pay $12,013 a month for eight months plus interest. This transaction became the beginning of financial matters that would bring about the fall of the Bowers empire.[52]

That spring, Sandy prepared for a prospecting expedition. Concerned that he might have an accident, he decided to prepare a will. The couple went to the Carson City home of J. Neely Johnson, their agent during the building of their mansion, to sign the will. Sandy left his entire estate to Eilley. After her death, their daughter, Persia, would inherit everything.[53]

Upon safely returning from his trip, Sandy moved back to Gold Hill to work and help save the failing Bowers Mine. On August 4, 1867, the new Imperial and Empire hoisting works were up and partially enclosed. By the end of the year, most of the original Little Gold Hill Mines tried to cut costs by using either the new Imperial and Empire or the improved Eclipse shafts and hoisting works.[54]

For several years, the Bank of California maintained an economic stranglehold on the Comstock. As 1867 ended, William Sharon and his financial institution had foreclosed on many mills, mines, and other properties on the Comstock. Much of the mining district had shifted from independent ownership to the monopolistic control of the "Bank Crowd."[55]

By the beginning of 1868, the Bowers and Plato Mine had completed work on a new shaft that took them months to excavate. It descended 150 feet and was almost eight feet wide. To add to their financial difficulties, they were delinquent in paying their property taxes. Complicating matters, heavy spring flooding in 1868 followed the brutal winter. Their "Thistle Mill" was inundated and temporarily stopped production. Sandy immediately began working to repair the building and its operation. Unfortunately, the cold, damp atmosphere added to an increasing lung complaint brought about by years of working in the mining industry.[56]

With his fortune lost and health failing fast, Sandy decided to sell the Bowers Mine. George Waters, to whom he was already in debt, offered to help. On April 9, 1868, local newspapers advertised the sale of all the ore from the five-hundred-foot level to the surface and half interest in the hoisting works. He also announced the lease of the newly repaired stamp mill with everything in complete running order. A few years earlier, this would have been an excellent opportunity.[57] In 1868, no one seemed interested in such an investment.

The sale of his mine did not come soon enough. At one o'clock in the morning on April 21, 1868, Lemuel Sanford Bowers, aged thirty-five, died at his home in Crown Point Ravine, Gold Hill, Nevada. As the local newspaper reported, "But alas for healthy hopes and expectations! Death—the conqueror of all mankind, has come and cut him down in the midst of

FIG. 17. Henry Riter donated a painting of Sandy Bowers to the mansion. The artist and date are unknown, but the painting still hangs in the north parlor. Courtesy the Bowers Mansion photo collection.

his usefulness, his hopes, and his ambitions—and our friend and neighbor is no more. A few short hours and all that is mortal of him will be covered with clods of the valley, and to sleep that long sleep that knows no waking."[58] His body lay in state at the Masonic Hall of the Silver Star Lodge No. 5 in Gold Hill, for he had been a member of the fraternal organization. After the Masonic Order performed its solemn funeral service, a half-mile-long "funeral cortege moved up Main Street to the Bullion at the junction of the Ophir Grade. Most of the procession was dismissed."[59] From there, Sandy crossed the Virginia Range, west into Washoe Valley and returned to his home where Eilley and Freemasons laid him to rest in the hill behind the mansion.

A reporter from the *Eastern Slope* newspaper recalled: "One of the fortunate few, he from poverty became an immensely wealthy man. He expended his money generously, perhaps lavishly, but never in the pride of prosperity has he forgotten or turned away from early friends. Honorable in his dealings, true to his friends, and accessible to all, he commanded the love of his neighbors during his life, their tears in his untimely death."[60]

CHAPTER 6

Bowers Mansion Resort

TWO WEEKS AFTER SANDY'S DEATH in the spring of 1868, an unrelated event occurred just twenty miles north of Eilley's home, forever changing her mansion. In April of that year, Myron C. Lake sold some land on the north side of the Truckee River to Charles Crocker, superintendent of the Central Pacific Railroad. The railroad then auctioned off lots, giving birth to Reno. Lake's Crossing had been a small community featuring a ferry service and toll bridge used by emigrants since 1859, but this new development eclipsed what went before.[1] With the railroad, western Nevada was now more closely connected to San Francisco, and within a year it would be linked to the rest of the nation via the transcontinental railroad.

Eilley had no time to consider the changes that were occurring around her. At forty-one, she needed to deal with Sandy's estate. On May 8, 1868, the court of the First Judicial District of Storey County gave notice that Alison S. Bowers had proposed that the last will and testament of Lemuel S. Bowers be admitted to probate. The judge declared Eilley as the sole executor of her husband's holdings.[2]

After settling Sandy's affairs, Eilley continued taking care of the family business. In July, she hired experienced amalgamator John W. Hogan to supervise the Bowers and Plato mine and mill. By early September, her efforts paid off when he exhibited three silver and gold bricks on the counter of the California Bank. The bullion, the product of eight days of work at the Bowers mill, had a value of $6,000. It was a welcome sight since the Bowers property had been unproductive for a month or two. Although Nevada was still suffering from its lingering depression, the Bowers Mine once again produced valuable ore.[3] Unfortunately, the mine's new success was not enough to repay Eilley's debts and mortgages, and she finished the year in financial decline.

Although the beginning of 1869 showed little improvement for Eilley and the mining community, February did bring new hope to Nevada with the construction of the Virginia & Truckee Railroad. William Sharon of the Bank of California controlled the finances behind the railway, which would connect the mines of Virginia with the Carson River Mills and Carson City and eventually with Reno and the transcontinental railroad.[4]

Eilley suffered another loss the morning of June 17 when the Thistle Mill was destroyed by fire. It only took a short time for the building to be ablaze. Nearby fire departments tried to rescue the building but were only able to save structures near the mill, which was unsalvageable. It had not been operational for several months and was only insured for $16,000. George Waters, a friend and financial backer of Sandy's, held a mortgage on the mill and helped Eilley by lending her $5,000 to make repairs. This loan only increased her debt to him.[5]

On November 12, 1869, a train appeared on the newly completed Crown Point Trestle, just east of the Bowers's old mill site. A grand celebration with champagne marked the occasion. Regular trains began traveling between Gold Hill and Carson City on December 21. This incredible engineering feat was astonishing. The curvy railroad right-of-way made the equivalent of seventeen complete circles as it covered twenty-one miles and rose 1,575 feet, with an average grade of 2.2 percent. Because of the hilly landscape, there were few like it in the United States.[6]

At the time, the railroad would have little effect on Eilley. Her financial situation was in such a state that she considered selling the Bowers Mine. In November 1869, she appeared in court and petitioned for the right to sell her mill, the Gold Hill home that she had shared with Sandy, and all other Gold Hill assets, including the mine. The court granted her request, although it delayed the sale for seven months.[7]

As she waited, her financial problems continued. With the mine no longer a source of income, she turned to Bowers Mansion as her only asset. By returning to her roots in keeping a boardinghouse, she understood how she could earn extra money by charging people and organizations for the use of her home. New Year's Eve brought hope for Eilley when she offered the mansion to the wealthy of Washoe County with a grand ball to promote women's rights.[8]

Participants arrived from the surrounding towns and farms in wagons and buggies. The elegant affair lasted until early in the morning, and many who attended gave it high praise. However, one newspaper correspondent showed his concerns about the occasion. He wrote, "If the doctrine of Woman's rights is carried to its utmost limit, instead of regarding woman 'as nearer angel than men,' we shall lose that regard for them which now almost invests them with divinity. If she is to be our rival in the forum, our competitor on this mark, she can scarcely strew with fresh flowers the narrow way of life, and be a comfort to solace at the same time."[9]

Despite the criticism, Eilley could count her effort a success, and she soon gave another dance, this one in honor of Washington's Birthday. Again, the ball was a thriving affair with about forty couples attending. The guests danced throughout the night, and the party finally retired at 6:30 a.m.[10]

With the mansion now serving as Eilley's primary source of income, she made improvements to allow her home to open as a resort and boarding house. By the 1870 census report, Eilley and Persia, now eight years old, had five other people living with them. Aside from returning to her previous occupation, she also entertained her guests with her psychic ability, as she was reported to have done during the early days of the territory. In late June, according to the *Territorial Enterprise*, a San Francisco correspondent gave Eilley the first-rate notice as a prophetess, but then the Nevada newspaper also made Eilley a victim of pre-tabloid news by publishing a story about her rise and fall.[11] From that point on, Eilley spent the rest of her life as an entertaining subject for idle newspaper reporters with nothing better to fill their columns.

Despite the adverse news reports, Eilley managed to use the papers to her advantage. She increased the use of her mansion by publishing advertisements. On July 3, a newspaper reported that her home was ready and open to the public as a place of resort.[12] Resting at the base of the foothills and surrounded by grand old pines, the beautifully landscaped grounds included greenhouse shrubbery and a flower garden. Guests used and admired two manufactured lakes, filled with natural hot and cold spring water, just a few steps from the mansion. Their mineral waters were reputed to have medicinal properties, and a physician made himself available for the benefit of ailing guests. The splendid mansion interior still included such luxuries as a delicate rosewood piano, an extensive library, a billiard table, and all the comforts of home. Eilley arranged the mansion suites for the convenience of families or single persons and served meals at any hour.

Eilley spared no expense in making the mansion the "Carlsbad of Nevada," as one reporter described it, referring to the famed spa in central Europe. The article indicated that "the medicinal properties of these mineral waters are unequaled. An experienced physician will be in attendance to wait upon such as many require his services. No pains or expenses will be spared."[13] To help exhibit her improvements, she planned a Fourth of July ball. Unable to complete the needed work, she postponed the celebration.[14]

While Eilley continued working on the mansion, her official career as a mine owner ended in July, when George Waters bought the Bowers Mining Company for $10,000. The money only paid a few debts. By this time, she owed nearly $43,000.[15] Eilley still held several small mining claims, but the famous Bowers Mine was no longer hers.

The beginning of the new decade proved gloomy for the Comstock and northern Nevada. Mine production slowed, stock prices fell, and stockholders withdrew their investments. Eilley and her surrounding community led a quiet existence for the next couple of years. Some mines paid, but the profit was not enough to build excitement. Eilley continued as resort hostess, restaurant manager, and boardinghouse keeper, but she only hosted two small picnics during the summer of 1872.[16]

Many Virginia City residents tried to rebuild and expand, to save their faltering community during those quiet years. With Reno growing as a new railway town, the V&T Railroad began the extension from Carson to the Truckee River. On August 24, 1872, workers drove the last spike.[17] The railroad now connected Virginia City, Carson City, Washoe Valley, Bowers Mansion, and Reno to each other and the rest of the nation. That October, passenger cars began running between Virginia City and Reno.

The train regularly left the Virginia City station and headed south through Gold Hill to Mound House, where it connected to the Carson River. There, it delivered ore to mills while taking passengers and other cargo along the route, which linked up with Empire and Carson City, then headed north to Washoe Valley. The train passed by the quiet community of Franktown, Bowers Mansion, and the dying towns of Ophir and Washoe City, their revenue cut off by cheaper milling along the Carson River. After forty miles of travel, it reached Steamboat Springs, which was only six miles to the west from Virginia City as the crow flies. The four-hour journey ended at the Reno Depot.[18]

As fall came to Washoe Valley, Eilley was again robbed, this time losing a $200 gold watch and seeming to symbolize her overall troubles. Eilley's finances continued sliding, and she soon found the need to sell

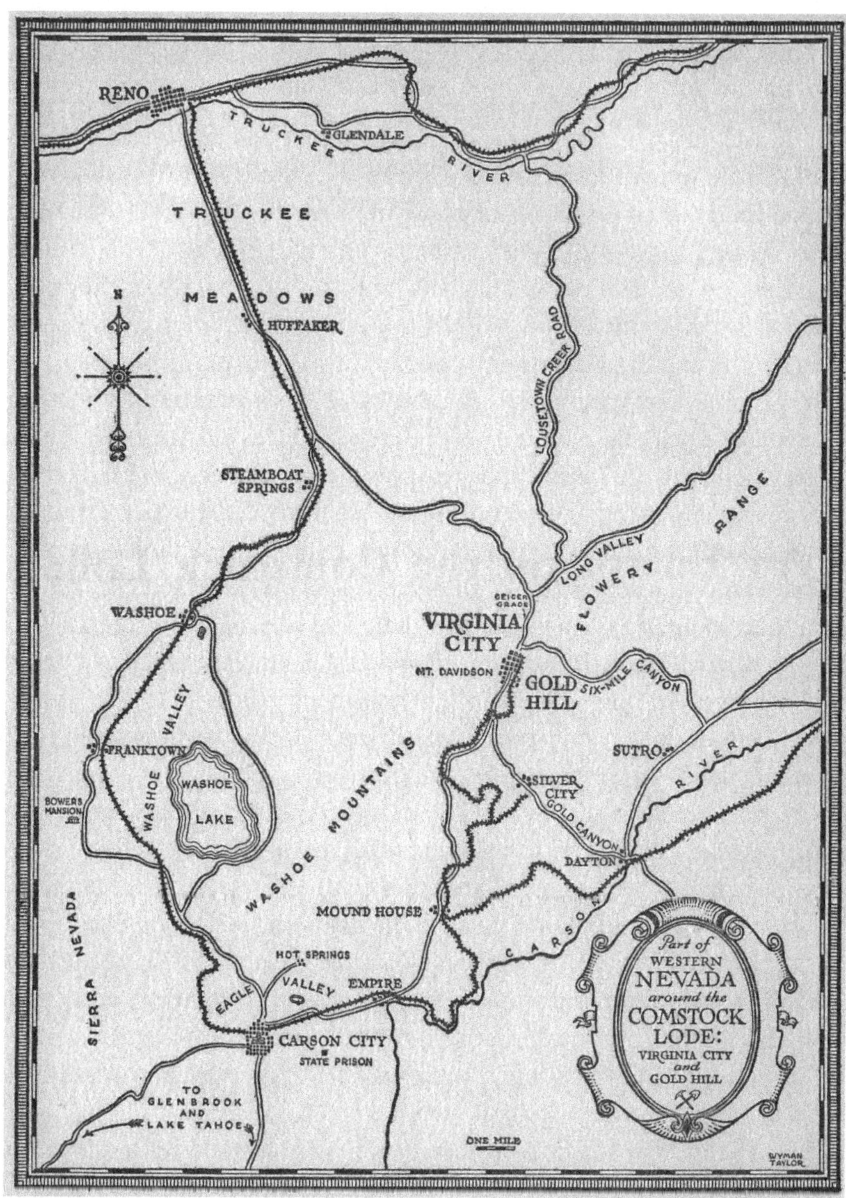

FIG. 18. The route of the Virginia & Truckee Railroad passed Bowers Mansion about a half mile to the east, allowing passengers easy access to the resort for picnics and swimming excursions. From Wells Drury, *An Editor on the Comstock Lode* (1948); courtesy Ronald M. James, private collection.

her beloved mansion. When the Nevada Legislature considered establishing a mental institution, Eilley offered to sell her home for $30,000. The legislature denied her proposal.[19]

March 1873 brought new life to northern Nevada when the Virginia Consolidated Mine found a fifteen-foot ore vein.[20] This discovery began the greatest boom in the colorful history of the Comstock Lode. The "Silver Kings," John Mackay, James Fair, James Flood, and William O'Brien, owned the mine, and with this and other strikes, they soon became wealthy mine owners and some of the richest men in the world. The days of the Big Bonanza had begun.

Virginia City was on the rise, even as Eilley's fortunes declined. At the end of April, she agreed to offer her mansion as a prize in a raffle, all to pay her debts.[21] Public raffles were popular at the time, making this a promising endeavor. Eilley and her manager needed to sell forty thousand tickets at $2.50 each to pay off the expenses of the raffle, cover her debts and begin a new life. With more than three hundred gifts offered at a total value of $350,000, Eilley's raffle was sure to be a success.

In May, William Thompson, Myron C. Lake's stepson-in-law became the "Bowers Mansion Grand Gift Entertainment" manager. He set September 1, 1873, as the day of the drawing. Prizes included seventy-seven coins ranging in value from $100 to $1,000, thirteen diamonds worth from $300 to $5,000, nineteen silver pieces ranging from $25 to $1,000, and twelve oil paintings with an estimated value of $1,000 to $3,000.[22] Other enticements included her piano, billiard table, sculptures, 148 acres of land, and most of her valuable belongings, with the mansion itself as the grand prize.

With the raffle being advertised, picnic weather in May led to the beginning of a successful entertaining season. Large outdoor gatherings were popular during the booming summer months. With the extension of the railroad and the newly completed water stop at Franktown, Eilley's home became a prime destination for grand excursions.

On Saturday, May 17, the season began with the Odd Fellows Picnic.[23] The following Saturday, a Reno Sunday School picnic visited the mansion. A band accompanied the celebrants who filled four train cars. They danced and ate plenty of delicious food. Newspapers reported that everyone had a splendid time. Eilley Bowers "exerted herself to make the scene one of perfect enchantment and proved herself the estimable hostess."[24]

Eilley began June by hosting another Odd Fellows Picnic, followed the next day by a gathering of the Emmett Guard, an Irish unit from Virginia

City. Both were great successes.[25] One guest was pleased with the beauty of the mansion, its splendid surroundings, and the possibility of winning it all: "Knowing as I do that this lottery is not a sham gotten up by a thieving company to swindle the public; that all the prizes are desirable, I shall surely invest."[26] At another picnic, Eilley opened the mansion to the guests. Several of those who attended enjoyed picking out the prizes that they would surely win.[27] The rest of June and July passed without any significant events except for an Episcopal Church picnic that used the mansion grounds. Eilley quietly ran her resort while advertising the Grand Gift Entertainment.

In early August, Eilley hosted another grand picnic, this one for the Washington Guard, a Cornish unit from the Comstock. Before the event, the *Gold Hill News* advertised that "Mrs. Bowers has been notified of the arrangements, and will entertain the members of the company and their friends in handsome style. The Bowers' *cuisine* is the best in the State, and at the mansion can always be found the finest of liquors, wines, and cigars."[28] Attendees prepared for the grandest event of the season thus far. When the day came, eight-passenger and platform cars left Gold Hill at 7:45 a.m. They carried about six hundred excursionists and a band. More picnickers joined them in Carson. At 11 a.m., the train pulled into Franktown Station, and the passengers disembarked. Eilley told the Guard officers that her house was at their disposal. She then ordered a magnificent lunch spread for the picnickers.[29]

Croquet grounds, foot racing, shooting, archery, and dancing were available for everyone's enjoyment. The *Gold Hill News* observed that the ladies "tripped the light fantastic" to their content. The men held a target-shooting contest. The women also joined an archery contest, although most had never shot a bow and arrow before. A Washoe Zephyr, a local name for ferocious winds, blew through the valley, complicating things as their targets fell to the ground.[30] As evening came, the happy excursionists reboarded the train and returned home. Eilley remained behind and began preparations for the next picnic that Saturday.

The Miner's Union Picnic was always the grandest of the season. Several days before the 1873 extravaganza, the *Gold Hill News* built up the excitement for the excursion by stating that the ladies were already preparing their garments and hats. Inexpensive picnic hats covered with white Swiss and green ribbons seemed most popular. The Belcher, Crown Point, Imperial, and several other large mines declared Saturday a holiday and granted their workers the day off. When Saturday arrived, men, women, children, and families crowded the main street with their lunch baskets as they waited for their departure. Two V&T trains arrived with fifteen elaborately decorated cars. The National Guard Band entertained the almost two thousand passengers. In Carson City, they added eleven more cars and joined the two trains. This addition created the longest train ever to pass through Washoe Valley.[31]

As celebrants arrived at the mansion, their "amicable and bustling hostess," Eilley Bowers, greeted them. Lunch was the first activity as picnickers quickly filled the grounds.[32] Again, Eilley opened her mansion to her guests so that they could admire the fine building with its magnificent furniture, beautiful pictures, and other splendid objects of interest.

The more adventuresome guests bathed in the swimming ponds, swung under the trees, waltzed on the dance floor, and generally had a good time. The only complaint was that Washoe Lake was too far away and very shallow. At five that evening, the almost three thousand guests boarded the twenty-six-car train, mounted their horses, or climbed into their wagons as they departed from the grandest event of the year.[33]

With the picnic season nearing its end, the Grand Gift Entertainment became the only major event on the calendar. When the day finally came, Thompson postponed the raffle. They had not reached the forty-thousand-ticket goal. He rescheduled the raffle for October 15 while continuing to run daily advertisements.[34] Eilley now needed the money more than ever. The *Nevada State Journal* announced that her tax bill was one of the largest in the county. She owed $12,065 in taxes. Later that month, she applied for a reduction of the assessed value on her property, lowering her bill to more than $9,000.[35]

October brought the end of any hope of a raffle when Thompson officially withdrew the Grand Gift Entertainment. He admitted that the enterprise failed and offered to pay dollar for dollar on every ticket purchased. The *Carson Daily Appeal* had a notion that Eilley would live to rejoice over the fact that she did not lose her home in the raffle.[36] Time proved them right in their assumption.

With borders and guests constantly at the mansion, the party-type atmosphere was unsuitable for raising an eleven-year-old child. Eilley sent Persia to live in Reno and attend public school.[37] Eilley spent the rest of the year alone.

Even with all her past difficulties, she retained possession of her

CAPITAL GIFT, $30,000!

(Being the Bowers' Mansion, Lands and Furniture.)

One Hundred other Gifts, Aggregating $70,000!

BOWERS' MANSION—$100,000 00

This TICKET entitles the holder to admission to the GRAND CONCERT AND GIFT ENTERTAINMENT, to be given at the

Bowers' Mansion, Washoe County, Nevada, September 1st, 1873.

And to such Gift as may be drawn by this number.

TICKETS, $2 50 Each. 37431 William Thompson Manager.

FIG. 19. Facing financial difficulties, Eilley Bowers sought to rid herself of the burden represented by the mansion. With the help of William Thompson, a Grand Gift Entertainment raffle was devised in 1873. This is one of the surviving tickets for the fundraiser that was eventually canceled, leaving her with the property for a while longer. Courtesy Nevada Historical Society.

mansion. As 1874 began, Eilley started making more improvements to attract additional guests to her home. She built a thirty-by-one-hundred-foot dance hall just north of the house and laid out new croquet grounds for the enjoyment of her visitors. In early May, she opened her mansion to the public. With refreshments of all kinds available and newly renovated picnic grounds accessible for all, local newspapers proclaimed the estate the loveliest and most accommodating resort on the Pacific Coast.[38]

At the time, Virginia City residents were enjoying the prosperity of the Big Bonanza. Excitement was high as wealth spread throughout the region, and people spent money freely. The Miners Union of Silver City wanted to celebrate by having a picnic at the mansion on May 9. They postponed it because of a spring snowstorm. The delay proved beneficial since crews had time to construct a new road between Bowers Mansion and Virginia City via the old Ophir Grade.[39]

When the city of Ophir died in the mid-1860s, the Dall's toll road and bridge closed, forcing people to travel from Virginia to Washoe Lake by way of Washoe City. The Marker and Bastian Road now took picnickers from Virginia to Bowers Mansion via Ophir Grade, making the distance only eleven miles, thus saving going around Washoe Lake. This accommodation allowed picnickers to get to the mansion by an easy, shorter route. On May 16, the Miner's Union became the first large group to use this road for its postponed picnic.[40]

On June 1, 1874, Eilley hosted the Champions of the Red Cross, a group that anticipated the modern American Red Cross, dedicated to emergency assistance for people in need. The Carson Brass Band provided the music for the dancers in the spacious pavilion, and the featured event was the grand dress parade. The *Nevada State Journal* reported that throughout the day, Eilley took great pride in making her guests comfortable.[41]

Two days later, the picnic of the Improved Order of Red Men, a fraternal organization, came to the valley. About six hundred members and guests left the Carson City depot at ten o'clock Saturday morning. They arrived at Franktown Station an hour and a half later. The *Carson Daily Appeal* reported that "the day was spent in dancing, promenading and love-making by the younger ones, while the older portion lolled lazily on the grass beneath the cool shade of the poplar and the pines." As usual, Eilley kindly opened her home to all who asked. The mansion and grounds were still impressive, yet some attendees noticed signs of neglect.[42]

The following Saturday brought Eilley's peers to the mansion when the Pacific Coast Pioneers with more than four thousand men, women, and children celebrated their First Grand Annual Picnic Excursion, intended to honor early settlers of Nevada and California. People came by horse, carriage, and train from Reno, Carson City, Gold Hill, and Virginia City to be part of the grand festivity. Picnickers ate and danced while the old-timers sang everything from the "The Star-Spangled Banner" to "Praise God from Whom All Blessings Flow." Participants declared the event was "the most enjoyable picnic ever given in this neighborhood," leaving the public indebted to the host pioneers.[43]

After the visit from her fellow pioneers, Eilley had more than three weeks to prepare for her next big event. During this time, her financial situation forced her to lease the mansion and grounds. William M. Cary, of the Cary House in Placerville, California, became the new manager of the resort, running it as Eilley had previously done. Although Eilley no longer operated the business that used her home, she continued living there and acted as hostess to her guests.[44]

A pleasant event occurred during the three-week break. Persia returned from Reno to visit her mother. At the time, the young girl lived with the Roff family on West Street between First and Second Streets.

FIG. 20. On the second story, Persia had a bedroom and a playroom. Her playroom was once filled with expensive toys and dolls. The small doll carriage in the background is an original toy currently being held at the Nevada Historical Society. Courtesy Bowers Mansion photo collection.

After a short visit, Eilley escorted Persia back to town.[45] Their goodbye was quick, as Eilley needed to prepare for another picnic that Sunday.

On June 12, the Montgomery Guard, yet another Irish unit from the Comstock, visited the mansion, and again the event proved successful. The crowd was not as large as usual, but the *Territorial Enterprise* reported that the guests enjoyed themselves tremendously. Eilley spread tables under the trees and provided a fine banquet. Members danced under the pavilion until five o'clock when the party ended. At the time, Eilley was unaware that her daughter had fallen ill.[46]

Persia had not been feeling well since her return to Reno. Nothing appeared to be serious until Sunday evening, July 12, when her pain became intense. Despite the efforts of the Roff family, nothing helped. The discomfort only worsened, and then on Tuesday evening, July 14, Persia quietly died.[47] Based on the newspaper description, Persia may have had a ruptured appendix, but doctors of the day gave no official cause of death.[48]

FIG. 21. This is the last known photo of Persia Bowers (*right*). Ella Worth (*left*) was a childhood friend of Persia's who lived in Gold Hill and had fond memories of playing together at her parents' home in Gold Hill. Bowers Mansion photo collection; donated by Helen Marye Thomas.

At the time of her passing, a reporter described Persia as "an affectionate and obedient daughter, one of the most congenial and generous of companions, and an obliging, true and devoted friend. Her noble heart and kind, happy disposition, was noticed by all who met her, and her sudden and untimely death saddened all who knew her."[49]

On Thursday, July 17, 1874, Eilley buried Margaret Persia Bowers next to her beloved father on the hillside behind the mansion. A source indicates that young Cora Cross was asked to sing "Holy Angels, Carry Me Home" at the funeral. She recalled the day years later in a letter to mansion superintendent Alice Addenbrooke, "I remember Mrs. Bowers reclining on a couch in the empty big dining room, clad in a calico gown of dark material and color, weeping, while the 'spiritual preacher-woman' bent over her." The Reverend William Lucas of Trinity Episcopal Church of Reno performed the rites, while a Mrs. Brown of Virginia City performed the "spiritual services."[50] At the age of forty-seven, Eilley had lost the last member of her immediate family.

CHAPTER 7

Seeress of Washoe

On August 5, 1874, the Sunday school children of Virginia City, Gold Hill, Reno, and Carson City held a picnic at Eilley's home. A newspaper account described the young people enjoying the day, overlooking the fact that it had been just three weeks since Persia's death. It is only possible to speculate about how the mistress of the mansion felt while watching the many children play in her yard.[1]

The annual Virginia Miners Union Picnic brought more than three thousand guests to the mansion three days later. Several serious incidents marred what should have been a grand event. A young girl's skull was fractured when a wooden swing seat struck her head. A boy almost drowned in the pond. A man trying to save the child cut his foot on a broken bottle. A Paiute man became the hero of the day when he assisted in rescuing the boy. No physician was on hand to help with the injuries.[2]

The following Saturday, the Union Sunday School and the Barbers of Reno visited the mansion. One newspaper reporter complained, half in jest, that the barbers' vacation was an inconvenience for the once-a-week bathers of Reno who only washed on Saturday.[3] This marked the end of the picnic season and any income resulting from picnics until spring. To add to her financial difficulties, Eilley soon found she was once again one of Washoe County's heaviest taxpayers, owing $7,705.[4]

A month later, a new phase of Eilley's life began when an article appearing in the *Territorial Enterprise* informed readers of Eilley's ability to see the future. For the next decade and a half, "The Seeress of Washoe" used her gift of foresight to impress, entertain, and frighten people.[5]

In Eilley's homeland, the Scots commonly practiced crystal ball readings and fortune-telling. During the witch craze two hundred years before Eilley's birth, King James I (who had been King James VI of Scotland)

FIG. 22. By 1874, Eilley's home had been fully transformed into a resort. Eilley's old bedroom and sitting room that once housed bedroom furniture from Europe and window coverings from Paris were now rented as suites for families. Courtesy Bowers Mansion photo collection.

declared crystal gazing a crime. This act almost extinguished the practice, but in the late 1800s, it again became fashionable within the context of the Spiritualism movement.[6]

Eilley's belief in her abilities as a seeress and in communicating with spirits was likely a survivor of Scottish tradition, rather than being born out of the Spiritualism movement. Nevertheless, that nineteenth century interest in the afterlife may have encouraged her belief in supernatural abilities and led people to her door. Employing more of a homegrown approach to the spiritual world, Eilley's "second sight," as the Scots would have called it, was something she might have been cultivating since an early age.[7]

As a seeress, Eilley believed she could contact people in the spirit world. From her point of view, these souls helped her see visions of the past, present, and future. From what is known of traditional practices, it seems that Eilley sat in front of her peepstone and meditated to conjure up a vision. With a question in mind, she concentrated on the idea itself. After a short period, as fortune tellers frequently describe, she might have perceived the orb beginning to cloud, after which she would have believed an image was appearing in the stone.[8] Eilley would then employ a level of intuition to arrive at an answer to the question posed by the client.

As winter approached at the end of 1874, Eilley was visiting some friends in Virginia City when she received a vision. She described an immense ore body at the north end of the Comstock Lode, near the Ophir Mine and beyond. She then said that if she had any money, she would put every cent of it into claims in that direction.[9] Three months later, the *Territorial Enterprise* verified the accuracy of her prediction. Discoveries were indeed pointing north.[10]

The following January, a reporter interviewed the "Washoe Seeress." Eilley said that while staying with a friend in Virginia City, a stranger came to visit. As he stood on the porch, a manifestation began to appear to her. The spirit identified himself as Old Chips, a friend of the man. Eilley described Chips as a jolly, good-natured, reckless, daredevil sort of fellow in his life. He was, however, untidy in dress, greasy, and dirty. The stranger asked her to go on a prospecting journey with him. To this, Eilley perceived that the spirit told her, "Go ahead. I will be with you. I always was a lucky dog, and whether I am in heaven, on earth, or in hell, I shall be lucky in discovering minerals that are hid in the ground." Eilley then saw the manifestations of another, a Dr. Gaston. He said, "We want you to serve us. Don't annoy yourself about your financial troubles. We will bring you out all right." Accompanied by her ethereal friends, she agreed to join the prospecting expedition.[11]

While traveling along what they said was an Indian trail in a northwesterly direction, Sandy's spirit came to her and said, "Ma, you are bearing too far to the northwest." The group consequently shifted the path and soon came to the spot identified by her spirit friends. She found the place that looked just as the spirits had described. About a mile and a half farther along, Eilley became fatigued and wished to rest. It is here where she seemed possessed by the spirit of a Catholic priest. She began singing a Catholic hymn in Latin and made the sign of the cross. This action seemed strange to her travel companions since she was not Catholic, nor did she know Latin.[12]

She predicted that they would establish an important mine named Wells Fargo and that there was ore underground from the Sierra Nevada to the Wells Fargo and beyond. She then declared plenty of ore all around and even underneath the Catholic cemetery. The reporter finally asked her why she did not make predictions for herself and get out of her financial situation. She said that her circumstances made it impossible to act on the insights gained from the spirit world. At one time, she tried to sell her silverware to earn enough money to buy some shares in the Ophir, but no broker was willing to purchase the items even at half its value. She also did not wish any of her friends to buy stock upon the strength of her prediction. She said, "I give them as they are given me. My only object is to benefit our people all I can."[13]

Six days after the *Territorial Enterprise* printed the interview, another article warned people to beware of such a prospecting method. "Give honor to whom it is due" was the headline that tried to bring people back to the reality of truth and science as a means of locating ore.[14] Despite this advice, some people continued to believe the prophetess.

In March 1875, Eilley was again in court over mining property. Sandy had owned a little over ten feet of the Atchinson claim when he died, and Eilley retained this interest as his executrix. Earlier, the Mexican Gold and Silver Mining Company ignored her ownership of the mining land and tried to possess it. The company owners refused to let her enter the property, and they denied her the rights to the profits from the ore. Eilley finally won the suit and maintained possession of her part of the Atchinson claim.[15]

Even with her notoriety as a fortune teller and her ownership of several small mining interests, Eilley's priority was her mansion. She remained optimistic and hired construction crews to begin renovating the mansion. This time, she spent $8,000 to change the entire structure of the building by adding a third floor. The expansion included fourteen extra rooms. Eight rooms were above the main house, and three others were over each of the wings projecting to the rear. Eilley hoped the spare rooms would bring in additional borders and income.[16]

Over the winter, she also prepared for the upcoming picnic season. Eilley's outdoor improvements included several new conveniences for her guests. She built a 110-by-165-foot dance floor surrounded by shade trees. She paid for a smooth, level road leading directly from the railroad to the mansion entrance. New walks covered the grounds, and she had them watered before each event to prevent her guests from getting dusty. Additional safety precautions included sheriff deputies attending her most significant events.[17]

FIG. 23. In 1875, Eilley concluded that fourteen additional rooms would increase revenue. A new third story (shown here in 1880) failed to solve the problem and only increased her debt, contributing to the eventual loss of the mansion. Courtesy Special Collections and University Archives Department, University of Nevada, Reno.

June was a successful month for large-scale events at the mansion. Organizations booked every Saturday and even one Thursday. Eilley made sure each celebration included fine music for dancing, plenty of food, and shady places to eat. When describing Eilley and the pioneer picnic, the *Carson Daily Appeal* wrote, "There is the cheer which comes from the heart of the good old wife that dwells by the trees that grace the scenes which surround the house that Sandy built. Of all the places in the world, Sandy Bowers' old home is the spot where this picnic should be held."[18]

While the picnic season flourished, rumors spread about the mansion's sale. The *Nevada State Journal* reported that the liquor firm of Kelly, Henderson, and Gilchrist bought the estate, but this proved untrue. Although Eilley still owned the mansion, it was under new management. A woman appearing in the records as "Mrs. Hunt" began managing the resort for John F. Kelly with C. F. Wootten acting as general manager. T. H. McClintock filed with the Justice Court of Reno to foreclose on a mechanic's lien. The suit included the "dwelling house and property known as the Bowers Mansion Ranch."[19]

Management of the estate aside, the parties served as happier times for Eilley. August brought the grand finale event of the season when the Miners Union returned for its annual holiday and picnic. Accounts described it as the largest and best of the season. The *Gold Hill News* reported that "those who did not spend a pleasant day had only themselves to blame."[20] The Miners Union picnic was the last significant event that Eilley would host while living at Bowers Mansion.

Looking back at that joyful past, Grant Smith wrote, "What boy or girl ever forgot their first picnic at Bowers' Mansion in Washoe Valley, where for the first time in their lives they saw clear running brooks, great pine trees, wide meadows spangled with flowers, and, beyond the meadows the shimmering expanse of Washoe Lake?" And he added his notable conclusion, "It was a trip to Paradise."[21]

On August 19, 1875, Eilley announced her plan to sell the furniture, personal property, and her beloved home.[22] With the picnic season over and her mansion all but lost, Eilley retreated to her spirit companions. Her next prediction brought her strong credibility as a prophetess. She apparently described a terrible disaster when she said Virginia City would burn, and burn it did.[23]

At 5:30 a.m. on October 26, 1875, a small fire started in a lodging house on A Street and spread quickly. The flames were soon out of control, driving people and the firefighters from one block to the next. As the air heated, the fire leaped over entire blocks. Fireproof buildings burned as readily as wooden structures. Flames quickly consumed mills and hoisting works. Explosions from stored blasting powder increased the horrors of the scene. A gale-force wind blew through town, knocking down walls and filling the air with ash and cinders. That night, the situation worsened when a severe snowstorm blanketed the devastated town with its many refugees camped on the mountainside.[24]

As Virginia City quickly began rebuilding, Eilley sent the "credulous and easily frightened" into spasms of terror when she predicted that an earthquake would soon destroy what remained of the Comstock. Many who believed in her "humbuggery," as one newspaper described it, made efforts to leave the city.[25] Even though this prediction never came true, many still believed in the aging woman, now almost fifty years old. Some, however, thought that her misfortunes and troubles had "crazed her brain." Nonetheless, no one disputed the fact that some of her predictions were "wonderfully and fearfully verified."[26]

The early months of 1876 brought new predictions. Eilley continued to believe in her previous prophecy that Wells Fargo would be the next rich bonanza, but there was more. In February, she said that the sudden death of a man named Thomas Donnelly was not accidental and that he was a victim of foul play. Donnelly's cabin in Franktown burned to the ground earlier that month with him still inside. On the same day that Eilley declared it was murder, the local coroner came to a similar conclusion without the help of a crystal ball. However, one man claimed, "she foretold the burning of Thomas Donnelly, in his cabin, a year or more beforehand."[27]

Another account in March described two men who visited Eilley. One was an old acquaintance of Sandy's, while the other was from San Francisco. Their conversation soon turned to spiritualism. Eilley asked the visitor from California, "Have you a brother in the spirit world by the name of Theodore? He died in Mexico. He wishes you to be careful of your money." She said, "I see a cloud gathering over Mr. Baldwin, and his horse cannot win the race if there is any truth in my spirit friends. . . ." The men did not believe the prediction and chose to go to the track and bet on the Baldwin horse. The horse did not win, and as Theodore's spirit had warned, they lost their money.[28]

In a late-twentieth-century oral history, Arnold Trimmer of Genoa recalled that Anna Frey remained near Genoa tending a ranch while her husband, Walter, worked at a butcher shop in Placerville, California. Whenever she visited Washoe Valley, she stopped by the mansion to have her fortune told. One time, Eilley "was lookin' in her ball, and she said she could see—'looked like a long table. No, I think it looks like a bar. Yes. I know it is 'cause it has a brass rail, and there's a number of men standing there . . . I'm sure one of them looks like your husband. He's raisin' up a glass as though they're having a toast to each other. I think you better go over and see what's happening.'"[29]

Frey went over to Placerville and found her husband just as Eilley had described. They closed the butcher shop, and the couple returned home to Genoa. Trimmer concluded by saying, "Course I think Mrs. Bowers knew the old-time butchers that they were all good when it came to drinking, that she didn't have to look too hard into the crystal ball herself. Cause she no doubt knew where her husband was working and what he was doing."[30]

A troubled decade in her forties seemed to affect Eilley's mind. Myra Sauer Ratay wrote that a young neighbor girl at the time recalled how

Eilley started having difficulty maintaining the mansion. "They allowed her to store her silverware in their parlor when she was particularly afraid someone would steal it. She would appear unannounced at the neighboring Twaddle Ranch doorstep either to bring her silver for safe-keeping or to take it back to the mansion."[31]

Firsthand accounts describe Eilley's final days in the mansion and how she was very concerned about collecting money from her guests. With each train's arrival, Eilley walked down to the gateway at the end of the road. She made sure that each person paid before entering her property. "She wasn't too worried whether they all got a meal or not, and . . . quite a few times they wound up at the adjoining ranch to get whatever they could eat for an evening lunch." Sometimes the food became so meager that they only had bread and milk. Every so often, a peddler would stop in front of the Twaddle Ranch and set up a fruit stand. This action angered Eilley, causing her to tip over his fruit stand and run the man off. This routine became a common occurrence at the mansion. Trimmer again recalled Alice Twaddle saying, "I think you could comb hell over with a fine-tooth comb, and you wouldn't find another person like her!"[32]

While Eilley was concerned over her affairs in Washoe Valley, her nephew, Robert Henderson, now thirty-three years old, found himself in trouble in Virginia City. On April 21, 1876, he maliciously and feloniously assaulted Joe Gavin with a loaded pistol. Arrested on June 14, he admitted his guilt, paid a fine, and disappeared from Nevada.[33]

By this time, Eilley was no longer able to hold off those who held her debts. In May, the District Court of Washoe County ruled against her and in favor of her creditors, John G. Fox, Charles Courtois, John Boyd, George T. Marye, R. W. Hold, D. B. Gates, T. H. McClintock, William M. Boardman, and John Kelley, for $13,622.17. On May 3, 1876, the courts auctioned off the remainder of her properties in front of the Washoe County Courthouse. Eight years after Sandy's death, Eilley lost everything. A $10,000 bid by Myron C. Lake, the founder of Reno, secured ownership of the Bowers property.[34]

The picnic season came and went, and no event took place at the mansion for the first time in four years. On August 6, the *Nevada State Journal* announced that "the Bowers Mansion will not be opened for the reception of guests during the present season. Mrs. Bowers still resides in the mansion."[35]

Although Eilley had lost the Bowers Mine in 1870, she still held an interest in several other operating mines. In September, her debts forced her to sell those mining rights. On September 16, 1876, again at public auction, John Kelley bought the controversial Atchison claim for $3,500. He also acquired sixteen and a half feet of both the Kinney Claim and the California Central Claim #2, paying ten dollars for each.[36] With that, Eilley's mining career ended.

That same year, William Sharon began combining all the original Little Gold Hill Mines into the Consolidated Imperial Mining Company to cut costs. This new company included the Bacon, Bowers, Consolidated, Eclipse, Empire, Imperial, Paiute, Rice & Co, and Triglone & Co claims, amounting to 451 feet along the Comstock Lode. The merger created a powerful mining company.[37]

While William Sharon consolidated his empire, Lake tried to reduce his assets. By the late 1870s, Virginia City mining declined, reducing the region's population. Grand picnics became a memory. Most organizations found other destinations for their annual events. Even Eilley's friends in both the Pacific Coast Pioneers and the Miners Union moved their gatherings to Treadway's Ranch in Carson City. In April 1877, Lake ran newspaper advertisements indicating that he hoped to sell the mansion and two hundred acres of land. No one accepted his offer.[38]

Lake then hired C. H. Sproule as the mansion's new manager. On June 10, Sproule reopened it as a "place of public resort," advertising it as having the finest swimming baths in the state, free passenger conveyance from the train stop, the best meals at all hours, and splendid rooms by day or week.[39] Sproule also made the trip to the mansion easier when he received permission to reopen the Dall's bridge and road which led from the base of Ophir Grade on the east side of Washoe Valley where it crossed the northern end of Washoe Lake. From there the road crossed a trestle built by the Ophir Company during the boom years. It was then an easy trek to Bowers Mansion. Picnickers received the key to the gate at the livery stables eliminating any delays.[40]

It had been almost thirty years since the first pioneers settled on the eastern slope of the Sierra Nevada and the legendary prospectors of Nevada roamed nearby desolate hills in search of gold. Most of the early settlers were already gone. With Eilley still in the public view, young Nevada residents, who had not been around to see her in her glory, began telling stories of her life and past.[41]

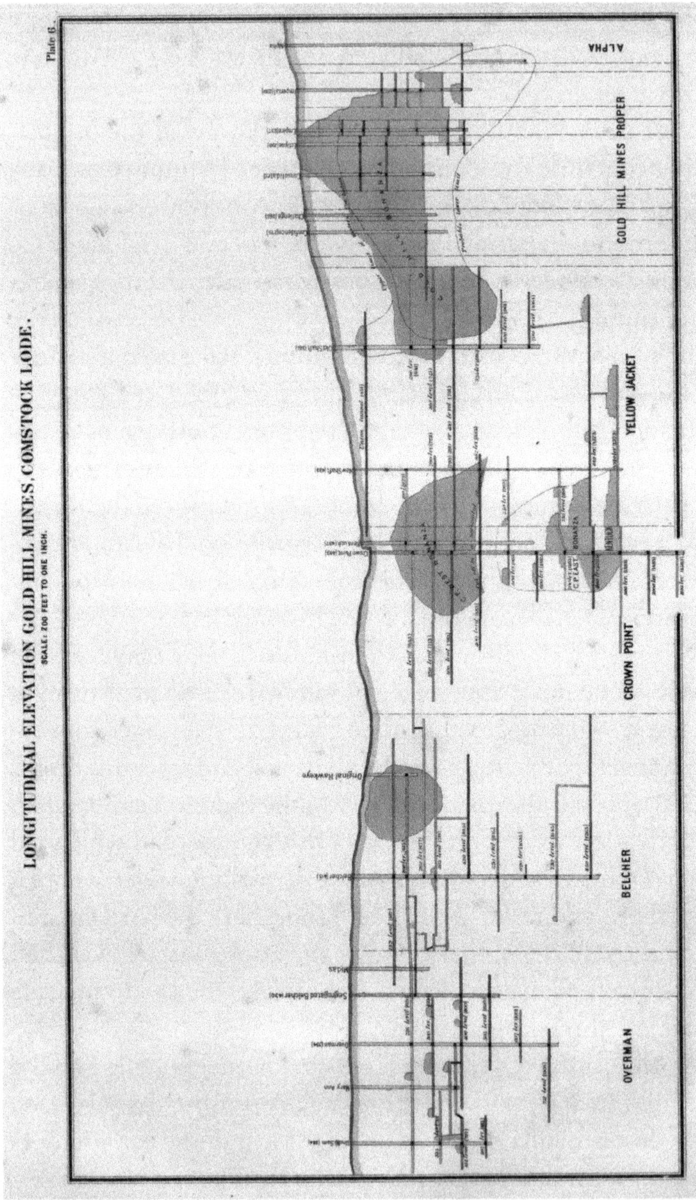

FIG. 24. A cross section of Gold Hill's share of the Comstock Lode, showing the principal mines and ore bodies. The Bowers Mine excavated a significant surface deposit, allowing the couple to become wealthy in a short amount of time. This is one of several detailed illustrations of the underground deposits completed in 1882 as part of a geological survey by George F. Becker. Courtesy Ronald M. James.

On January 1, 1878, less than two years after Eilley lost her mansion, the *Nevada State Journal* wrote of "Sandy's Folly." The reporter told how Sandy and Eilley had gained their riches and built their mansion. He maintained that the "change from poverty to affluence was too great and too sudden, and the result was that Sandy's head was turned."[42] The reporter blamed their financial troubles on the mismanagement of their money. He told how Sandy left Eilley with an enormous debt when he died. The reporter then blamed her subsequent losses on her having no capacity for business.[43]

The *Journal* also published a letter from Father Thomas McGrath, who had known the Bowers since 1862. He spoke highly of Eilley when he said:

> Times change; fortunes fluctuate; true womanhood never changes, even in the rapid changes of life in grand old Washoe. . . . [Now] the wife and mother is lingering on the shores of time homeless and melancholy. Where are the people who were friends (?) of Mrs. Bowers, who were entertained in her mansion only a few years ago? Are we to respect the wealth only? Has true friendship become a lost treasure? Can the poor "Washoe Seeress" tell us where to find the lost jewel? Oh, Heavens! "A friend in need is a friend indeed." Where is such a friend? But no matter; the lady has merit, and what if her friends (?) have proved themselves to be sycophants? The real is true all the time.[44]

During the first part of February 1878, Eilley stopped by the house of her old friend and fellow pioneer, Laura Dettenreider. Laura claimed a belief in spiritualism through the years, and she had met with fellow spiritualists on different occasions.[45] Now she offered to help Eilley. Laura allowed Eilley to stay at her boardinghouse in Virginia City and give readings for money, an offer Eilley had previously refused.[46] There were many skeptics about spiritualism when Eilley was giving readings. Although her predictions were not always accurate, many people came to her for advice, and she made a decent living off their curiosity.

Eilley spent most of her time traveling between Reno and Virginia City, telling fortunes and, in the process, earning notoriety. To make her stay on the Comstock more convenient, she rented a house on South C Street, next door to Dettenreider's boarding house.[47] As the *Territorial Enterprise* reported of her work in Virginia City, Eilley was often "besieged with persons who desired to consult her concerning various matters, her room . . . being crowded for hours."[48] Echoing her early days in the 1850s, many of her clients asked for help in finding lost or stolen items.

A man named G. L. Whitney told of losing a valuable gold watch chain. He believed that a Chinese man, an employee, had stolen the item. After a diligent but fruitless search, he chose to ask Eilley for help. Eilley told him to look in a pile of rubbish in one of the rooms in his house. Although Whitney did not have confidence in her prediction, he did as he was told. After a couple of hours of searching, he found the lost chain.[49]

A woman living on D Street lost a diamond ring worth $450, ten thousand or more dollars in today's currency. She had received it in a package from San Francisco. Soon after that, it was stolen from her pocket. She told Sam Wagner, the town crier, to offer a reward of $100. The culprit did not return it. Finally, she went to Eilley, who told her not to worry about the diamond. A few days later, the woman heard a ring at the door. When she answered it, there was no one there, but in a small package on her doorstep was the missing jewelry.[50]

Out of curiosity, a woman named E. L. Hickok visited Eilley after losing an insurance policy. Eilley described the culprit, a woman who had taken it and some money, and then she told Hickok how to recover her stolen property. Following the instructions, Hickok found the lost policy. The woman who had stolen it apologized humbly and promised to pay back the money she had also taken.[51]

Under the headline "Senseless Proceedings," the *Territorial Enterprise* reported on a prediction by Eilley Bowers that one of the big prizes in the Havana Lottery was to come to Nevada. This caused a constant crowd of people to ask what number they should buy. The reporter asked these to "take a sensible view" of the matter. Besides, as the newspaper pointed out "if she knows what ticket is going to draw a prize, she most certainly is not going to tell anyone, but will secure it herself."[52]

Once Eilley became famous, it was inevitable that rumors would spread about her predictions. One of the stories maintained that she foretold of an accident caused by a train breaking down on Gold Hill's Crown Point Trestle while carrying children to a school picnic. Eilley wrote to the public through the *Territorial Enterprise* that this was false, and she believed that the picnic excursion would be a safe and pleasant trip. John Taylor Waldorf described this prediction in his recollection, *A Kid on the Comstock*. "She scotched the 'great scare' by blandly trusting herself to the Virginia and Truckee. Rounding the Gold Hill depot,

FIG. 25. In 1878, false rumors began spreading that Eilley had predicted a train would break down on this trestle causing an accident. Completed in 1869, the wooden structure spanned Crown Point Ravine just east of the Bowers's Thistle Mill and Gold Hill home. After crossing the ravine, the Virginia & Truckee Railroad continued onto Carson City, Washoe Valley, and Reno. Courtesy Special Collections and University Archives Department, University of Nevada, Reno, Libraries.

the excursion train crept through a cut in the wall of Gold Canyon and approached the Crown Point Trestle. Spanning the ravine where the Crown Point mine works lay, the trestle was 350 feet long and ninety feet high, though it must have looked far longer and higher to all on board that day. But it proved to be as strong as Mrs. Bowers' faith, and the train went on its winding way."[53]

Aside from telling predictions for money, Eilley continued to have visions that troubled her. One time, she saw the body of a dead man lying underwater with a foot extending above the waterline. He wore one slipper, and the side of his head was crushed in as though by a blow with a blunt instrument. Unfortunately, she could not fix his exact location and could only say it was in the eastern part of town.[54] Disposing of a murdered body in an abandoned shaft was a not uncommon event, making it predictable that someone would eventually find a corpse lying in the water at the bottom of a shaft. After her prediction, men began searching abandoned mining shafts. They found nothing. Almost two months later, some workers cleaning rubbish in a mine discovered a body wrapped in a gunnysack. Like Eilley's prediction, the partially decomposed remains lay in two feet of water.[55]

Two separate accounts show how people saw Eilley's gift differently. The *Gold Hill News* reported that on a dark night in October 1878, Eilley's fortune-telling career almost ended. A man visited her and said that he was seeking information regarding some mining land. She said that she saw the area of interest as being rich with ore, chlorides, bromides, ruby silver, and gold. As she continued with the prediction, a strong wind came along, forced the door open, and blew her candle out. She then left the room to get something to relight it, but the man and her crystal ball had vanished when she returned. She mourned her loss all night and then decided to send her spirit friends after the thief. The following night a neighbor found the ball at his door.[56]

The *Territorial Enterprise* gave a less melodramatic version of the same story when it described the man as so excited over his good fortune that he jumped in joy and swung his hat all around, extinguishing the candle. With Eilley out of the room, he took the crystal ball and ran. The newspaper also reported that the man was unhappy with the stolen stone since he could not get a reading from it and, therefore, returned it on his own.[57]

The *Territorial Enterprise* also reported that while visiting Reno, "Mrs. Bowers has captured Truckee. We might be inclined to ridicule fortune-telling if many of our leading families and citizens of the town had not contributed their dollar to have their fortunes told. . . . All who have had good fortunes say there's something about the woman they 'can't understand,' while those who are going to die (according to her predictions) immediately say she is a bilk."[58] Nevertheless, the report continued, "many have visited her again and again to ask her advice, on finding her predictions true and verified."[59]

During her many years as a seeress, Eilley's predictions were often correct, but she was just as likely to be wrong. Waldorf's mother received one of the erroneous forecasts. Waldorf recalled Eilley telling his mother that a treasure lay buried under their house. He spent many unrewarded hours digging in the basement. "I can still recall my blistered hands, but I have no regrets because for days I spent imaginary millions and was richer then than I have ever been since."[60]

Another failed prophecy involved Hannah Powers of Silver City who was troubled by Eilley's prediction that her one-year-old daughter would die when she was two. The mother worried herself until her daughter turned three. The daughter, Mabel Powers Kelley, lived to be seventy-eight years old.[61] Failed divinations combined with engrained cynicism to cause skepticism about Eilley's abilities. Even with disbelief, many were curious about what she was doing and saying.

Eilley spent 1878 making just enough money to survive; others on the Comstock were also struggling. Once again, a mining boom was fading and depression appeared inevitable. In June, a big strike in Bodie, California, inspired a new rush, this one away from Nevada. Many northern Nevadans moved to the mining town with a promising future.[62]

Bowers Mansion manager C. H. Sproule was now living in Virginia City, publishing a financial newspaper, the *Stock Report*. Nat Holmes had taken the job as mansion proprietor in May 1878. Holmes purchased new furniture, hoping to bring back its early splendor, but what opened to the public was a pale shadow of earlier days; many groups continued to find other destinations for their events.[63] The *Territorial Enterprise* reported: "The times are not now as they were then." The Pacific Coast Pioneers were the only major group to return that summer.[64]

As a result of these changing times, private outings facilitated by the railroad became popular. During the summer of 1878, the V&T offered a Sunday excursion special for anyone who was interested. The train ran between Virginia City, Gold Hill, Carson City, Bowers Mansion, and Steamboat Springs. Virginia and Gold Hill residents could conveniently picnic at any of the stops and return later that evening for $1.50 or less. Children under 13 rode for free. Bowers Mansion was no longer the preeminent destination. Emerging favorites included Dall's Grove in Washoe Valley, the National Guard Hall in Virginia City, the Masonic Hall in Gold Hill, and the most popular, Treadway's Ranch in Carson City.

Eilley continued wandering between Reno, Franktown, and Virginia City, telling fortunes for the next few years. In early 1880, she moved into a house on the southwest corner of A and Sutton Streets in Virginia City.[65] From there, she continued fortune telling for money.

Finally, Eilley moved into a little white dwelling, which stood in a grove of tall pine trees just west of Franktown.[66] In early 1881, she became concerned about the new Little Valley Dam just above her house. She told Elias Owens, a neighbor, that she wanted to go there and show him a defect, but at the time, the snow was too deep to travel to the site. Even with her prediction of the dam breaking, she did not have time to save her own home and furniture when it did, in fact, give way. At two o'clock in the afternoon on February 2, the Little Valley Dam broke, and the resulting flood swept away nearly all of Franktown. With the disaster anticipated, all the women and children had safely moved to Bowers Mansion and other ranches south of town before the flood. When the mud settled, Eilley's little house lay ruined. The slide tore off its front, and the side frame gave way, causing the roof to drop to the ground. Eilley also lost $200 worth of furniture.[67]

As Myron Angel's *History of Nevada 1881* recognized, Eilley was a part of the state's incredible story. The unknown writer hired by Angel to conduct an interview saw her "as the 'Washoe Seeress; a woman now 52 years of age, down whose cheeks a tribute in sadness trickled as the writer's questions uncovered the memorial ashes of past hopes dead, revealing the wreck of a long and eventful life, verging upon its close."[68] Eilley, by then aging and carrying a large ear horn to help with her failing hearing, described her life as she wanted others to remember her.

She described her birth in the Scottish Highlands, her marriage at fifteen, and her journey to Salt Lake City in 1850. She explained how she left her first husband, Stephen Hunter, because he was a polygamist even though she neglected to mention that he remained unmarried for two years after their separation. She moved on to her second marriage, to Alexander Cowan, and then told of their journey to Washoe, and their ranch in the valley. She also recounted that when Brigham Young summoned the Mormons in 1857, Eilley refused to return to Salt Lake and the domain of polygamy.[69]

Eilley then continued her story for the interview, describing her marriage to Sandy Bowers, her mining land, and her wealth. She glorified their European trip by saying they traveled through the Old World for three years. Angel's history did not report on whether she mentioned her daughter, Persia, or the circumstance of her birth. She also doubled the mansion's value by claiming it was initially worth $407,000. In addition she claimed that the mine and mill superintendent ran up a $30,000 debt after Sandy's death, causing the balance of her possessions to be taken.[70] These exaggerations and explanations may or may not have been how Eilley recalled her life. However, it is apparently the way she wished others to remember her. After she told her story, Eilley, like many pioneers before her, left Nevada.

CHAPTER 8

The Final Years

THE 1880S BEGAN WITH THE mansion's future in jeopardy. Myron C. Lake again tried to rid himself of the burden it represented. William Thompson, Lake's stepson-in-law, intervened to give the property to the State of Nevada for use as a mental institution. Others opposed the plan. Illustrating how the property was being allowed to deteriorate, an article in the *Reno Evening Gazette* included the observation, "A more desolate and dreary place could not be found."[1] A legislative committee tabled a bill to make it a mental institution and never addressed it again. With the mansion still in Lake's hands, Dave H. Lodge took over as manager. He also assumed the payment of the estate's taxes.[2]

By 1883, Eilley, now fifty-seven, lived in a small basement flat on O'Farrell and Larkin Streets in San Francisco, conducting her business as an astrologer and fortune teller.[3] It had been nearly a quarter century since she struck it rich on the Comstock, and the generation that remembered the old days was largely gone. In Nevada, her family was all but forgotten. The *Reno Evening Gazette* felt the need to remind people of the story behind Bowers Mansion and Sandy's grave:

> Wealth rolled into his pockets in a stream, but he neither had the education nor common sense to enjoy his good fortune . . . Bowers, like hundreds of others, struck a porphyry horse and went through the hole when the 'bottom dropped out in 64'. . . . The grave was dug due east and west, and six feet depth [*sic*]. Coarse sand crumbling from the granite mountainside hide from view the mortal remains of Bowers. At one time, a picket fence protected the spot from cattle and hogs, but one by one the palings have dropped from the rail, until now about all there is left to mark the place is a little mound of

dirt. His widow, after holding communion with Sandy's ghost and other friendly spooks for a month or two, moved into a little cabin hard by, where she made her living by telling fortunes . . . The little mound and the building known as Bowers Mansion, now owned by M. C. Lake, is all that is left to indicate that Sandy Bowers ever lived.[4]

Alfred Doten, by then the former editor of the *Gold Hill News*, defended Eilley by describing her difficult years. He wrote a letter to the *Territorial Enterprise*:

> The *Reno Gazette* does Mrs. Sandy Bowers a rank injustice in stating that she deserted the famous Bowers Mansion a month or two after her husband died, and "moved into a little cabin hard by, where she made her living telling fortunes." Hundreds of people can tell the *Gazette* that the old lady did nothing of the sort. She occupied the mansion itself for years afterward as a landlady, receiving paying visitors, renting it out to picnic parties, and making it a source of private revenue to a considerable extent. And many a thirsty picnicker remembers the cups of tea and coffee they succeeded in procuring from her, as a special favor, at two bits each; water free, but predominant. If Sandy Bowers had left his financial affairs better regulated, the old lady would be in the same line of business yet. It is true that she has, since evacuated the mansion, established quite a lively reputation as a spiritualistic fortuneteller, Seeress and all that sort of thing, and is still at the same, but she picks up plenty of pocket money at it, and anything but a 'precarious living.' Some of her predictions have been literally, squarely (and unavoidably) verified, but numerous others have not, by a long chalk, and never can be, but then she is very hard of hearing, not being able to distinguish a jingle of a quarter from the ringing of a church bell for the last thirty years.[5]

November 1883 brought Eilley's return to Nevada. She read her crystal ball during her stay and became even more famous as a fortune teller. Local reporters again filled articles with predictions and stories of the "Washoe Seeress." One prophecy made on January 9, 1884, took four months to see how it would unfold. Eilley had been quietly warning her friends to prepare for a fire that would destroy Reno during the last part of April or early May. Many business owners, who believed in her ability, increased their fire insurance. Others waited patiently to see if the impoverished woman might be involved with the insurance companies.[6]

Eilley claimed to have found the youth who she believed would start the fire. The boy only went to Eilley to have his fortune read. She told him, "Young man, you are the one that is going to set fire to Reno next April," but he denied the accusation. Eilley continued, "You are in the habit of reading late at night by the light of a candle after going to bed." The youth agreed that he sometimes did, though not often. "I knew it, I knew it, and you will fall asleep leaving the candle burning, which will burn down, set fire to the building and from that the whole town will be destroyed and you with it. You may think you will stop the practice, but you will not, and before the first of May, what I now tell you will come to pass."[7]

On March 14, a fire alarm sounded in Reno, causing many to panic until they realized they still had over a month before Eilley's big fire. People quickly calmed down and extinguished the flames.[8] On April 30, the *Nevada State Journal* reported only one more day before "the fire." It looked as if the prediction was not going to come true. The boy who was to start the fire had moved soon after Eilley's prediction, and residents boarded up the house where it was to start. Recent snows had dampened every other prospect of the fulfillment of the prophecy.[9] In another letter to the *Territorial Enterprise*, Doten wrote that Eilley was only "about forty miles out of the way on her prediction that Reno would burn toward the end of April; Wadsworth burned instead."[10]

In June 1884, disaster struck Eilley again when her tiny home, the place she was living at the time in Franktown, burned to the ground. Thieves first stripped the cabin of valuables and then set it on fire. The *Journal* asked the people of Nevada to come to the relief of Bowers.[11] Some helped. Others refused because they believed Eilley set the fire herself.

Eilley's misfortune was echoed by that of the owner of her former home in Washoe Valley. Eight years after Lake acquired the mansion from Eilley, she saw him lose everything. On June 20, 1884, Lake died only four months after she predicted his death. Lake's demise came after the passing of a local lawyer and one-term Reno district attorney named William Cain, whom Eilley also predicted would die.[12] Even though Eilley had foretold many deaths that did not occur, her prediction of these two caused quite a stir. In an attempt to calm the town, the *Reno Evening Gazette* published the following article:

> Encouraging Superstition—Those who have not been taught to reason from cause to effect may find in the sudden death of two prominent citizens of Reno encouragement in their superstitious fancies by the haphazard assertion made by Mrs. Bowers, last February, that both William Cain and M. C. Lake would die in April. She said Mr. Lake would be the first and Mr. Cain would follow in a few days. It seemed an idle remark at first, and when Mr. Cain reproached the would-be Seeress for disturbing the peace of his wife and family, she is reported to have said, 'Well, Mr. Cain ain't it well to be always ready?' To those who are making themselves uncomfortable about such an impossible matter as the foretelling of events, it is well to remind them of the thousands of instances that fail. The fortune-teller is simply a relic of the dark ages, and is not at all creditable to this century. They should be discouraged by all sensible people.[13]

Eilley returned to San Francisco in the fall of 1884.

Three years before Lake's death, his wife, Jane Lake, divorced him on the grounds of cruelty. He managed to retain all his property, which included Bowers Mansion. After his death, his new wife, Mary Ann McFarland Lake, acquired all his real and personal properties. This prompted Jane to take action. Her lawyer was able to have Lake's last will and testament dismissed. McFarland settled for $15,000 and deeded Myron Lake's real and personal property to his ex-wife and William Thompson, Jane Lake's son-in-law. On December 2, 1885, they officially became the owners of Bowers Mansion.[14]

In late 1886, Thompson proposed to have the mansion dismantled and taken to Reno's business district. A reporter for the *Carson Morning Appeal* commented that "but now Thompson, that old iconoclast, has his utilitarian grip on the building and will knock out all its romance and fragrant memories by lugging the stone over to Reno and building a prosaic business house where he can get huge rents for it."[15]

With the possibility of Thompson moving her mansion, Eilley returned to Nevada for a short time in July 1887. While trying to regain her failing health at Shaw's Hot Springs, just north of Carson City, she attempted to secure the removal of Sandy, Persia, and her first two children's graves. Eilley is believed to have moved the babies from Gold Hill to the hillside behind the mansion after Persia's death. With word that the mansion might be moved, she now wished her family to "rest in a live town."[16]

Neither move was realized, and instead the mansion showed new life as the 1887 season proceeded with events. The most significant of these came in early August with the Caledonia picnic. Their special guest was Eilley Bowers, who was still visiting from San Francisco. A *Reno Evening Gazette* reporter met with her as she sat surrounded by friends, all of whom shared stories of the past. As the former mistress of the mansion adjusted her ear horn, the reporter asked her how she was doing. She replied, "I'm not in the best of spirits when I come to Sandy Bower's Mansion as a guest, especially when I consider I was once queen of the whole of Washoe Valley. Ah, it makes my heart weary when I look up to the hill yonder and see the fence that surrounds the remains of my dead Sandy."[17] Following the bittersweet gathering, Eilley returned to San Francisco and continued work as a seeress, living in several locations.[18]

By the summer of 1888, the mansion had become dilapidated. A *Reno Evening Gazette* reporter wrote that "the spot which was made noted by the sudden streak of good fortune, followed by an extravagance that savors of the fabulous, shows signs of neglect, and unless it should fall into hands that will resurrect its former greatness will soon lose the interest it once had."[19] J. B. Frances, agent for Wieland Beer, believed that even if the mansion itself could not be preserved, its image could. He then hired William Behringer, an emigrant artist from Munich, to paint a thirty-six-by-fifty-six-inch portrait to adorn the walls of the Wieland Saloon in the McFarlin building on the corner of Sierra and Third Street in Reno. In late July, Frances, J. L. McFarlin, attorney D. Allen, and the artist traveled to the mansion to work on a sketch that would become an oil painting.

When finished, the colorful landscape highlighted the three-story mansion surrounded by shade trees and backed by the ever-rising Carson Range of the Sierra Nevada. McFarlin and Allen are shown conversing by the enlarged fountain while a horse quietly grazes behind them. An unknown figure exits the silent dance hall to the right while an unidentified woman, perhaps Eilley herself, watches over the events from the mansion's veranda.[20]

That fall, Jane Lake sold the mansion to longtime Washoe Valley resident Theodore Winters on October 22, 1888, for $70,000.[21] In an overview of the local history, Myra Sauer Ratay observed, "At this time Winters owned about four thousand acres of farm land from Washoe City to Franktown in Washoe Valley."[22] Like Eilley Bowers and her second husband at the time, Winters purchased land in Washoe Valley before the

FIG. 26. In 1888, a Reno bar manager hired William Behringer to create a painting of Bowers Mansion, in celebration of local history. Henry Riter later bought the painting, which inspired him to purchase Bowers Mansion in 1903. When Riter sold the property in 1946, he left the painting in the mansion where it still hangs. Courtesy Bowers Mansion photo collection.

Comstock gold and silver strikes. Winters, too, made his initial fortune in mining as one of the principal stockholders of the Mexican Mine in Virginia City. He also built a large house in Washoe Valley at the same time as the construction of Bowers Mansion, but unlike Sandy and Eilley Bowers, Winters expanded his empire by becoming a rancher, dairyman, and famed breeder of racehorses.[23]

At the time of the purchase, Eilley had been visiting Reno when a *Gazette* reporter again confronted her, this time as she waited for the train to take her back to San Francisco. He asked her what she thought about Winters purchasing the mansion. She replied, "It has fallen into good hands. Theodore Winters is a good man. If I were in need of a home I know of no old friend I would rather ask it of than him."[24] The Winters family never lived in the mansion, preferring to remain at their ranch house just to the northeast.

Winters did, however, allow his sister Harriett Reid and her family to occupy the mansion for a time. The Reid boys were rough on the house, nearly destroying parts of the old structure. In addition, Winters cannibalized the outdoor dance hall flooring to build a sizeable gothic-type barn for his racehorses near his track. He also dismantled other outbuildings, including the old barn south of the mansion.[25]

In 1890, Winters ran as the Democratic candidate for governor. He financed his campaign as well as the expenses of other party candidates. In the end, Winters lost to the Republican, R. K. Colcord, and ultimately found himself in debt, owing roughly $80,000. One of his debtors was longtime Carson City resident and former attorney general, Robert Clarke. Faced with these obligations, Winters found the mansion to be too much of a burden. He needed to rid himself of the property, but with no buyers, he again tried to make it a valuable asset.[26]

In 1892, he announced plans to return it to its original glory by making it a casino, "a new Monte Carlo." He donated the mansion and grounds to a syndicate of investors. J. Cairn Simpson, editor of the *Breeder and Sportsman*, had grand plans for the old mansion as a sporting resort. He even intended to construct an electrified transport system to Lake Tahoe, only eleven miles over the Sierra Nevada from the mansion.[27] These grandiose plans never materialized.

During Winters's four and a half years of ownership, he attempted to give the property away as a home for disabled miners and then as a mental institution, but the state refused him each time.[28] With another summer approaching, he finally gave the mansion and seventy-five acres of land to Clarke on July 10, 1893, for $100, friendship, esteem, and professional services and advice.[29] Clarke planned to turn the estate into a summer home for himself and his family, but this never became a reality, and the mansion remained unused. Like Eilley, Bowers Mansion had fallen on hard times.

According to an 1894 article in the *Midwinter Appeal and Journal of Forty-Nine*, an old gate, tied closed, blocked the entrance to the once glorious home that now housed only jackrabbits and various birds. The empty dance hall remained quiet. The property was only sporadically disturbed by a few passing drifters who used the old bathhouses for temporary lodging. Unpruned trees lined the weed-covered walks, while long grass and a dry fountain decorated the mansion's front garden. The reporter observed

FIG. 27. Now restored, the kitchen still shows signs of brave service. Located at the rear of the south wing, this room acted as a private kitchen when the Bowers lived in the house. During the boarding house years, Eilley offered meals at any hour. When Henry Riter ran the mansion as a resort, his wife, Edna, ran a restaurant out of this room while guests dined in the courtyard. Courtesy Bowers Mansion collection.

that a lonely black snake lay coiled on the masonry edge, seemingly undisturbed by several lizards darting through open stone crevices. The doors were nailed tight, but he could see uncarpeted floors, bare walls, and ghastly white ceilings through the cracked windows. In one corner of the kitchen lay a "ragged plaid apron whose stains told of its brave service in the interest of cleanliness." Masses of coarse ivy with leaves as large as one's hand hung from the exterior walls, and the weed-filled swimming pond had become the home of many turtles, frogs, and snakes.[30]

As her home lay in ruin, Eilley was given the opportunity to relive her days in a mining camp when she attended San Francisco's Midwinter Fair. On January 27, 1894, San Francisco opened the gates to an exposition created to rival the Chicago World's Columbian Exposition of 1893. One exhibit, on the north slope of Strawberry Hill, was the '49 Mining Camp. Organizers searched all over California to collect relics that could

FIG. 28. This photograph appears to have captured Eilley Bowers standing in the doorway of an old miner's cabin at the '49 Mining Camp exhibit of the 1894 San Francisco Exposition. She spent time there, telling fortunes, cooking for the old miners, and recalling stories of her own life in a mining camp. Courtesy *Harper's Weekly*, February 24, 1894; Bowers Mansion collection.

tell the story of those early days of the 1849 Gold Rush. They transported or reconstructed several old mining cabins, including two they claimed belong to J. W. Mackay and Eilley Bowers.[31]

Eilley joined other old-timers as they shared their experiences with visitors. The camp reminded her of life many years before in her own primitive cabin. Being enthusiastic over camp life, she proposed staying a while to tell the visitors fortunes and cook for the miners. This idea was welcomed by the men who enjoyed the excellent cooking and motherly attention bestowed on them by the older woman.[32] During her time at the camp, another reporter asked her to tell her life story. In the interview, she defended Sandy's business sense by declaring that it was not his fault she was broke. "It is not true, as everyone supposes, that Sandy left me in poverty. I had a hundred thousand dollars and the house, besides some mining stock, but I took bad advice, and lost everything."[33]

After leaving the miner's camp, Eilley quietly lived out the rest of the century in San Francisco. The pioneer age had ended, and the next generation of Nevadans focused on their future. There was talk of paving the roads in Reno, and General Electric planned to open a power plant in the area. A few horseless carriages traveled the streets, and residents could make long-distance phone calls with the help of an operator. A rumor circulated that two brothers from Dayton, Ohio, were trying to fly.

With all the excitement, most people probably anticipated the future more than pondering former times. For Eilley, the past was all she had left. She tried to persuade the Nevada government to pay her $1,000 in return for the $14,000 the Sandy and Eilley Bowers had given the volunteers to help finance the Pyramid Lake War of 1860. Unfortunately, a fire destroyed her receipts long before she decided to file her claim, making it difficult to verify her donation. Eilley continually wrote to old Nevada residents and asked for their help proving that she and Sandy had given the money.[34] In a letter to Hannah Clapp, an educator in Carson City, Eilley wrote, "It is very hard for me to be so dependent on others in my old age. . . . All I ask from the government is a small amount, in fact only enough to bury me decently, and I know truly I am entitled to it. . . . If you find I have still any old friends, give my kind regards to them, and my kindest regards and love for yourself." Before she signed the letter, she predicted that diggers would find oil in Washoe Valley.[35]

After receiving a letter from Eilley, a widow named Mrs. W. M. Cary visited her in San Francisco. She found Bowers in a home on Larkin Street near Golden Gate Avenue, living "in a pitiful condition—she has been sick for about a year and has no one to care for her—her deafness has increased—she cannot see well enough to read the paper—and is almost helpless—as she cannot comb her hair—it had not been combed for four days."[36]

Eilley even contacted US Senator William M. Stewart of Nevada, who was a Virginia City mining litigation lawyer in 1860, regarding reimbursement of money she and Sandy lent to the community during the 1860 Paiute Indian War. She finally received a response in July 1899. It was not the response for which she had hoped. He said that the date for filing her claim had passed, and there was no longer a designated board to examine her presentation, making it impossible to do anything for her.[37]

While Eilley wrote to her old Nevada friends, she may have also reached out to her first husband's daughters from his second marriage.

According to family history, they had kept in touch with Eilley for many years. Before Stephen Hunter's death, he asked them to stop their correspondence. They did not know why, but the reasons may have been a concern that she would ask for money.[38]

Eilley's last involvement with Nevada began in February 1901. While still living in San Francisco, Eilley made a final published prophecy. She wrote a letter to an old friend from the early Nevada days about coal oil near Bowers Mansion in Washoe Valley. She wanted him to search for it because it was worth millions of dollars, and she hoped to have it discovered before she died.[39]

That summer, Eilley again returned to Nevada. She arrived in Reno on the night of July 8, poor, ill, and almost friendless. A local reporter wrote, "Mrs. Bowers has come back to the scene of her former triumphs, an old decrepit woman, to await the summons to another world."[40] The once famous Queen of the Comstock found no welcoming reception. No one offered her a place to stay as she had done for others when she was the acclaimed "Mistress of the Mansion." The reporter further asked, "Where are the people who enjoyed the hospitality of the Seeress in the good old days . . . ?" With no friends to help, Eilley was sent to the poor house while "the icy hands of death . . . outreached above her face."[41] There she awaited her death and burial in the potter's field.

At the same time, F. D. King, a Reno attorney, tried to raise the $1,000 to repay the Bowers donation for the conflict with the Northern Paiutes in 1860. He wrote people and asked for contributions to allow Eilley to live in the Crocker Mansion of San Francisco. He raised some money, but not enough to secure her a place in the home.[42]

During her final visit to Nevada, California newspapers played up the story of the Washoe Seeress. Within a few weeks, reporters from the San Francisco newspapers, the *Chronicle*, and the *Call Bulletin* reimagined details of her life and created the beginnings of the misleading stories that became the legend of Eilley Bowers. They wrote of a young Mormon girl coming to Nevada, where she met Sandy, whom one reporter referred to as Leon, at a grand ball that lasted three days. Although engaged to another woman, he agreed to marry Eilley. The mine that they had acquired was soon paying $10,000 a day. With riches at hand, he located some land in the dreary and lonely Washoe Valley and built a glamorous mansion that Eilley wanted. They took their young daughter, Persia, with them on their three-year excursion to Europe, where they met with

Queen Victoria of England. The reporters even took a famous tale from Mark Twain's *Roughing It* and made Twain's John Smith, a simple man who struck it rich on the Comstock and traveled to Europe, into Sandy Bowers.[43] They described trunks filled with elaborate gowns and Sandy's many waistcoats with fancy frills. They killed Sandy three years earlier than he died and said he left her with a fortune. They claimed she squandered the money until it was gone. The only prediction they reported was the one about the school picnic train crossing the Crown Point Trestle, a prophecy she never made.[44]

While the San Francisco newspapers were busy rewriting history, Sandy's brotherhood of Freemasons, the affiliated women of the Eastern Star, and the Washoe County Commissioners tried to figure out what to do with the impoverished woman. No one wanted to take on the responsibility of a poor, sick, homeless widow. Linda Odett, the wife of the manager of the county hospital, said that Eilley had grown childish, needed great care, and was more trouble "than all the other county wards in the paupers' home."[45]

It seemed that the residents of Nevada had determined that they could not care for this fallen queen. On August 19, 1901, Eilley Bowers prepared for her return trip to San Francisco, where she could drop "out of sight in the city's busy life by the Golden Gate," as a reporter for the *Reno Evening Gazette* described.[46] A *Nevada State Journal* reporter recorded her final words as, "Farewell Nevada! Farewell!" spoken in a husky voice "that faltered from old age and saddened, lonely heart." Eilley boarded the westbound train, and that was the last time she would stand on Nevada soil. A few kind friends had given her about thirty dollars, and the county paid for her transportation out of the state.[47]

A *Nevada State Journal* reporter wrote, "The irony of things worldly! Forsaken Mrs. Bowers! To whom can she turn? Where are those friends of the past? . . . Thus Nevada shakes off the responsibility of the destitute Washoe Seeress. Western hospitality, me thinks, has taken on itself wings and fled. But fare you well, Mrs. Bowers, and our blessings (if nothing else) be with you."[48]

On March 11, 1902, seven months after returning to San Francisco, Eilley moved into the King's Daughters Home on Broadway Street in Oakland, California.[49] Its stated mission was "to minister to those most unfortunate of God's creatures—the incurable. Such are entitled to the deepest pity, for they exist without hope and suffer with no prospect of permanent alleviation. The very hopelessness of their condition removes them to a certain extent from the active sympathies of philanthropy." This charitable medical facility allowed guests to pay only for their needed services, making it affordable for the aged fortune teller to spend the rest of her days.[50]

FIG. 29. Bowers Mansion was in a state of neglect and decay when this photograph was taken in 1902. Henry Riter purchased the mansion a year later after hearing the Bowers story and seeing the Behringer painting. He had no idea it had fallen into disrepair. Undeterred, he hired workers to bring the mansion back to its original glory. Courtesy Special Collections and University Archives Department, University of Nevada, Reno, Libraries.

CHAPTER 9

A Resort for a New Century

As Eilley lived out her final years, her beloved home's fate remained uncertain. On February 11, 1900, six years after purchasing the mansion, Robert Clarke died, leaving his widow to handle his estate. In December 1901, Carson City newspaperman Philip Mighels paid Ida Clarke, the former attorney general's widow, $800 to relieve her of the mansion's burden and to make it his new home.[1] Rather than moving into the mansion, Mighels left it abandoned and ignored, allowing trees and brush to remain overgrown and untrimmed. A newspaper account told how "windows were open and doors hung from their hinges, while cows and sheep as well as skunks wandered in and out."[2]

A year before Eilley moved into the King's Daughters Home, brewer Henry Riter came across the previously mentioned Behringer painting of Bowers Mansion in the Wieland Saloon. Years later, Henry recalled falling in love with the painting and purchasing it for $10. He hung the artwork in his Elite Brewery in Reno. In the spring of 1903, local newspaperman Sam Davis visited Riter's bar and saw the painting. At the time, Davis's stepson Philip Mighels was willing to sell the mansion. According to Riter, he had never visited the place depicted in the painting when Davis indicated that the estate could be purchased. Riter later recalled to a *Gazette* reporter, "I couldn't see what I would do with the old property, but when he said I could have it for $1,000, I dug into my pocket and turned over that money in bills."[3] A week or so later, Riter received a deed for Bowers Mansion and forty-six acres of land.[4] Doten wrote in his diary, "Great events taking place in the world—Prest Roosevelt is to be in Carson May 19 on a trip to Pacific Coast—The purchase of the Panama Canal has been decided in Congress—Henry Riter of Reno has bought the old Bowers Mansion in Washoe Valley."[5]

Born into a farming family at Klinger, in the region of Pfalz, Germany, on October 8, 1863, the Reno brewer was one of Philip and Barbara Riter's nine children. At sixteen, he boarded the steamer *Rotterdam* and headed for New York. Soon after arriving, Henry Riter traveled by train to Sacramento, California, where he found work in several trades, including ranching, butchering, and cattle driving. After four years in the Sacramento area, he moved to Reno in March 1884. It was here where Riter met California native Lila Dixon. The two married on June 13, 1888.

In 1895, Riter settled into the beer business when he acquired the old Hoffman Brewery. He soon conducted his enterprise under the name Elite Brewery. Advertisements in the *Nevada State Journal* stated that "Elite Steam Beer is a beautiful, amber colored beverage. It is creamy and delicious and wholesome. This beer is made from the purest materials, and does not contain a headache. It is now on tap at the leading saloons." With his steam beer, Riter had established himself as a prosperous Nevada entrepreneur.[6]

Soon after Riter purchased Bowers Mansion, the *Nevada State Journal* reported that he had hired a force of men to work on the estate. The plan was to return the mansion and grounds to the days before Sandy Bowers died. Riter hired George Lindsay to manage the property as a picnic destination.[7]

On June 6, 1903, the *Nevada State Journal* announced the completion of the renovation while publicizing the grand reopening: "This is the finest picnic grounds accessible from Reno and will doubtless be extensively patronized this season. Arrangements have been made with the Virginia & Truckee railroad company by which tickets will be sold for $1 round trip, good for three days . . . All holders of these tickets are entitled to a free bath in the warm mineral plunge and swimming baths. Bathers are required however to bring their suits with them and are requested also to bring their luncheons as the mansion is not fitted up as yet to furnish meals."[8] The *Reno Evening Gazette* added that one possible issue for patrons was the hike from the railroad to the grounds, and yet the newspaper also described the trek as pleasant for anyone who loved nature. Bluebells, violets, wild roses, honeysuckle, and hundreds of other plants made the path pleasing and refreshing. The walk ended near a water fountain spraying spring water twenty-five feet into the air. A short stroll around the fountain led to five granite steps leading to the building proper. A grand stairway with two luxurious parlors on each side greeted the guests when they went inside. Many rooms throughout the house were not yet completed but were being fitted attractively. Even Sandy's old library had been "transferred into a general assembly for those who are thirsty and weary laden."[9]

Throughout the summer, guests visited the mansion as they did in the glory days of the Comstock Mining District. Then August brought the first of many moonlight picnics, as they were called. The Knights of Pythias hosted this inaugural event selling almost four hundred tickets for the evening affair. A seven-car excursion train entered the valley as the full moon slowly rose over the eastern foothills. Guests dismounted and carried lanterns illuminating the path as they walked toward the mansion. Friends from Carson City and the Comstock quickly joined the Reno Knights. Swimming and dancing were among the favorite activities throughout the evening. As the midnight hour approached, no one wished to leave, and it was not until the early morning hours that the guests finally agreed to return home. The *Nevada State Journal* concluded its description of the event by reporting that "hearty cheers for Proprietor Henry Riter were given before the departure of the throng."[10]

As summer days grew short and children returned to school, the *Nevada State Journal* announced a Sunday event for everyone: "The picnic season is drawing to a close. In a short while you will be climbing under a load of blankets that would make a mule kick while at the present time nothing can be offered more enticing than an outing at a place with the historic elements of Bowers Mansion. Of course the swimming ponds will be filled with the younger generation but there will be room for the older folk if they want to take a chance."[11] The *Journal* continued by reminding locals that there would be singing, dancing, races, laughter, and jests of the children that will remind the older generation of their youth and will "bring memories that have long since become rusty from disuse."[12]

Henry Riter had returned Bowers Mansion to its original splendor. His first season was a success. Unfortunately, a sad ending brought everything back to where it all began when Henry received word from Oakland regarding Eilley's health. A few weeks earlier, the wife of a relative, whom Eilley did not know, came to visit. Jeanette was married to Harry Livingston, a so-called nephew of the Bowers family, although his lineage remains unclear. There is little doubt that Jeanette and Eilley's conversation centered on the recent purchase, restoration, and reopening of her once beautiful mansion. Jeanette is the last known Nevadan to see Eilley alive.

On October 27, 1903, seventy-seven-year-old Eilley Oram Bowers died at the King's Daughters Home in Oakland. Part of the facility had recently burned, making the life of the failing queen of the mining frontier even more miserable. Her death certificate listed the cause of death as senility and chronic rheumatism.[13] Riter arranged to "fulfill the dream of a loving and faithful woman and wife" by having her buried beside her family.[14] On November 4, George Gillophy, an unknown man from San Francisco, claimed her cremated remains, allowing Eilley to take her last train ride to Nevada.[15] The final event held at Bowers Mansion that season came on Sunday, November 15, when the mistress of the mansion returned to her beloved home.[16]

As a young woman, Eilley followed an unusual path. She crossed the Atlantic and the United States before modern transportation made the trip easy. She outlived all three of her children and all but one of her husbands. She was one of the first women to arrive on the eastern slope of the Sierra Nevada during the Utah Territorial period. She was also exceptional for her gender as someone who struck it rich by owning mining land. She saw Nevada rise in power as she rose in wealth. She lived to see the West change and grow as she became old and forgotten. If Eilley had died at a young age, people would only remember the adventure, the glory, the wealth, and the hospitality of the young pioneer.

The *Sacramento Union* announced: "The last honors will be paid to the memory of the Washoe Seeress as her ashes find sepulture beneath the trees that cast their evening shadows across the roof of the Bowers Mansion."[17] On November 16, 1903, the *Reno Evening Gazette* reported:

> The last chapter in a romantic history is thus closed and the woman whose career has been so strange and turbulent has at last found rest. The interment was under the control of the ladies of the Eastern Star of which order the deceased was an honored member. Mrs. Rank Stewart and Mrs. Leslie Jamison of this city officiated, and the beautiful ceremony of the order was carried out. The wild and wintry day was emblematic of the long span of her life. Few people were present at the ceremony owing to the wind and rain. Nevertheless, the last sad rites were impressive.[18]

The reporter for the *Sacramento Union* elaborated about the character and history of the Bowers couple. The *Union's* two-column article paid a kind tribute to her and her husband. Dr. Simeon Bishop was quoted as recounting that:

> Two better people than Sandy Bowers and his wife never lived . . . I believe that two persons never lived together as husband and wife in any more perfect harmony and undeserved affection . . . They were homey folks, both of them, though she was somewhat more pretentious than he, and had the advantage of a better education . . . Their tastes were much the same, for the main idea of both appeared to be that life consisted of doing good for the mere happiness that was to be had in kind deeds. . . .
>
> While Mrs. Bowers was not noted for beauty, she was comely and a good physique, and her respect and affection for her husband were such that when she spoke of him her face glowed with a joy that was charming. . . . [Sandy] was a gentlemen without trying and without knowing why—just because he couldn't help it. Besides, he was one of the handsomest men as well as most modest that I ever knew. . . .
>
> Sickness was eagerly seized on by them as a valid excuse for an outpouring of their bounty, and most any day, even in the coldest winter weather, Mrs. Bowers might be seen traveling the snowdrifts of Bullion Ravine or Slippery Gulch, in which the town of Gold Hill was distributed, laden with packages and bundles of good things to eat, and generally Sandy Bowers would be found following close in her footsteps carrying some choice cordial or expensive wine, for he was a great believer in good things to drink, though himself almost an abstainer.[19]

Bishop further remembered about Sandy that "the hospitality of Sandy Bowers was ideal. It was cordial without being insistent; free handed, open, frank . . . he never refused to help a friend who needed his assistance and would accept his good offices."[20]

As the Bowers family found peace on the hillside behind the mansion, new life came to the resort. Lindsay and his wife, Nellie, continued running the resort while making improvements over the next two seasons. During the summer of 1904, the Lindsays and Riter himself hosted numerous grand-scale picnics with a steady flow of private picnickers and swimmers.

In 1905 at age forty-two, Riter decided to return to his home country for a visit. His parents were planning their fiftieth wedding anniversary, and he wanted his wife to meet them. Henry and Lila Riter together with her niece Edna Williams left for their European journey on April 6 of that year, boarding the eastbound train for New York. In June, the travelers returned, and Riter assumed the personal management of Bowers Mansion.[21]

After a summer of entertaining guests, Riter again arranged for someone else to run the resort. This time the goal was to promote the water there as having medicinal properties to help ailing guests and tourists. Near the end of October, Dr. J. C. C. Price, a veterinary surgeon, took over the mansion's lease, but Riter remained central to the management of the estate.[22]

As the 1906 picnic season neared its end, Riter found a new way to promote the mansion during hunting season. He began running advertisements in both the *Reno Evening Gazette* and the *Nevada State Journal* announcing the opening of Bowers Mansion Game Reserve. According to the newspapers, Washoe Lake offered the "Best duck shooting in the State." Hunting permits could be purchased at the mansion, and boats and decoys were available for hire. Each advertisement ended with the phrase "All trains stop at the mansion."[23]

In keeping with the mansion's history of promoting health, Riter incorporated the Reno Mineral Water Company in October 1909. With this, locals could purchase "sterilized by nature and absolutely pure" Shoshone Mineral Water and Royal Ginger Ale, both bottled at Bowers Mansion. Advertisements claimed the springs at Bowers Mansion were the only hot soda springs known in the region. The company also offered stock in the mineral company for only $1 per share.[24]

Tragedy struck during the fall of 1911 when Riter's wife died in San Francisco.[25] The following summer, he negotiated a three-year lease of the mansion with J. M. Mawer and F. S. Perrine. They quickly began remodeling the house and furnishing it as a hotel where guests were entertained by the day, week, or month. They also renovated the hot spring pools and baths and lined them with cement, allowing for easier and more frequent cleanings. They served meals and provided lunches for picnics and parties in keeping with tradition.[26]

Responding to a changing world, they purchased a new E-M-F five-passenger automobile from Steinheimer Brothers of Reno. This innovative means of transportation brought guests from the Virginia & Truckee station at Franktown to the park. A newly installed telephone allowed

FIG. 30. After acquiring Bowers Mansion in 1903, Henry Riter added many attractions to bring visitors to Washoe Valley. This group was part of a hunting excursion in 1912. Courtesy Nevada Historical Society.

parties to make advanced arrangements for automobile transportation to the resort. The railroad company agreed to make a special round-trip rate of $1 from Reno to Bowers, suitable for Saturdays, Sundays, and Mondays.[27]

In mid-April 1915, Henry Riter unexpectedly left Reno without explanation, a journey that forced him to miss the grand reopening of the mansion hosted by the new managers, J. P. and Anna Ketsdever. They promoted first-class meals and rooms, advertising the picnic grounds for all "Societies and Lodges" and offering a dancing platform together with the finest swimming pools in the state. Special dinners and banquets were available upon sufficient notice.[28]

Riter returned a few weeks later, accompanied by a new wife, a young woman named Edna. At the time of their elopement, Riter was fifty-two, and Edna was fifteen years his junior. By this time, locals had already received word of the nuptials. Edna sent a wire to her parents soon after the wedding. Born to prominent Nevada pioneers George and Martha Robison, the Wabuska native graduated from the University of Nevada's Normal Department in 1898, earning her the degree necessary to become a public school teacher. Before her marriage, she taught school for three years at Ione and Washoe City.[29]

It was not long before the Riters sold their little bungalow in Reno and moved into Bowers Mansion.[30] In the summer of 1917, the place that Sandy and Eilley Bowers had built was once again a home. With Henry and Edna's care, the resort remained a summer destination and playground for anyone wishing to make the journey to the remarkable place.

The next few years were difficult for the country. The entrance of the United States into World War I, an influenza pandemic, and the ratification of the Eighteenth Amendment banning the manufacture, transportation and sale of intoxicating liquors all combined to make for sober times, literally as well as figuratively. Nonetheless, journeys to Bowers Mansion continued to be an inexpensive escape where everyone could enjoy the relaxing atmosphere. Riter turned his library bar into a soda fountain and encouraged families to drive to the mansion, where "the older folk sat on the lawn, and recalled the past. The younger groups arranged the lunches and games, while the children scampered over the hill or played in the water."[31] During the long winter months, when it was too cold to picnic, guests were still welcome to spend time in the hot spring baths. In February 1921, locals could even see the mansion at the Rialto Theater in Reno in the form of the silent movie. *The Jucklins*, based on Opie Read's 1896 novel, was set in rural North Carolina, but the producers used both Bowers Mansion and Donner Lake, California, for shooting locations.[32]

Like many locals, Riter found a way to profit from the Nevada divorce trade. Ruth Weatherstone had been living at Bowers Mansion while awaiting her six-month residency to obtain a divorce from a mystery man she had married three years earlier. Weatherstone, a native of Norway, met her future husband in New York soon after her arrival. After an impulsive marriage, the two traveled throughout the country while living a luxurious lifestyle. When she questioned where he acquired his wealth, he replied, "I am caring for you and that is all that should concern you." Soon after the birth of a child in California, her husband left. His last words to her were, "You will never see or hear of me again."[33] An uncontested divorce was her only means to emancipate herself from the unhappy bond.

It is unclear if others seeking divorces lived at the mansion as Riter continued to promote a family atmosphere. His efforts were tainted when, on May 11, 1922, the former brewer was arrested for violating the Volstead Act of 1919, prohibiting the manufacture and sale of alcoholic beverages. He pled his innocence but was convicted by a jury seven months later. Although he appealed his case, in the end, he agreed to serve four months in the county jail. His arrest and conviction continued to plague the resort when drunk teenagers, returning home, informed their parents that they had secured the liquor at the mansion. Henry took out advertisements assuring people that the resort did not and would not sell alcohol on the premises.[34]

As times changed and motorized vehicles became more popular, the concept of a transcontinental highway was formed. West of Fallon, the new Lincoln Highway divided, giving westbound drivers a choice to cross the Sierra Nevada by driving through Reno and over Donner Summit or by way of Carson City and South Tahoe. Riter used his business influence to persuade Governor Emmet Boyle to link the Reno and Carson routes of the Lincoln Highway by building the proposed road on the west side of Washoe Lake.[35] Riter and longtime Washoe Valley ranch families, the Winters, Sauers, and Twaddles, all deeded the right of way through their land for the new highway. On September 15, 1922, the Reno–Carson City Highway opened, allowing traffic to travel the new concrete road along the west side of Washoe Lake. Before the improvements, Carson City resident Everett White Harris recalled that the trip from Reno to Bowers Mansion took two hours or more, depending on how many flat tires needed repairing. It was now a smooth journey. With the completion of the highway, Riter saw the need to provide additional auto services, so he converted his old carriage house into a garage and began selling Quick Starting Red Crown Gasoline in 1924.[36]

That same year brought another innovative addition to the mansion when Riter built a powerhouse with a Pelton Wheel on Franktown Creek about one mile northwest of the grounds. This new power source provided electricity for laundry and kitchen appliances and interior lighting for a few hours each night. Walter Van Tilburg Clark described the outdoor lighting in his novel, *The City of Trembling Leaves*, published in 1945. He recalled, "The little lights on lines around the pools and the dance platform . . . made the sky as dark as the valley."[37] Soon after the mansion became electrified, the *Nevada State Journal* noted that the lights were burning low. A winter drought left little of the water needed to generate power. There was only enough electricity for lighting.[38]

It had been more than a half century since Eilley lost the mansion and almost three decades since her passing. Few locals could now claim to have known her personally, and her story was almost forgotten outside of anecdotes told around picnic tables on the grounds where she once hosted lavish parties. This all changed in early 1929 when Eilley's life story became the subject of a novel. Written by former University of Nevada English professor Gustavus Swift Paine, the fictional biography, *Eilley Orrum, Queen of the Comstock*, became a huge success. At the time, Paine was living in New York, but he had recently visited Virginia City, where he spoke to longtime residents and meticulously read local newspapers. *The New York Times* provided a flattering summary of the novel: "The fabulous story of Eilley Orrum is elegant entertainment throughout."[39] The novel wove together fact and fiction to create a long-lasting tale that would forever influence people's perception of Eilley's life.

Another new chapter for the mansion began on May 20, 1931, when Maurice J. Sullivan, an attorney representing some Los Angeles investors, set up a meeting with Riter to discuss the purchase of the estate. Sullivan presented Riter with plans for a new resort and offered to pay him $125,000. It was a fair price, considering that Riter had previously invested about $50,000 on improvements. The proposal was no doubt inspired by actions taken by the state that year to legalize gambling and to make Nevada a tourism destination. Conceiving of a sizeable investment in the area amid the Great Depression underscores the importance of the growing gaming industry.

The tentative proposal included returning the mansion interior to its 1860s appearance and constructing a large modern hotel, casino, and sanitarium. Sullivan's investors also planned to subdivide the fifty-six acres of land into home sites in addition to building summer cottages on the northern section of the property. Each cottage would include a steam bath. They believed the springs and powerhouse provided ample water and electricity for ten thousand people. It was a difficult decision and a potential opportunity for Riter, now sixty-seven years old, to retire. Nevertheless, a deal was never reached, and he continued operating the resort himself.[40]

After almost a decade of picnics, dances, and parties, a seemingly ordinary event found its way into Nevada history. On July 31, 1932, a picnic held in honor of men and women who had lived in the state for more than fifty years, was hosted by the Nevadans' and the Nevada Native Daughters societies. At the appointed hour, almost four hundred guests gathered on the grounds in front of Bowers Mansion. Shade from the pine-covered hills and a gentle wind cooled the guests. The scent of pine and sage revived their childhood memories of being raised in Nevada. Honored speakers of the day, Morley Griswold, the state's lieutenant governor, Felice Cohn, president of the Nevadans', and R. K. Colcord, a former Nevada governor, echoed their sentiment. After the speeches, organizers placed a square grand piano on the front balcony. Bertha Raffetto concluded the program with a simple yet poetic melody she had finished composing earlier that morning. For the first time, Nevada's sons and daughters heard the now iconic song, "Home Means Nevada," eventually destined to serve as the state's anthem. Bertha later recalled, "I wanted to express in a simple, natural style, those enduring and homely qualities I had found in Nevada—the same qualities one finds in a good home—beauty, joy and security."[41]

Another successful decade passed, and in the fall of 1943, Riter celebrated his eightieth birthday. After spending half his life caring for the mansion, it was time to find new owners. He had two offers of $75,000, but each came from individuals wanting to turn the resort into a "Gambling Palace," as the *Reno Evening Gazette* reported. Riter was not opposed to gambling, but the newspaper added that he felt that "Bowers has too long been a playground for children to have it now turned into a gaming resort and roadhouse of the old days."[42]

Instead, Riter began negotiations to turn Bowers into a state park, so future generations of children could enjoy the grounds as their parents and grandparents once had.[43] A *Reno Evening Gazette* reporter endorsed the plan when he wrote:

> Nevadans—especially of those whose memories are rich with recollections of all-day pilgrimages there for family picnics. Some of the oldsters recalled the horse-and-buggy days when travel consumed a large part of the day and left little time for youngsters to "explore" and swim. Even when the early model automobiles came into use—before the paving was laid—the trip homeward was usually made in the dusk, with the acetylene lamps sending feeble shafts of light up the graveled, but rutty, road. But all of the youngsters who participated in those expeditions absorbed a great deal of early Nevada history, from the anecdotes passed back and forth over the picnic table.[44]

FIG. 31. This photograph captured Henry and Edna Riter at Henry's eightieth birthday party in 1943. After forty years of running the mansion as a resort and making it their home for almost three decades, the couple was ready to retire and made plans to sell the estate.

He went on to add that Henry Riter and state parks superintendent Robert A. Allen "are entirely correct in stating that this property should be preserved for all time, as a historical site and as a recreational center. Nevadans everywhere will hope that the negotiations now reported under way will be culminated with the state's acquisition of the property."[45] The state declined the opportunity, and the mansion's future remained unresolved for the next few years.

The threat of losing Bowers Mansion as a summer destination loomed on a cold January morning when five members of the Reno Women's Civic Club drove to Bowers Mansion, hoping to speak to Riter personally. Dorothy Allen, Ella Gottschalck, Elvira Fox, Ethel Parker, and Villa Peckham arrived to find him talking to some California investors prepared to give him a $25,000 down payment for the sale of the property. Riter told the men that they would have to wait a moment so he could speak to the new arrivals. He is reported to have said, "Ladies, I don't want them to have it. It belongs to Nevada and Nevada's children. What kind of offer can you make me?" The five representatives huddled for a minute or two, then Dorothy Allen returned with one dollar and an option to produce $25,000 in three months. They promised to take care of the additional $75,000 needed to pay Riter a total of $100,000 later.[46]

On January 26, 1946, the Bowers Mansion Association's inaugural members met at Parker's home. They promptly appointed officers with Allen as chair; Harriett Spann, co-chair; Alice Addenbrooke, secretary and historian; Trudy Fowler, corresponding secretary; and Frances Beaupeurt, treasurer. Lloydine Clayton, Harriet Gelder, Gottschalck, Parker, Peckham, Anna Belle Washburn, and Joyce Williams were additional Reno Women's Civic Club members who assisted the officers. Dozens more quickly joined the newly formed Bowers Mansion Association.[47]

At their fourth meeting on February 11, they coined the phrase "In Memory of the Past—Buy Bowers Mansion for the Future." With the campaign moving forward rapidly, they reached out to local governments, schools, lodges, organizations, newspapers, and radio stations to help spread the word. They placed old coffee cans in local stores, libraries, and the mansion. No donation was too small. Children gave coins during school penny drives, and locals from all over northern Nevada began sending what they could to the committee. Forty-seven children from the Carson Orphans Home raised a total of $23.50. The organizers were grateful for every contribution, noting that "the three pennies that came from a little boy were just as important as larger sums."[48]

Unfortunately, many local businesses, which the women were confident would make large donations, said the mansion was not worth saving. They also questioned who would manage the park and take care of maintenance. Many believed it was a hopeless endeavor. Then on February 20,

FIG. 32. A group of women representing the Reno Women's Civic Club began a campaign to save Bowers Mansion from being sold in 1946. This image depicts the first group to be known as the Bowers Mansion Association. (*Left to right, standing*) Ethel Parker, Ella Gottschalck, Anna Belle Washburn, Harriett Spann, Villa Peckham, Harriet Gelder. (*Left to right, sitting*) Lloydine Clayton, Joyce Williams, Dorothy Allen, Alice Addenbrooke, Frances Beaupeurt. Not pictured: Trudy Fowler. Courtesy Bowers Mansion photo collection; donated by Frances Beaupeurt.

Addenbrooke, Gelder, and Spann appeared before the Washoe County Commission and asked for assistance. The commissioners agreed to help in any way they could, even though the Bowers Mansion Association had only collected $1,035 by March 8. Later that month, the commissioners agreed to investigate the legality of the county purchasing the grounds to serve as a public recreation park.[49]

Addenbrooke began writing newspaper articles reminding locals of the mansion's long and eventful history. The women spoke at meetings of any organization that would hear them. At the end of each gathering, they passed the collection plate. They even asked for donations in motion picture theaters before each film. They organized luncheons at the Mapes Hotel and offered picnic excursions as fundraisers. A large banner reading, "Help buy Bowers Mansion," hung over Virginia Street.

FIG. 33. According to Hymers family history, this bedroom set was purchased in London during the Bowers's European excursion in 1862. During the 1946 campaign to save the mansion, the set was displayed in a Reno furniture store with a sign saying, "Help Save Bowers Mansion." It was donated back to the mansion in 2023 by the Hymers family. Courtesy Bowers Mansion photo collection.

They ran full-page newspaper ads listing those who had already donated money. Lew Hymers, a Nevada artist and political cartoonist, lent a bedroom set, initially owned by Sandy and Eilley Bowers, to be displayed in the window of a local furniture store.[50]

In April 1946, the group met with the county Chamber of Commerce. They were nowhere near their goal, with only $3,090 in the bank. The committee, feeling defeated, knew that collecting an additional $75,000 from local citizens would be impossible. Everything changed when Spann, Gelder, and Addenbrooke entered the room with news from the county commissioners, who were now convinced that the public wanted Bowers Mansion saved. Since they believed the women could collect the down payment, the commissioners agreed to take over the balance themselves and dedicate Bowers Mansion Park to honor the sons and daughters of Nevada veterans of World War II. With renewed faith in the drive, locals made additional donations to the cause.[51]

On April 20, the *Reno Evening Gazette* announced that the Washoe County Commission had appointed three disinterested persons to appraise the mansion's value. They returned with a figure of $100,005. Five days later, local newspapers reported that the campaign had hit the halfway mark with only $12,500 of the down payment left to raise. As the women inched closer to their goal, more locals believed this small group of local women might pull off this seemingly impossible task. New donations arrived daily.[52]

At the end of April, the Washoe County Commission and other interested parties joined the women for a meeting at the district court to discuss the future of Bowers Mansion. The commissioners suggested two goals: developing the recreation aspect of the grounds and preserving the historic atmosphere of the park. The picnic grounds and swimming pools did not present a problem, but the use of the building was a concern. Addenbrooke proposed collecting material from the period, even if the items did not belong to the Bowers family, to give the interior an authentic appearance. Spann suggested that the original group of twelve women from the Bowers Mansion Association oversee restoring and furnishing the home. Commissioner Carl Shelly reminded the women that the mansion had been purchased "without strings." Addenbrooke agreed but added, "The original Bowers Mansion group still was interested and intended to support the Commissioners in their efforts to improve and develop the project as a county park."[53] Commissioners agreed that the Bowers Mansion Association would continue to work with the county to refurbish and run the mansion as a museum.

As the deadline neared, the women worked tirelessly to collect the remaining funds, and by the end of the month, they had $13,353 in the bank. On the evening of April 30, the drive ended. The campaign was still short of its goal, but donations continued to trickle in. On May 1, Riter, his attorneys, and the county commissioners went ahead with their scheduled meeting to discuss details of the transfer of property. There was no mention or worry that the Bowers Mansion Association was still short of its goal.[54]

Then on May 6, 1946, at the twenty-ninth meeting of the Bowers Mansion Association, Beaupeurt and Addenbrooke drafted a check for $20,000 and presented it to the Washoe County Commissioners. They agreed to pay the additional $5,000 within weeks. During the final push, Henry and Edna Riter donated $2,500. Ultimately, the Bowers Mansion

Association raised $25,400.78 from more than 1,500 organizations, businesses, and individual subscriptions.[55]

With Bowers Mansion now belonging to Washoe County and Nevada's children, Riter could retire. He and Edna left their home in the valley and moved into a little Tudor on Lander Street in Reno, where they could live quietly. Three years later, Henry Riter began feeling ill. At eighty-five, he died peacefully in a local hospital on September 1, 1949. Many locals and Washoe Valley residents attended his funeral.[56]

Riter had found rest, but the Bowers Mansion Refurbishing Committee's work had just begun. Addenbrooke was named superintendent in April 1950 with a salary of $250 plus transportation.[57] Her first task was to collect original and period furniture that would take Bowers Mansion back to Nevada's heyday. The Refurbishing Committee once again put out a call to locals who began donating Victorian-era items. On June 18, 1950, the doors of Bowers Mansion were once again open to the public, allowing locals to journey back in time and experience how millionaires Sandy and Eilley Bowers lived in the glory days of the Comstock Lode.[58]

CHAPTER 10

Restoration

As 1964 APPROACHED, NEVADANS PREPARED to celebrate their one-hundredth anniversary of statehood. The Nevada Centennial Commission called on all counties to create a flag to display at commemorative events.[1] In response, the Washoe County Parks Commission spent many hours discussing possible designs. The final drawing came from Washoe County Parks Commission member Dorothy Stafford.[2] Her sage green banner included the image of Bowers Mansion at the center. Behind the mansion lay snowcapped mountains, pine trees, Pyramid Lake, and Lake Tahoe. Commission Chairman J. C. McKenzie told a *Reno Evening Gazette* reporter that "the flag stands for Washoe County and Nevada one hundred percent."[3]

Bowers Mansion had become an official symbol of Washoe County, and its ever-popular pools were attracting almost twenty-five thousand swimmers each summer.[4] A century had passed since Sandy and Eilley first welcomed friends to their home for a relaxing retreat. During those early days, guests quietly napped under tall shade trees and took soothing dips in one of two hand-excavated swimming ponds fed with clear, natural spring water. The grounds had changed little from the days when the Miner's Union first brought their families to the mansion for a memorable day of picnicking, swimming, dancing, playing games, or just escaping the fast-paced world of Virginia City. The giant poplar trees planted by Henry Riter remained, lining the mansion drive, and childhood memories were still forged each summer. Nevertheless, thousands of visitors and a hundred years of weather had taken a toll on the pools and grounds.

Over the years, Riter made many improvements, including modernizing the pools before the 1925 season. He contemplated removing the islands that had graced each pool's center for decades, but he ultimately

FIG. 34. Created to help celebrate Nevada's state centennial in 1964, a flag bearing this emblem featured what the county commissioners felt was important about Washoe County. The sage green banner includes the image of Bowers Mansion at the center. Behind the mansion lie snowcapped mountains, pine trees, Pyramid Lake, and Lake Tahoe. Courtesy Washoe County Commission.

left them in place for the enjoyment of swimmers and sunbathers. However, he deepened the cold pool's east half and built a concrete wall around each swimming pool with steps on the west and east sides.[5] Even with these improvements, the swimming ponds continued to deteriorate. Adding to Riter's problems, the state's health department required him to sterilize the pools using a chlorine additive. Unfortunately, water still flowed from the reservoirs and into a nearby field where the chemicals killed surrounding plants.[6]

When Washoe County purchased the grounds and pools in 1946, park officials also struggled with the state's regulations. A year after the purchase, county health officer Dr. A. R. DaCosta allowed the pool to remain open but stated there would be no renewal the following year. State health official W. Wallace White determined the historic ponds needed to be entirely rebuilt. In a *Nevada State Journal* report detailing the dire situation, County Commissioner James Peckham said, "It looks like the day of the old swimming hole is being replaced by a new era of rigidly controlled sanitary swimming pools."[7]

In the meantime, commissioners concluded that cementing the base of the pools would work as a short-term solution. The original stone-lined swimming ponds had sandy white bottoms that allowed water and chemical additives to ooze through and flow into the eastern meadow. The restoration project covered the natural bottom with rough concrete. White determined that a smooth floor was slippery and dangerous for swimmers. He chose to use a broom finish to reduce slippage. After receiving several complaints about it being too abrasive and easily cutting people's feet, he lessened the problem by grinding the surface, but the white sand floor never returned.[8]

Almost twenty years later, maintaining and cleaning the concrete ponds had become overwhelming. Once a week, workers drained and scrubbed each pool. The problem persisted even with new scum gutters, used to help filter water, and sundecks to reduce debris entering the pools. In addition, they needed an entirely new water treatment system. In the end, county commissioners determined that the pools were unsalvageable. They then ordered County Manager C. B. Kinnison to build new facilities using money from a million-dollar bond approved by Washoe County voters in 1962.[9]

The summer of 1964 marked the final season for the original swimming holes. The parks commission approved plans to construct a modern swimming facility north of the old ponds. After reviewing several bids, A. Dee Construction Company won the $143,449 contract.[10] Its proposal included a forty-foot wide and one-hundred-and-forty-foot long, almost Olympic-sized pool in the shape of a Z. The southwestern end housed two diving boards. The low board was three feet high, with a high dive at nearly ten feet. A shallow play area occupied the northeastern portion of the Z. The second pool offered a fifteen-by-twenty-five-foot wading pool for tots. An adjacent building rose to house a new water filtration system.[11] Soil removed to excavate the new pools filled the historic cold pond. Crews worked through the spring, and the facility was ready before schools released students for summer vacation.

Water for the new pools came from two sources. Riter improved the original Bowers Springs in 1927 when he excavated a new water supply in Kelly Canyon behind the mansion. Riter Springs, 5,500 feet northwest of Bowers Mansion, produced a low dissolved mineral content that flowed at a frigid 54 degrees Fahrenheit. This was too cold for swimming, but it was very desirable for drinking. As noted earlier, Riter created the Reno Mineral Company, where he bottled and sold water under the name Shoshone Mineral Water starting in 1909.[12]

An attempt to drill for cold water in 1962 encountered a 117 degrees Fahrenheit water source at a 207-foot depth. This hot Bowers Well offered an ideal thermal water supply for the new pool and wading pond, but it was too hot for swimming. To solve this problem, they combined hot and cold water for a comfortable 76 to 78 degrees Fahrenheit, a perfect swimming experience. Eilley's original hot spring pond became a reservoir and cooling pond for the new irrigation system.[13]

The next generation of Bowers swimmers entered the new complex on June 19, 1965, and county officials dedicated the facility on August 7, 1965. In addition to the swimming pools and bathhouse, the renovated Bowers Mansion Park and Recreation Complex included public restrooms, reworked landscaping, a children's playground, group picnic areas, and individual picnic sites, each with a concrete pad, barbecue, and table. To make this area more accessible, they also provided a large, paved parking area.[14]

Bowers Mansion Park and its pools were now modern, but the mansion itself showed signs of age. The Bowers Mansion Restoration Group, an organization affiliated with the Nevada Federation of Women's Clubs, maintained the interior and offered tours through the house, but the exterior required attention. In the fall of 1965, workers discovered a large crack in the south wall, bringing into question the stability of the structure.[15] Eilley's ninety-year-old boarding house no longer gave travelers a quiet place to rest their weary heads. The top floor had become an empty shell that was unsafe and could ruin the entire structure. The old mansion needed restoring, but the project was too massive for the county's master plan.

February 1966 brought renewed hope for the old building when the Washoe County Commission agreed to place its master park plan on the ballot as a bond proposal.[16] Washoe County Parks Commissioner Thomas A. Cooke and others pushed hard for voter approval of the bond. Cooke was born in San Francisco but was raised in Nevada. Before serving in World War II, he studied history at the University of Nevada and studied law at the Hastings College of the Law in San Francisco. From a young age, he believed in preserving the past, but he also felt strongly about slowing urban growth and establishing parks and recreation areas so residents could experience Nevada's open spaces. His father, also a lawyer, had a thriving mining practice that allowed young Cooke to learn about the importance of Nevada's industrial history. He combined all his experience and energy into educating voters about the importance of the 1966 parks and recreation bond issue.

The bond proposal put the mansion's future in the hands of the public, but it would also fund work at many other local parks, including Hidden Valley, Galena Creek, Crystal Peak, Empire-Gerlach, Peavine Mountain, Davis Creek, Pyramid Lake, Spanish Springs, Mogul, Geiger Grade, and

Paradise Park, as well as a Washoe Lake boat landing, and a golf course at Stead Air Force Base. On November 8, 1966, voters went to the polls to decide Bowers Mansion's fate. An overwhelming majority passed the $1.75 million parks and recreation bond. More than fourteen thousand voted for the bond, while fewer than eight thousand opposed it.[17] In appreciation of Cooke's efforts in helping to preserve Bowers Mansion and Park and the other recreation centers, the newly constructed playground north of the pool was named in his honor.

The parks commission then awarded the $90,000 Bowers improvement contract to architect Edward Shier Parsons. Parsons was born in Tonopah, Nevada, on April 23, 1907. As a child, he spent time in both Nevada and Utah. While he attended Reno High School, one of his teachers, Effie Mona Mack, noticed his talents and encouraged him to pursue a career in architecture.[18] Parsons began his formal education at the University of Southern California. After one year, he transferred to the University of Pennsylvania, graduating with an architecture degree in 1932. While living in Philadelphia, Parsons became fascinated with "the beautiful two-story houses with native slate stone, dormer windows with lace curtains and a Bible on the stand."[19] This experience may have inspired his future in preservation.

Parsons returned to Nevada, where he took on his first post-graduation job working for well-known Nevada architect Frederic DeLongchamps, who was just finishing his design for the Reno Post Office on the south bank of the Truckee River. Parsons spent summer vacations working for DeLongchamps, finding him an inspiration. During the Great Depression, Parsons spent some time working in San Francisco before returning to Reno to accept a job with Russell Mills and the Home Owners Loan Corporation.[20]

Finally, in 1938, Parsons opened his first office and launched his long and memorable private architectural career. But his work was soon abruptly interrupted when he joined the army during World War II. After the war, Parsons began designing various local buildings, including private homes, commercial and recreational facilities, churches, hospitals, educational institutions, and public buildings. When confronted with the opportunity to restore Bowers Mansion, he eagerly met the challenge. Parsons believed he knew enough of that period to restore Bowers Mansion to its original appearance.[21] This was not his first preservation project, but it is one of his most noteworthy.

On May 2, 1967, county workers began inventorying and removing furniture from the mansion in anticipation of the restoration work. When the project began, the mansion was in a state of deterioration, but it retained its majesty and charm. Parsons and contractor Leonard Smith eagerly endeavored to restore the mansion. Smith, a Colorado native, spent his early years on a Wyoming ranch where his mother taught students in a one-room schoolhouse, and his father worked as a contractor. Smith's family moved to Fallon when he was nine years old, and after serving in World War II, he relocated to Reno. There he began his career as a contractor. Smith had fond memories of taking his children to Bowers Mansion for family reunions and summer picnics. His daughter, Patti McClelland, indicated that he was proud to be part of this historic project.[22]

The two men worked closely together as they devised a plan to restore the old building. They adjusted their approach many times as each day brought new concerns that needed different solutions. For example, natural spring water posed a major obstacle. The hot and cold springs were advantageous when Alexander Cowan and Eilley first purchased the property. When Sandy and Eilley Bowers constructed the building, a cold spring flowed beneath the north wing cellar. Water seeped through the floor stones, keeping the cellar cool. More than 110 years later, that same spring water had disintegrated the mortar, creating an unsound foundation. Severe cracks and settling in the south wing's south wall were not as evident but this was still a threat. After the project began, Parsons and Smith realized the damage was worse than expected. After discussing the situation, they agreed that jacking up the ground floor and placing a steel beam along the foundation would stabilize the building.[23]

The next phase included reinforcing the stone exterior. The original rubble-filled walls had been covered in plaster and were scored to take on the appearance of cut stone resembling the dressed granite on the east side of the building. The engineer with whom Parsons worked, Harold V. Lamberti, suggested they remove the existing plaster, cover the walls with chicken wire and then spray it with concrete using a process known as guniting. After many attempts to find the correct consistency of concrete, sand, and aggregates, they managed to reinforce the entire building using a compressor and a long snakelike hose that resembled one used by firemen of the day. They then rescored the exterior, taking it back to its original appearance.[24]

Parsons next created a new front door using duplicate moldings from the original entry. It was then time to finish off the exterior with paint. Some of the original pigment remained, offering a glimpse into its color. Sand had been mixed in with the light, fawn-brown paint, mimicking the actual granite blocks of the east wall. With that information, the mansion was returned to its original color scheme.[25]

From the beginning, Parsons realized that the third-story addition was going to be his biggest obstacle. Rather than constructing a proper floor in 1875, carpenters used the second-floor ceiling joists to support the floor for the additional story. The construction was cheap and shoddy by any standard. According to Parsons, it was little better than a tenement-type rooming house. Because of its poor design and lack of care throughout the decades, Parsons and Smith recommended removing the mansard roof and returning the mansion to its original flat roof. Only a few Nevadans in their nineties remembered Eilley's original two-story house with its eight-sided windowed cupula, widow's walk, and three-quarter porch and balcony. The change back to the mansion's two stories with a cupula displeased many locals, even though it was historically accurate as well as needed to restore the integrity of the structure. That summer brought rainstorms, so the workers began building the new roof under the old mansard addition. When they were finished, the components of the boardinghouse were cut into large sections, allowing a crane to lower each piece to the ground where some sections simply shattered and fell apart.[26]

With the foundation leveled, the exterior walls covered and painted, and the old roof removed, the next project was re-creating the iconic wooden porch and balcony. Parsons was having difficulty spacing the columns to the dimensions that could be seen in an 1860s photograph. He then decided to excavate one corner of the twelve-foot-wide porch where he discovered the original eight-foot-wide porch foundation still in existence. By the time Riter purchased the mansion, much of the 1860s verandah suffered from wood rot. Rather than repair the damage, presumably in the mid-1920s, Riter chose to tear it down and fill the porch foundation with concrete to create a solid patio. Parsons believed that rebuilding a wood porch only to have it deteriorate again was not an option. Leveling the preexisting concrete pad and adding wood planks to resemble an old wooden porch seemed more practical.[27]

FIG. 35. By 1967, it was determined that the mansion's third story was unsalvageable and needed to be demolished. This photo shows a crane removing one section of the mansard roof. Once the old roof hit the ground, it shattered into pieces. Courtesy Bowers Mansion photo collection; donated by Leonard Smith.

With that project complete, he was able to space the new columns to resemble the original balcony. The porch was then painted to match the house, and the ceiling was painted sky blue, consistent with common practice in the nineteenth century.[28]

Now came the process of re-creating the cupula. Constructing an eight-sided room surrounded by glass windows seemed easy enough, but many questions arose, including how people originally entered the structure. Parsons had access to the 1868 inventory showing a center table, four chairs, and a rocking chair in the small octagonal room, and he had read an old letter that described Persia and friends climbing to the cupula. He took this to mean that they climbed a ladder and not the staircase guests had taken to the third-floor boarding rooms after Persia's death. Never being able to solve the mystery, Parsons removed the staircase and added a hatch door in the center hallway to allow access to the cupula by ladder.[29]

The mansion's interior needed less attention, but restoring everything to the Bowers Restoration Group's satisfaction proved a little more

FIG. 36. When Washoe County hired Ed Parsons to restore Bowers Mansion to its original appearance, he only had one image to use as his guide. He relied on this 1860s photo of the building, taken soon after construction, to reproduce the cupola and porch that had been removed many years before. Courtesy Bowers Mansion photo collection.

difficult. While repairing the plaster, Parsons discovered the original paint to be a mustard yellow color. Gladys Mapes said it looked like something from a low-rent apartment complex and declared, "I'll have no tenement yellow in this building."[30] Since they were not receiving historic preservation funds, which would have restricted the restoration to more rigorous standards, the interior was painted with an off-white tint.

After additional complaints from this group, Parsons responded in a two-page letter dated May 16, 1968. In his frustration, he explained that he did his best to restore Bowers Mansion to its original design based on historical and factual knowledge of the house. Silver doorknobs, wallpaper, and a spiral staircase to the cupula appeared to be more myth than fact. As far as decorating was concerned, anything they picked out would be based on "personal ideas of what might have been in the mansion, rather than fact."[31] With that, the Bowers Restoration Project was completed.

Furniture and other donated items were returned to the mansion as they prepared for the grand reopening. Before the dedication ceremony

FIG. 37. In 1968, Bowers Mansion exhibited its original design after the third story was removed. Courtesy Bowers Mansion photo collection; donated by Ed Parsons.

on July 27, 1968, a plaque was placed near the front entrance acknowledging all the people responsible for the restoration of Bowers Mansion. It read, "Bowers Mansion Restoration July 20, 1868. Dedicated to those who have helped make the preservation of this historical landmark possible." It then went on to list the names of all involved including county commissioners, park commissioners, architect Edward S. Parsons, and contractor Leonard W. Smith. However, there was no mention of the women who had worked tirelessly to save, preserve and restore Bowers Mansion.

To avoid an embarrassing situation, Cooke, speaking on behalf of the parks commission, altered his dedication speech to include the steadfast women. He stated,

> If it had not been for the indomitable and gallant persistence of these extraordinary women, we, and generations of Nevadans to follow, would have been deprived of this opportunity of recapturing the past. Like so many symbols of our history, it too would have been lost, and today would exist only as a vague and fanciful memory or in books. Now with the restoration complete, it isn't difficult to visualize once

> again, in our imagination, Sandy Bowers, and his friends perhaps, enjoying a late party in the billiard room, where he kept a fine stock of imported ale and liquer [*sic*]. . . . or Eilley Orrum, [*sic*] sitting in one of her throne chairs, receiving her friends from Virginia City, or perchance, catching a glimpse of her as she strolled through her garden on a summers evening. . . . Bowers Mansion, more vividly and poignantly than any history book can, tells us how it was. . . . While we should always look forward to great tomorrows, we must sometimes look back to great yesterdays . . .[32]

He added that a bronze plaque noting the names of the most significant group was being created and would be placed in the courtyard next to the plaque recognizing the original twelve women of the Reno Women's Civic Club.[33]

One month later, on August 28, 1968, Washoe County Manager Kinnison sent a letter to Frances Creek, chair of the Bowers Restoration Group, ending the women's official involvement with Bowers Mansion. The group had recently accepted a donation from the William Fife family with the agreement that the downstairs bedroom be dedicated to the Fife family. Kinnison wrote, "It is the County Commissioners' direction that this situation be remedied by furnishing all rooms in the Mansion in keeping with the Bowers tradition." He recognized the "magnificent contribution" that had been made by the group, but he informed them that they would now take on a role as an advisory committee to assist county-paid curator Ruth Eason.[34] The following season, on May 10, 1969, Betty Hood took on the role of mansion curator, a title she would hold for forty seasons.

Over the years, the advisory committee became less involved until almost all the members had died. On April 7, 2006, Gloria Mapes Walker wrote a letter to Doug Doolittle, director of Washoe County Department of Parks and Recreation, as it was then called. She enclosed a donation, a check for $3,915.12 made out to the Bowers Mansion Restoration Group. In the letter, she wrote, "Washoe County is indeed fortunate to have historic Bowers Mansion for the enlightenment and pleasure of visitors as well as residents of our state. Betty Hood with her personal dedication to the Mansion, her knowledge of the history, and her friendly concern for the visitors has done an exceptional job as curator. We are indeed fortunate to have her to showcase this jewel of our history."[35] This is the last known correspondence between Washoe County and the Bowers

FIG. 38. This is a photograph of Martin Clayton taken the winter of 1946. Lloydine Clayton brought her son to Bowers Mansion on the snowy afternoon to see for herself that it needed to be preserved. After spending the day there, she began working with other women from the Reno Women's Civic Club to keep the property from being sold to a private interest and to preserve it for Nevada's children. Courtesy Bowers Mansion photo Collection; donated by Lloydine Clayton.

Mansion Restoration Group. Hood ended her tenure at Bowers Mansion with the close of the 2008 tour season. Thanks to her devotion, enthusiasm, and determination to preserve this important story, Bowers Mansion continues to thrive as a summer destination and remembrance of the glory days of Nevada when two little-known dreamers struck it rich on the Comstock Lode.

• • •

The best view of Nevada's nineteenth century heyday can still be seen from the Bowers Mansion porch. On a warm summer afternoon, you can use your imagination to picture guests arriving for a celebrated picnic. The women in their Victorian-era dresses wear inexpensive picnic hats covered with white and green ribbons. Visitors arrive from every direction by train and horse-drawn buggy. They lay out their blankets and prepare their picnic baskets. They play games, swim in the ponds and dance throughout the day. If you listen closely, you can hear more than a century of children's laughter, for Bowers Mansion has always been a place where childhood memories come to life.

An Architectural History

Michael A. "Bert" Bedeau

The first step an architectural historian takes with a structure such as Bowers Mansion is to describe it in coldly detached, objective terms. This is needed to understand how the structure fits into the history of design over the span of centuries. The mansion is a two-story dwelling at the foot of the eastern slope of the Sierra Nevada in the extreme south of Washoe County, Nevada. It faces east, overlooking Washoe Valley and Washoe Lake with a view of the Virginia Range. The house was on the main road between Lake's Crossing of the Truckee River (later to become Reno) to the north and the territorial capital of Carson City to the south. It was near Sandy and Eilley Bowers's main gold-processing mill, which was connected to their Gold Hill mining properties by road over the Virginia Range to the east.

The house as built (and as restored) consists of a main rectangular block and two rear one-story ells forming a courtyard which originally contained a large greenhouse. The entire structure is rendered in rough-cut, locally quarried sandstone. The primary elevation is organized into five sections, or bays, with a central entry door. The building is capped by a heavily bracketed roof, topped by a decorative octagonal feature known as a belvedere.

The building is a classic example of a center hall plan. It features large parlors flanking a main stair hall with smaller chambers to the rear. The hall is dominated by a single flight staircase which provides access to a rear landing and the second floor. The southern rear ell provides service functions for the house, such as kitchen. The other ell is home to a library.

This general plan, while executed in the 1860s, has roots much further back in American and European architectural tradition.

The five-bay center hall plan originated with the European Renaissance, traveling with the general revival of interest in all things classical from Italy to France and thence to England in the sixteenth and seventeenth centuries. When Europeans began to settle and build in North America, these forms and fashions were transplanted across the Atlantic. Before the American Revolution at the end of the eighteenth century, the five-bay center hall form dominated what was known as the Georgian period in American domestic architecture, particularly in the northern colonies. This form, and the accompanying classical styling derived from ancient Greece and Rome, persisted past the establishment of the new republic and into the early nineteenth century.[1]

It was only with the emergence of Romanticism in the nineteenth century that the dominant classical style of architecture began to change in America. More whimsical styling began to take hold of architectural taste in the form of the Gothic, derived from medieval European design, and the Italianate. Italianate or bracketed style also has its origins in the Italian Renaissance. Unlike Georgian classicism however, it is not based on a fairly restrained and formal Greek and Roman precedent, but rather the more exuberant decorative traditions of Italy in the Renaissance period, particularly the rococo. The Italianate was first popularized in the United States via the published works and plans of architect A. J. Downing. His work, covering both the Gothic and the Italianate styles, became highly popular beginning in the late 1830s and came to dominate domestic fashion in the United States for the next two decades.[2]

Bowers Mansion can, then, be regarded as having a Georgian floorplan with an Italianate execution when it came to the rest of the structure. In all, the house is a typical example of a large domestic dwelling rendered in the Italianate style. Because it is built of stone rather than brick or wood, it may appear a bit more restrained than other more decorative examples. Nevertheless, it possesses all the elements of a finely crafted and *au courant* Italianate house of the early 1860s. This is demonstrated by the typically heavy, carved eave brackets which dominate the building's roof line. Other typical Italianate features are the enhanced stone blocks, or quoins, at the corners of the building, as well as a wide full porch with highly decorative turned posts and brackets, tall window openings with thick decorative hoods, and the octagonal belvedere at the roof peak.

The design for Bowers Mansion remains lost to history. No original plans have been located. Nor are there any sources from the period before or during construction in the early 1860s that reference the origins of the building's architectural design. All there is to go on is rumor, myth, and speculation. What is known is that Sandy and Eilley Bowers commissioned the dwelling to be built before their departure for their grand tour of Europe in the spring of 1862. It is clear that a set of plans did exist because they are referenced in committee proceedings from the 1873 Nevada Legislature when it considered and rejected purchasing the property for a mental hospital, as discussed below.

What is also known is that the couple left supervision of construction, along with the rest of their affairs, in the hands of their attorney, J. Neely Johnson of Carson City. He has at times been credited as the designer of the house; however, this is not likely. Johnson was an attorney, businessman, and politician. There is no indication that he had any training as a builder, let alone as a designer with the training to execute a house this complex and stylistically sophisticated. Johnson had emigrated to California during the Gold Rush, set up a law practice in Sacramento, and became involved in state politics. In 1855, he was elected governor as the Know-Nothing Party candidate and served one tumultuous two-year term dominated by strikes and political infighting. He then found it desirable to decamp to Nevada in 1860, still part of Utah Territory. He quickly established a law practice in Carson City and became involved in local politics, eventually winning an appointment to the Nevada Supreme Court in 1867.[3]

The Johnson connection, however, does lead to a possible designer. It has been rumored that Bowers Mansion was the work of a California architect. During his time as governor of California, Johnson began the construction of the new state capitol building in Sacramento. For this work, Reuben S. Clark of San Francisco was hired as supervising architect. He would have worked closely with the governor during his time in office and may well have been asked to design a house for Johnson's clients in Nevada. Clark had previously partnered with Henry Kenitzer operating a prominent architectural practice in San Francisco beginning in 1854. By 1860, Clark had moved to Sacramento to supervise construction of the state capitol where he remained until he was committed to the State Insane Asylum in Stockton, California, dying in 1866.[4]

It is also possible that Kenitzer may have assisted in the design of the Bowers dwelling. Following the dissolution of his partnership with Clark in

1860, he formed the firm of Kenitzer and Farquharson and then Kenitzer and Raun from 1870 to 1880. These firms were among the most prominent and prolific in the region during this period and can count among their commissions the Storey County Courthouse in Virginia City, completed in 1877.[5] Of course, there are other possibilities as well. Research into architectural history of San Francisco for this period is particularly difficult because many records were lost during the fire resulting from the 1906 earthquake.

Another possible source for the original design of the Bowers dwelling is a plan book or mail order plan service. These were quite popular in the United States in the nineteenth century, particularly in smaller communities without professional architects and builders. Indeed, a very prominent Nevada landmark was probably built from published plans initially used for a building nearly two thousand miles away. In 1872, the town of Lincoln, Illinois, built a large four-story brick school building. The plans for this structure were subsequently published in a popular plan book.[6] In 1875, Virginia City sought to construct a school for its Fourth Ward political subdivision. The project was begun before that year's Great Fire, which destroyed much of the center of the town, but the partially erected school survived, to be completed and opened in early 1877. For this project, the school district may have used the published plans for the Illinois school, substituting wood for brick.

It is possible that Sandy and Eilley Bowers used a similar plan book or service for their new home. One definite possibility exists in published plans by architect John Riddell of Philadelphia in 1861. Popular when released, this could have easily come to the attention of the couple. While none of the designs in the book match their mansion, there is a striking similarity, particularly with Design #22 for a mansion. This could be the inspiration or source of the plan for the house.[7]

In the early 1870s, following the death of her husband in 1868 and a decline in revenue from the Bowers mining enterprises, Eilley Bowers explored ways to generate income from her home. She began to take in lodgers and to open the house and grounds for picnics and other events. In 1873, she approached the State of Nevada to see if the property might be purchased for a state mental hospital. While the legislature ultimately declined, hearing records indicate that a set of plans were examined and that the house had originally been designed with a third story in mind.[8] Ultimately, this third floor was added by Mrs. Bowers herself to expand

FIG. 39. In 1861, John Riddell published an architectural plan book. It includes an option, Design #22, which might have inspired the approach to Bowers Mansion. Courtesy of the Smithsonian Institute.

her guest accommodations. This did not provide adequate long-term revenue, and she was forced to sell the house and its contents in 1878.

Following its sale, the house continued to function as a boarding establishment and resort on and off for the next six decades. By the late 1940s, it had fallen into disrepair and was acquired by Washoe County to be used as a park and historical museum. The county retained Edward Parsons, a prominent architect and early preservationist from Reno, to renovate the house. The decision was made to return the building to its original exterior appearance by removing the third-floor addition and replicating the original roof and belvedere. The interior of the building was essentially gutted and reinforced. The result is the structure as we know it today.

A National Context

Ronald M. James

For more than one and a half centuries, the story of Sandy and Eilley Bowers has enthralled visitors to their mansion. After its construction in 1863, the estate became an icon of the wealth made possible by the territory's Comstock mines. For many years, this was likely the most expensive house built in Nevada, and because it was opened to the public within the first decade of completion, the Bowers home and grounds became a well-known local favorite for recreation.

That is a way to understand the Bowers legacy in the context of northern Nevada, but the history of the Bowers family and their mansion also calls for a regional and national perspective. Following the 1848 gold strike at Sutter's Creek, California, fortune seekers were drawn to the West by the hundreds of thousands, hopeful of making their "pile." Many saw this subjectively defined term to be about $10,000, typically judged to be enough to purchase a farm or to start a business "back home." Most failed to secure enough gold to establish this imagined prosperous life, and, in fact, most did not return to the places of their birth.[1]

The famed 1849 California Gold Rush had many successors: Thousands of prospectors eventually fanned out beyond the western slope of the Sierra to discover new opportunities, trying to find their own boundless treasure. Subsequent rushes to new mining districts and boomtowns flamed imaginations, occasionally fulfilling dreams, but more often dashing hopes. This process continued through the end of the century with the gold rush to Yukon Territory in northwestern Canada followed by the Klondike excitement in Alaska. With the end of the rush to Goldfield,

Nevada, in the first years of the twentieth century, a chapter of North American history closed, having lasted six decades.[2]

Early on, a crucial change in the mining West occurred as placering and other approaches to extract from surface deposits yielded to underground hard rock excavations, also known as quartz mining. Placer works—the washing of soil or gravel to reveal heavier particles of gold—could, on a good day, yield significant proceeds in the hundreds of dollars. Importantly, placer miners often relied on a low-level, inexpensive technology, increasing possible profit. The simplicity of the method meant that virtually anyone could participate. That said, it was next to impossible to become a millionaire washing placer deposits because the gold was scattered in relatively small amounts over a large territory. Nevertheless, it was much easier than underground mining, which was dangerous and required investment, technology, and expertise. Digging underground was only justified if there was a concentrated vein of precious metal that could yield considerable wealth.[3]

During the late 1850s, the pursuit of underground mining in the West resulted in new possibilities, both in the retrieval of precious metals, but also in the rise of the mine-owning millionaires. At the same time, this transformation turned many dream-seeking placer miners into salaried laborers. Gone was the hope for many of making one's "pile" and retiring to an independent, comfortable life. The mining West was becoming corporate.[4]

With underground excavations begun in the 1850s, the Empire Mine near Grass Valley, California, provides an early example of how subsurface gold mining would change the West. This transformation is most clearly exhibited, however, by the discovery of the Comstock Lode in the far western reach of the Great Basin in what was then Utah Territory. Strikes in 1859 revealed significant deposits of gold, and then an assay demonstrated that silver was also present in remarkable amounts. Surface excavations represented the first chapter of the new mining district, but it was quickly clear that underground work was needed. The Comstock Mining District became an international symbol of how subsurface extraction could be engineered in the technologically driven industry during the second half of the nineteenth century.[5]

When it came to mining in the American West, the quest for a phenomenal fortune was rarely realized. Some did strike it rich, although too often success was fleeting. Imagining what to do with sudden wealth undoubtedly took countless individual paths, but for those few newly minted millionaires, patterns emerged. Their stories, grounded in Western, precious metal, hard rock mining, often included the construction of fabulous homes removed from the excavations that furnished the wealth and fueled the legends.

This can seem counterintuitive for modern tourists since historic mining districts often boast houses that are referred to as mansions. Virginia City, Nevada, has celebrated examples of so-called mansions associated with the Savage, Chollar, and Mackay mines, but these did not usually accommodate the owners. Instead, local structures served as the offices and homes of the corporate superintendents.[6]

It is a simple fact that the word "mansion" is thrown around in the West with no consistency. Accommodations for mine superintendents were places of business with space for an office as well as rooms for living, affording executives with dignified places to live and work. Mine owners when visiting the area might lodge there, but their visits were often brief. After making their fortune, they usually lived elsewhere. While sometimes extravagant for their mining-town context, houses designed for mine superintendents were humble compared with what the mining barons typically built in places removed from the mining district.

Those familiar with Virginia City may also recall the impressive structures along the famed "Millionaire's Row." Grand though some of these may be, they were not normally erected by mine owners. Instead, the remarkable houses surviving along B Street and the other upper streets of Virginia City were constructed by entrepreneurs who made their fortunes operating stores and a variety of other businesses. The fine local homes were needed so merchants, bankers, and others could tend to their enterprises in the community. Many of these structures are splendid, but again, the palaces built by those who became millionaires thanks to the mines were consistently of a greater scale.[7]

Often, mine owners did have a house near the source of their wealth. These were sometimes where they lived before making their fortune: Sandy Bowers maintained the humble dwelling he had shared with his wife in the earliest days while living and working in Bowers Ravine in Gold Hill. After the erection of their mansion, the older house served as a place where he could stay when tending to his business. John Mackay (1831–1902) used his early, unpretentious home in Virginia City in the same way until the Great Fire on October 26, 1875, turned to it ashes. After that, he may have lived for several months at the so-called "Mackay Mansion," his superintendent's house, but as soon as the International Hotel was rebuilt, Mackay moved to a suite there for many of the following years.[8]

James Fair (1831–1894), Mackay's business partner, built a significant house in Virginia City, but importantly, his magnificent mansion was in San Francisco. While only an investor in Comstock mines, James C. Flood (1826–1889), an affiliate of Fair and Mackay, built his famous brownstone mansion on San Francisco's Nob Hill. Constructed in 1886 near Fair's palatial home, the Flood Mansion is now home to the elite Pacific-Union Club. Before that, Flood expressed his wealth to the south of San Francisco at Menlo Park. His Linden Towers, nicknamed the Wedding Cake or the White Castle, was a fabulous forty-room structure approaching seven stories situated on six hundred acres. By building just south of the city, Flood was able to combine the benefits of urbanity with the luxury of living in a semirural country setting.[9]

John P. Jones (1829–1912), a Nevada superintendent of mines, a mine owner, and eventually a US senator, had a significant home in Gold Hill. Colloquially called the "Jones Mansion," the house is large, but it is hardly as grand as the structures he built elsewhere. Indeed in 1887, Jones erected a palace, which he named Miramar, in Santa Monica, California. With seventeen bedrooms, it was a mansion worthy of the name.[10]

In addition, Adolph Sutro (1830–1898) was a Comstock entrepreneur who made it rich by selling interests in his famed Sutro Tunnel shortly after its completion in 1878. His mansion on the San Francisco Peninsula near Seal Rock and the Cliff House was glamorous, combining a rural setting with easy access to the city. To facilitate the trip back and forth—for himself as well as for patrons to his famed nearby Sutro Baths—Sutro built a rail system between the largely undeveloped land along of the western shore and the city to the east. His mansion sat on what became known as Sutro Heights, enjoying a commanding view of miles of seashore, nearby rocky islets, and the expanse of the Pacific Ocean.[11]

Before considering mansions built by mine owners elsewhere, there needs to be a quick look at the house that the Winters family built very near Bowers Mansion. While the Winters brothers were early investors in the Virginia City mines and returned to Washoe Valley with substantial profit, they were at the outset ranchers and that was what they remained. They had not staked their fortune on mining even though they did seek to exploit the opportunity it offered through investments and employment.

The process of investing and profiting is distinct from the cycle of a poor miner who strikes it rich and then seeks to build his dream home or of a woman who follows much the same pattern, placing her hopes in a young mining community, making her fortune, and then building a mansion. These stories are unlike the path the Winters family followed.[12]

The mansion that the Bowers couple built in the early 1860s was removed from the mining district, but not by far. Aside from when the couple traveled to Europe, Sandy Bowers remained an active owner, participating directly in the retrieval and milling of ore, and that required being close to his claim. Later, Mackay took much the same approach, but his wife left the mining district for a lavish life in New York and Europe. She lived in palatial grandeur, while her husband only occasionally visited. Nevertheless, the Mackays exhibited the approach of a fabulous lifestyle expressed far removed from the mines. This is the pattern that mine owners typically followed as numerous examples demonstrate.

Besides the evidence of Comstock mining barons building big in San Francisco, that remarkable city provides at least one additional example. The peninsula's Pacific Heights, to the west of Nob Hill, featured Bourn Mansion, built in 1896. William Bowers Bourn II (1857–1936) had inherited the Empire Mine from his father, who died in 1874. He then turned opportunity into enormous wealth. Besides the fortune in gold from California's Empire Mine in Grass Valley, which yielded bullion for decades, the younger Bourn also invested in the San Francisco Gas Company and the Spring Valley Water Company.

With Bourn there is, again, a pattern of a local house being eclipsed by its urban counterpart: The so-called "Bourn Cottage" at the site of the mine was constructed in 1897, using rock taken from the mine. This gave the mine owner a comfortable place to stay when visiting his property in the lush, rural setting of the Empire Mine. That said, extravagant scale was reserved for elsewhere, first with San Francisco's Bourn Mansion and then with his famed Filoli, the impressive estate built between 1915 and 1917 on a sprawling 715 acres to the south of San Francisco at Woodside. The name for this exaggerated expression of wealth combines the words, "Fight, Love, Live" taken from Bourn's credo, "To fight for a just cause; to love your fellow man; to live a good life."[13]

Turning from the Pacific Coast, it is possible to see the tendency for wealthy mine owners to build on a grand scale in a city, removed from the source of their millions. Patrick "Patsy" Clark (1852–1915) had been a superintendent at a Comstock mine before becoming associated with Marcus Daly, managing the copper mines of Butte, Montana. He operated and controlled mines in Coeur d'Alene, Idaho, and in British Columbia, using these opportunities to rise among the ranks of millionaires. Clark had built a mansion in Spokane, Washington. After the house burned in 1889, he built another, an almost twelve-thousand-square-foot palace completed in 1898. At three and a half stories and together with furnishings, it was reputed to have cost $13 million.[14]

Thomas Kearns (1862–1918), co-owner of the Silver King Mine Company in Park City, Utah, moved more than thirty miles to Salt Lake City to build his elaborate Kearns Mansion, completed in 1902. Now serving as the Governor's Mansion, it cost an estimated $250,000 and was designed by a professional architect, Carl M. Neuhausen. Kearns eventually owned the *Salt Lake Tribune* and was elected to the US Senate for one term beginning in 1901. Salt Lake City is not far from Park City, but by the same token, Kearns could have remained in the mining town or nearby in its attractive rural setting. Instead, he transferred his fortune to the largest nearby urban center and that became the location for his palatial home.[15]

Margaret "Maggie" Brown (1867–1932) has become a well-known expression of the history of women and mining, largely because she was the subject of the famous play, *The Unsinkable Molly Brown*. This promoted her story, which included a rescue from the sinking *Titanic*, an event captured in several popular films, further promoting her name. Setting aside the inaccuracies of those depictions, it is possible to consider the choices that Brown and her husband, James Joseph "J. J." Brown (1854–1922), made when it was clear that they had become wealthy. They had an impoverished start in the mining town of Leadville, Colorado. His talent as a miner inspired owners of the Little Jonny Mine to give him shares in the enterprise and a seat on the board. With their fortune made, the Browns sought an impressive place to live in an urban center, in this case, purchasing a sizeable house in Denver.[16]

As a humble couple who struck it rich, their story recalls that of Sandy and Eilley Bowers. Nevertheless, the analogy quickly fails. J. J. Brown continued to work the mine far removed from their house in Denver. Maggie Brown preferred to live an urban life of the arts, culture, and travel. She went on to make significant contributions to social reforms, including juvenile justice, and advancing the rights of women. Because of the growing divide, the couple eventually separated.

The tendency for successful precious metal miners of the West to build elaborate mansions in large cities was not necessarily echoed in coal country or in other mining endeavors that pursued extensive lower-value deposits. Bramwell, West Virginia, sat in the middle of coal fields, and yet it boasted elaborate homes built by millionaires who made their wealth in that industry. Similarly, E. E. White built his mansion in Glen White, West Virginia, close to his coal-bearing property.[17]

Founded on copper mining, Douglas Mansion was built in 1916 near the source of the family's revenue in Jerome, Arizona. Similarly, William A. Clark (1839–1925) located a mansion in the 1880s near his copper mines in Butte, Montana.[18] Here, the pivotal factor is, perhaps, the fact that to be profitable, copper like coal must be mined with an extensive operation. Wealth is generated by means of years of managing a marginally profitable resource. A hard rock gold mine pursuing a narrow seam of the precious metal may yield bullion for years, but its path to a fortune was either obvious in a short time or the district was likely abandoned, deemed unworthy of the effort and expense.

The approach to building one's palatial residence near the source of wealth appears to extend to other extractive industries that depended on lower-value products requiring the processing of large quantities of material. Thus, lumber barons also tended to build their mansions in the communities where their mills processed logs. The famed Carson Mansion in Eureka in northern California is an excellent example of this approach to grandeur. Built by lumber magnate William Carson (1825–1912) in the early 1880s, the monument to craftsmanship in wood allowed for proximity to the industry that earned Carson his fortune.[19]

Industries that depended on extensive low-profit extraction of resources established a pattern of mansion construction distinct from choices of owners of successful precious metal mines of the West. To find their ostentatious exhibitions of wealth, it is usually necessary to travel away from the centers of industry, the source of their fortune. Occasionally, second-generation mansions were built in more pastoral settings: Bourn's Filoli leaps to mind. Hearst Mansion can be seen as another second-generation mansion with a link to mining. George Hearst (1820–1891) founded his dynasty on gold and silver in the West, but his son,

William Randolph Hearst (1863–1951) built upon that with his trade in media. Regardless of the roots of the fortune, the younger Hearst's fabulous mansion in San Simeon, California, is an expression of what subsequent generations sought to do with their wealth.[20]

Similarly, George Whittell Jr. (1881–1969) built the Thunderbird Lodge on the shore of Lake Tahoe, Nevada. He was a third-generation scion of San Francisco wealth, generated beginning in the 1850s by exploiting the mercantile needs of the California Gold Rush. He used his rural mansion as a retreat, while his principal residence was a palatial estate in Woodside, south of San Francisco, a neighbor of Filoli.[21]

Given this context, it is reasonable to consider why Sandy and Eilley Bowers chose to build in Washoe Valley, separate from the mine that produced their riches but also removed from any city. It is important to point out that they made their fortune early in the history of hard rock mining in the West, so they did not have examples to imitate. Those who followed, winning fortunes in Western mining, tended to build mansions in cities, often far removed from the source of their wealth. This tendency may have been influenced by the observation that precious metal mining districts invariably failed, so locating a magnificent house there would not be prudent. It also seems that many of these *nouveau riche* imagined having a palace in an important city, and that was usually somewhere else.

Tens of thousands came to the West, worked hard at mining, and dreamed of winning this nineteenth-century lottery. Just as people today fantasize about what they would do if they held a winning ticket, those who labored in the mines, retrieving precious metals from the ground, considered what they would do if they found a huge treasure. It is easy to picture fortune seekers exchanging ideas with one another in the evening after a day of exhausting work.

Given all this, the question remains as to why Sandy and Eilley Bowers decided to build their mansion where they did. Perhaps they were simply not good at being rich and did not know what to do with their fortune. Their prosperity did, after all, evaporate before their eyes, leaving Eilley impoverished in her final decades. Ultimately, the reason why Sandy and Eilley Bowers did not move to a city is largely unknowable and must be set aside. There may also have been obvious reasons for avoiding Gold Hill: Although it was the source of their good fortune, the Comstock is arid and runs counter to any idealized bucolic setting that existed on the western slope of the Sierra at the Empire Mine, for example. In addition, in the early 1860s, Virginia City and Gold Hill were booming, but they were not anywhere near the scale of San Francisco of opulence.

It is tempting to conclude that Eilley wished to express sudden good fortune with a country estate, the sort of thing she knew from her homeland in Scotland. As with so much of what was behind the choice of Sandy and Eilley Bowers, there is no way to know if this ideal was a legacy of her earliest experiences. Of course, the decision was easy to make since she owned land in Washoe Valley, in what was a beautiful, lush setting. Perhaps that aspect of the property served as sufficient enticement to build there. Like the copper and coal barons and like John Mackay a decade later, Sandy Bowers clearly felt the need to be close enough to manage his mine. At the same time, Eilley may have been the driving force to exploit the pastoral setting of her real estate for her dream home, but this second point remains unverifiable. Whatever inspired the couple, their choice did not serve as a model for subsequent precious metal mining barons. In this sense, Bowers Mansion represents an important example of how the earliest of the *nouveau riche* of the mining West expressed sudden good fortune.

It is perhaps ironic that many children of Western tycoons sought pastoral settings for their mansions. Bowers Mansion represents a choice that was unusual for the newly minted mining moguls who followed, making it largely a historical dead-end for these first-generation millionaires. Still, it was a pattern followed by the children of newfound wealth.

In addition, while Bowers Mansion was built on a grand scale, it is also important to remember that this house was quickly outdone by those that followed in the cities of the West. The mansion is monumental, but the true American mining palaces were yet to be erected. Nevertheless, the home of Sandy and Eilley Bowers provides insight into the spectrum of hopes and ambitions of the earliest fortune seekers in the region, should they fulfill their dreams by striking it rich.

Notes

Chapter 1: Emigrating to America

1. *Nevada State Journal*, August 20, 1901, 1:7.
2. Oakland, California, Death Records. #11 in October deaths. (FHL Film #1577750).
3. Oram family records from Andrew Crawford, great grandnephew of Eilley, living in Scotland.
4. Mormon Church Endowment House, Sealing and Endowment Records. Book A and A1, 1851–1854, 37–38, February 29, 1852 (FHL Film # 1255545).
5. British Marriage Records, Church of Scotland, Clackmannan Parish, 196 (FHL Film #102092).
6. Mormon Church Endowment House, Sealing and Endowment Records. Book A and A1, 1851–1854, 37–38, February 29, 1852 (FHL Film # 1255545).
7. Conway B. Sonne, *Ships, Saints and Mariners, 1830–1890* (Salt Lake City: University of Utah Press, 1987) 204; New Orleans Shipping records—Passenger list of *Zetland*, embarked from Liverpool, England, arrived April 3, 1849, #160 (FHL Film #0200161); Stephen Hunter's name is barely readable, but Ellison is clear; customs report (FHL Film # 0200240) and passenger list index verifies that Stephen Hunter was on *Zetland*.
8. Atkin, *Journal of Emigration*, 13.
9. Pratt, *Life on Board a Mormon Emigrant Ship*, 4.
10. *Millennial Star* (Manchester, UK), June 15, 1849, 40:12, 182–85.
11. Pratt, *Life on Board a Mormon Emigrant Ship*, 10.
12. Pratt, *Life on Board a Mormon Emigrant Ship*, 3.
13. Pratt, *Life on Board a Mormon Emigrant Ship*, 9.
14. Pratt, *Life on Board a Mormon Emigrant Ship*, 10.
15. Atkin, *Journal of Emigration*, 15.
16. Atkin, *Journal of Emigration*, 15.
17. *Millennial Star*, June 15, 1849, 40:12, 183.

18. Atkin, *Journal of Emigration*, 15.
19. *Millennial Star*, June 15, 1849, 40:12, 184.
20. Atkin, *Journal of Emigration*, 16.
21. Miller, *The Journal of Reuben Miller, 1811–1882*, 1.
22. Atkin, *Journal of Emigration*, 24.
23. Atkin, *Journal of Emigration*, 24.
24. Miller, *The Journal of Reuben Miller, 1811–1882*, 67.
25. Atkin, *Journal of Emigration*, 25.
26. 1850, 7th United States Manuscript Census, Great Salt Lake County, Utah Territory, 35, house #155.
27. *Acts, Resolutions and Memorials, passed at the several annual sessions of the legislative assembly of the Territory of Utah* (Salt Lake City: Joseph Cain, 1855), chapter 18, p. 162, "An Act in relation to Bills of Divorce," approved March 6, 1852.
28. *Deseret Evening News* (Salt Lake City), November 7, 1860, 8:4; Family Group Records Collection. FHL Film Genealogy Society, Stephen Hunter (FHL Film #1274383); 7th Ward Pioneer Stake 1904–1922, Record of Members 1849–1913, Salt Lake City Church Archives Historical Department. Record of Members Collection (#16).
29. Salt Lake Death Register (Salt Lake City), Book B, 127 #1814 (FHL Film #0026554); *Deseret News* (Salt Lake City), August 21, 1900, 2:1–2.

Chapter 2: Carson County

1. Cowan, "History of Alexander Cowan."
2. Cowan, "History of Alexander Cowan."
3. 1850 Salt Lake City Street Map; 1850 Pioneer Map: Great Salt Lake City, Great Basin, North America compiled by Nicholas G. Morgan Sr.; map work by J. B. Ireland. Family History Library, Salt Lake City.
4. Cowan, "History of Alexander Cowan."
5. Divorce *Alison Cowin* [*sic*] v. *Alexander Cowin* [*sic*], Probate Court Records 1855, Utah Territory, June 4, 1860, 56–57.
6. *Mormon Church Journal History*, December 1, 1853, 3.
7. Albert R. Page, *Orson Hyde and the Carson Valley Mission* (Reno: thesis, University of Nevada, Reno, history department, 1970), 35; see also Makley, *Imposing Order without Law*.
8. *Mormon Church Journal History*, May 31, 1855.
9. Richard O. Cowan, "John Cowan's Family," Cowan Family History, 3.
10. *Mormon Church Journal History*, May 31, 1855; Will Bagley, *So Rugged and Mountainous: Blazing the Trails to Oregon and California. 1840–1848* (Norman: University of Oklahoma Press, 2010); John D. Unruh, *The Plains Across: The Overland Emigrants and the Trans-Mississippi West, 1840–60* (Champaign: University of Illinois Press, 1993).

11. Angel, *History of Nevada 1881*, 35; James and Stewart, *The Gold Rush Letters of E. Allen Grosh and Hosea B. Grosh*; James, *The Roar and the Silence.*
12. "What Mrs. Dettenreider Remembers of 1853" in Bancroft, *History of Nevada, 1540–1888*, n. 74; women sometimes engaged in mining, but there is no evidence of this occurring in Gold Canyon in the 1850s: James and Raymond, *Comstock Women*; Sally Zanjani, *A Mine of Her Own: Women Prospectors in the American West, 1850–1950* (Lincoln: Bison Books, University of Nebraska Press, 2000).
13. *Mormon Church Journal History*, May 31, 1855.
14. Page, *Orson Hyde and the Carson Valley Mission*, 42; Makley, *Imposing Order without Law.*
15. Page, *Orson Hyde and the Carson Valley Mission*, 49.
16. Agreement with Reese Brothers and Alexander Cowan. 10/10/1855 in Terr-0093, #30.
17. Page, *Orson Hyde and the Carson Valley Mission*, 53.
18. Page, *Orson Hyde and the Carson Valley Mission*, 49, letter from Hyde to Young.
19. Page, *Orson Hyde and the Carson Valley Mission*, 47.
20. Page, *Orson Hyde and the Carson Valley Mission*, 53.
21. Page, *Orson Hyde and the Carson Valley Mission*, 59, letter from Hyde to Young.
22. Page, *Orson Hyde and the Carson Valley Mission*, 67.
23. Transfer of Property, John Cambell to Alexander Cowan, Carson County, Utah Territory Records, Early Maps, Book A. 1855–1860 (Nevada State Library and Archives), May 19, 1856, 15.
24. *Reno Evening Gazette*, May 31, 1930, 5:2.
25. Page, *Orson Hyde and the Carson Valley Mission*, 68, Olive Branch Millburn, *William Henry Branch, Sr.* (Salt Lake City: Paragon, 1950), 26–27
26. *Deseret News*, March 12, 1856.
27. Carter, *Heart Throbs of the West*, 456, describing the Richard Bentley, Autobiography, Mormon Church Archives, Salt Lake City.
28. Carter, *Heart Throbs of the West*, 456, describing the Richard Bentley, Autobiography, Mormon Church Archives, Salt Lake City.
29. Page, *Orson Hyde and the Carson Valley Mission*, 79.
30. Page, *Orson Hyde and the Carson Valley Mission*, 79, 82, 85, 87, 92–93.
31. Page, *Orson Hyde and the Carson Valley Mission*, 96, letter from Young to Loveland; Zanjani, *Devils Will Reign*, 75–77.
32. Angel, *History of Nevada.*
33. Page, *Orson Hyde and the Carson Valley Mission*, 99; *Western Standard*, February 14, 1857.
34. Angel, *History of Nevada*, 624, "Petition to the County Court"; Page, *Orson Hyde and the Carson Valley Mission*, 106.

35. Page, *Orson Hyde and the Carson Valley Mission*, 105, Letter from Loveland to Young.
36. Carter, *Heart Throbs of the West*, vol 7, 454, diary of Abraham Hunsaker.
37. Page, *Orson Hyde and the Carson Valley Mission*, 107, 111; letter from Young to Loveland.
38. Page, *Orson Hyde and the Carson Valley Mission*, 112; *Western Standard*, July 31, Aug 7, Aug 28, 1857.
39. Zanjani, *Devils Will Reign*, 75.
40. Page, *Orson Hyde and the Carson Valley Mission*, 115; message from Young.
41. Norman F. Furniss, *The Mormon Conflict: 1850–1859* (New Haven, CT: Yale University Press, 2005); Leonard J. Arrington, *Great Basin Kingdom: An Economic History of the Latter-day Saints, 1830–1900* (Cambridge, MA: Harvard University Press, 1958); Leroy R. Hafen and Ann W. Hafen, editors, *Mormon Resistance: A Documentary Account of the Utah Expedition, 1857–1858* (Lincoln: University of Nebraska Press, 2006).
42. "Orson Hyde's Curse," Angel, *History of Nevada*, 41.

Chapter 3: Life in a Mining Camp

1. Wright, *History of the Big Bonanza*, 11; James and Stewart, *The Gold Rush Letters of E. Allen Grosh and Hosea B. Grosh*; Hutcheson, *Before the Comstock, 1857–1858*, 14; Zanjani, *Devils Will Reign*; Makley, *Imposing Order without Law*.
2. Angel, *History of Nevada*, 104.
3. Hutcheson, *Before the Comstock, 1857–1858*, 25.
4. Makley, *Imposing Order without Law*, 124. Ambrose also appears as Ambrosia.
5. Probate court records, 1855, Application for Divorce: *Alison O. Cowin v. Alexander Cowin*, April 18, 1860, 52–54.
6. Bancroft, *History of Nevada*, 99; James and Stewart, *The Gold Rush Letters of E. Allen Grosh and Hosea B. Grosh*.
7. Wright, *History of the Big Bonanza*, 20; Angel, *History of Nevada*, 51.
8. Probate court records, 1855, Application for Divorce: *Alison O. Cowin* v. *Alexander Cowin*, April 18, 1860. 52–54.
9. Wright, *Snow-shoe Thompson*, 42.
10. Wright, *A History of the Comstock Silver Lode and Mines*, 46; Wright, *Snow-shoe Thompson*, 48–49.
11. Crowell, *A technical review of the early Comstock mining methods*, 2.
12. *Territorial Enterprise*, April 21, 1859. 1:2.
13. J. Ross Browne, *Mineral Resources of the Pacific States and Territories, 1868* (Washington, DC: Government Printing Office, 1868), Section IX, 327.
14. Henry DeGroot, *Mining & Scientific Press*. November 5, 1876, as cited in Smith, *The History of the Comstock Lode*, 95; Angel, *History of Nevada*, 571.

15. Hutcheson, *Before the Comstock*; Ronald M. James, *Monumental Lies*.
16. New York City Passport Record. US Records, Washington, DC # 6041, May 29, 1862, Vol. 229 (FHL Film #1432606); 1860, 8th US manuscript census Utah Territory, Carson County, 36, line 1; *Sacramento Daily Union*, April 24, 1868, 3:3, obituary of Sandy Bowers; Gold Hill Mining Records, May 21, 1859, Storey County 65, Book AB, 2, 3, 5, 10, 13, 15.
17. *Sacramento Daily Union*, October 9, 1863, 4:7.
18. Young, *Western Mining*.
19. James, *The Roar and the Silence*.
20. Wright, *Snow-shoe Thompson*, 46.
21. Crowell, *A Technical Review of the early Comstock mining methods*, 3.
22. James, *The Roar and the Silence*.
23. Angel, *History of Nevada*, 61.
24. *Territorial Enterprise* (Genoa), June 25, 1859, 2:3; Wright, *History of the Big Bonanza*; Eliot Lord, *Comstock Mines and Miners* (Berkeley, CA: Howell-North Press, 1959 [1883]).
25. Angel, *History of Nevada*, 571.
26. Bancroft, *History of Nevada*, 108.
27. *Territorial Enterprise*, July 9, 1859, 2:5; *Sacramento Daily Union*, October 9, 1863, 4:7; Ansari, *Mines and Mills of the Comstock Region*, 40.
28. Gold Hill Mining Records June 28, 1859. Storey County 64, Book AB, 14, 50.
29. *Sacramento Bee*, August 18, 1859, 3:3.
30. Mortgage November 2, 1863, Storey County 48, Book C, 442.
31. Smith, *The History of the Comstock Lode*, 23, 94, 96–97.
32. Paher, *Nevada Ghost Towns and Mining Camps*, 29; James, *The Roar and the Silence*.
33. Wright, *History of the Big Bonanza*, 37.
34. Angel, *History of Nevada*, 61.
35. Angel, *History of Nevada*.
36. Power of Attorney, Storey County 73, Book A, 290.

Chapter 4: The Comstock Lode

1. Bancroft, *History of Nevada*, 207.
2. Wright, *History of the Big Bonanza*, 76.
3. J. Ross Browne and James Taylor, *Mineral Resources of the United States* (Washington, DC: Government Printing Office, 1867) 28.
4. Storey County Mining Records, Book B, 359 and Book D, 154, both February 20, 1860; Book A, 652, April 12, 1860.
5. Deed, Mining & Real Estate, vol. B, Carson County, Utah Territory, Genoa, April 23, 1860; February 10, 1860, Power of Attorney, 359–60, Nevada State Library and Archives, Carson City.
6. Surveys, Carson County, Utah Territory Records, Early Maps, Book A, 388.

7. *Territorial Enterprise*, April 14, 1860, 2:4.
8. Records of Carson County, Utah Territory, 1855–1861, Application of Divorce, April 18, 1860, 52–54, and June 4, 1860, 56–57.
9. Deed, Mining & Real Estate, vol. B, Carson County U.T., Genoa, April 23, 1860, July 14, 1860, Real Estate, 361–62; July 14, 1860 Real Estate, 361–62.
10. Cowan, "History of Alexander Cowan."
11. Cowan, "History of Alexander Cowan."
12. Frank Esshom, *Pioneers and Prominent Men of Utah* (Salt Lake City: Western Epics, 1966) 823.
13. Angel, *History of Nevada*, 567.
14. Angel, *History of Nevada*, 151; Zanjani, *Devils Will Reign*; Egan Ferol, *Sand in a Whirlwind: The Paiute Indian War of 1860* (Reno: University of Nevada Press, 1985).
15. Stewart Letters, Box 4/9, July 2, 1899, letter from M. J. Henley to William Stewart, Nevada Historical Society.
16. Bowers Family Bible (held in a private collection, Virginia City, Nevada).
17. Angel, *History of Nevada*, 74, 192, 571; James, *The Roar and the Silence*.
18. Storey County Mining and Deed Records Books B, D, A, G, F, and J.
19. Angel, *History of Nevada*, 68.
20. Angel, *History of Nevada*, 68.
21. Angel, *History of Nevada*, 68.
22. Bowers Family Bible (held in a private collection, Virginia City, Nevada).
23. These figures do not include the Indigenous people. 1862 Nevada Territorial Census; James, *The Roar and the Silence*; Ronald M. James, "A Tale of Two Wests: A New Census Report for Nevada in 1860," *Nevada Historical Society Quarterly*, 53:1 (Spring 2010).
24. Smith, *The History of the Comstock Lode*, 27.
25. Some mines paid this amount before 1864, but at that point a miners union was established, and its demand for a $4 per day minimum became the Comstock standard for over a decade.
26. Addenbrooke, *Mistress of the Mansion*, 16; *Sacramento Union*, November 16, 1903, 5:3–4.
27. *Territorial Enterprise*, May 18, 1861, reprinted from the *San Francisco Herald*, May 25, 1861, 2:2.
28. *Territorial Enterprise*, June 15, 1861, reprinted from the *Marysville Daily National Democrat*, June 21, 1861, 2:3.
29. Ansari, *Mines and Mills of the Comstock Region*, 47.
30. Bowers Family Bible (held in a private collection, Virginia City, Nevada).
31. Wright, *History of the Big Bonanza*, 90; Smith, *The History of the Comstock Lode*, 23–24.
32. Storey County Mining Records and Deeds Books B, I, and H.

33. David Thompson, *Nevada Events, 1776–1985* (Douglas County, Nevada: Grace Dangberg Foundation, 1987) 14.
34. Kelly, *First Directory of Nevada Territory, 1862*, 107–108.
35. Kelly, *First Directory of Nevada Territory, 1862*, 183.
36. Transfer of Deeds, Storey County 72, Book B, 517, March 31, 1861.

Chapter 5: Comstock Millionaires

1. Deeds, Storey County 20, Book C, March 28, 1862, 173.
2. Angel, *History of Nevada*, 622.
3. Angel, *History of Nevada*, 622.
4. Storey County Mining Records Book J, April 19, 1862, 367, Book of Deeds Book C, April 30, 1862, 207.
5. Supreme Court of California #1015, Hardenbergh vs. Bacon and Woodruff, section 267.
6. Harry Parker and Frank C. Bowen, *Mail and Passenger Ships of XIX Century* (London: Sampson Low, Marston and Company, 1928), 125; Parker, Macpherson, and Bowen, *Mail and Passenger Ships of Nineteenth Century*, illustration #123; James P. Delgado, *To California by Sea* (Columbia: University of South Carolina Press, 1990), 57, 165; North Star passenger list (FHL Film #0175575); *The New York Times*, May 24, 1862, 2:1; *Daily Alta California*, May 25, 1962, 1:2.
7. Passport Application, May 29, 1862, #6041 Volume 229 (FHL Film #1432606).
8. *The New York Times*, June 18, 1962, 7, shipping advertisements; the actual shipping records for this time were destroyed by fire in London.
9. Henderson File; Storey County Courthouse.
10. Washoe County District Court Records, January 16, 1863, April 13, 1863, June 1863. The name "Poffle" is unclear.
11. Oram Family Records from Andrew Crawford, great-grand nephew of Eilley, Scotland.
12. Letter from Sandy Bowers to John Oram, Nevada Historical Society.
13. Parker, Macpherson, and Bowen, *Mail and Passenger Ships of Nineteenth Century*, 62–63; Passenger List, "City of Manchester" (FHL Film #0175582); *Hardenbergh v. Bacon and Woodruff*, section 273. The court case shows that they were in Nevada in March 1863. San Francisco passenger lists for this period were destroyed by fire.
14. Bowers Family Bible (held in a private collection, Virginia City, Nevada); Ratay, *Pioneers of the Ponderosa*, 224, 241.
15. Bowers Family Bible (held in a private collection, Virginia City, Nevada).
16. *The New York Times*, June 18, 1962, 7, shipping advertisements.
17. Letter from Sandy Bowers to John Oram, Nevada Historical Society.
18. City of Manchester Passenger List: Family History Library, Salt Lake City (FHL Film #0175582).

19. *Washoe Times*, February 28, 1863, 4:5.
20. Angel, *History of Nevada*, 15–16, 582.
21. The Bowers family may have moved into the mansion as early as August, but other than a story from Ella Bishop Drury, this is without confirming documentation. November is the first time they used Washoe Valley as their place of residence in a recorded mining transaction. Several sources provide the final cost of the mansion, but this seems to be the most accurate estimate; *Territorial Enterprise*, April 22, 1868, 3:1.
22. Furnishings are inferred from details associated with the probate Sandy's estate in 1868.
23. Paher, *Nevada Ghost Towns and Mining Camps*, 43, 45.
24. Outline map of Washoe District, Nevada: showing Comstock Lode, locations of mineral claims, shafts, mills, mining towns, etc. Washington: The Surveys (Special Collections Library and Archives, University of Nevada, Reno, 1879).
25. Paher, *Nevada Ghost Towns and Mining Camps*, 43.
26. Wells Drury, *An Editor on the Comstock Lode* (Palo Alto, CA: Pacific Books, 1948) xii–xiii.
27. 1870 Federal manuscript census, Washoe County, Nevada, 278.
28. Kelly, *First Directory of Nevada Territory, 1862*, 183,
29. Mining Records and Deeds, Storey County 28, Book P, 52; Book M, April 21, 1863, 299; Storey County 27, Book Q, April 21, 1863, 270.
30. Ansari, *Mines and Mills of the Comstock Region*, 40.
31. Convention at the time was to express monthly rather than annual percentage rates for loans, so this was likely 3 percent monthly interest due. Mortgages, Storey County 48, Book C, November 2, 1863, 442.
32. *Gold Hill News*, November 25, 1863.
33. Wright, *History of the Big Bonanza*, 99–100.
34. *Sacramento Daily Union*, December 2, 1863, 2:1.
35. Deed, Storey County, Book X, June 2, 1864, 289; Mortgages, Storey County 48, Book C, June 4, 1864, 446. Luning was the maternal grandfather of George Whittell, Jr., who would later purchase much of the Nevada side of Lake Tahoe and build a famous mansion there. James and James, *Castle in the Sky*, 11–12.
36. *Gold Hill News*, October 26, 1864, 2:1.
37. *Gold Hill News*, October 31, 1864, 2:1.
38. *Gold Hill News*, October 26, 1864, 2:1.
39. *Gold Hill News*, November 11, 1864, 2:2.
40. Elliott, *History of Nevada*, 125; James, *The Roar and the Silence*.
41. *Gold Hill News*, December 29, 1864—January 9, 1865.
42. Power of Attorney, Storey County, Book C, February 15, 1865, 259.
43. Doten, *The Journals of Alfred Doten, 1849–1903*, 824; *Gold Hill News*, March 6, 1865, 3:1.

44. Doten, *The Journals of Alfred Doten*, 830.
45. Doten, *The Journals of Alfred Doten*, 831.
46. Samuel Clemens [Mark Twain], *The Works of Mark Twain, Early Tales and Sketches, Volume 1, 1851–1864*, Edgar Marquess Branch and Robert H. Hirst, editors (Berkeley: University of California Press, 1979), chapter 41.
47. Angel, *History of Nevada*, 594.
48. Storey County, Storey County Deeds Book 27, December 20, 1866, 59.
49. *Gold Hill News*, June 15, 1865, 3:1; *Carson Daily Appeal*, June 16, 1865, 2:2.
50. *Gold Hill News*, November 23, 1865, 3:1; January 17, 1866, 3:1; November 22, 1866, 3:1.
51. Storey County 32, Storey County Deeds Book, December 20, 1866, 59.
52. Power of Attorney (January 7, 1867), Storey County, Book D, 403.
53. Last Will and Testament of L.S. Bowers, Power of Attorney, Storey County, Book D, November 2, 1869, 522–30.
54. *Territorial Enterprise*, August 4, 1867, 3:1; Nevada Bureau of Mines, *Individual Histories of the Mines of the Comstock*, No.23 (Reno: Nevada State Bureau of Mines, 1942) 2.
55. Elliott, *History of Nevada*, 125; Makley, *The Infamous King of the Comstock*.
56. *Territorial Enterprise*, October 22, 1867, 2:5 and January 19, 1868, 3:2; *Eastern Slope* (Washoe City, Nevada), February 8, 1868, 2:4; *Gold Hill News*, January 11, 1868, 3:2.
57. *Territorial Enterprise*, April 9–21, 1868, advertisement.
58. *Gold Hill News*, April 21, 1868, 3:2.
59. *Territorial Enterprise*, April 23, 1868, 3:1; *Gold Hill News*, April 22, 1868, 3:1.
60. Eastern Slope, April 25, 1868, 3:1.

Chapter 6: Bowers Mansion Resort

1. Elliott, *History of Nevada*, 113; William D. Rowley, *Reno: Hub of the Washoe Country* (Woodland Hills, CA: Windsor Publications, 1984).
2. *Territorial Enterprise*, May 9, 1868, 2:5 and November 5, 1869, 2:6.
3. *Gold Hill News*, July 22, 1868, 3:2; *Gold Hill News*, September 7, 1868, 3:1; *Territorial Enterprise*, September 8, 1868, 3:2.
4. Smith, *The History of the Comstock Lode*, 122; Elliott, *History of Nevada*, 127.
5. In the Matter of the Estate of L. S. Bowers, Storey County, Book D, November 2, 1869, 522.
6. Elliott, *History of Nevada*, 127; *Carson Daily Appeal*, November 12, 1869, 3:1; Myrick, *Railroads of Nevada and Eastern California, Vol. 1*, 138.
7. *Territorial Enterprise*, November 5, 1869, 2:6.
8. *Carson Daily Appeal*, January 4, 1870, 3:2; *Territorial Enterprise*, January 8, 1870, 3:1.
9. *Territorial Enterprise*, January 8, 1870, 3:1.

10. *Territorial Enterprise*, February 24, 1870, 3:2.
11. *Territorial Enterprise*, June 28, 1870, 2:1.
12. *Carson Daily Appeal*, July 3, 1870; advertisement.
13. *Carson Daily Appeal*, June 21, 1870, 3:1; *Territorial Enterprise*, June 29, 1870, 3:2.
14. *Carson Daily Appeal*, June 30, 1870, 3:1.
15. Order of Confirmation in the Matter of the Estate of L. S. Bowers Power of Attorney, Storey County, Book D, December 7, 1869, 522–30.
16. Smith, *The History of the Comstock Lode*, 126; *Nevada State Journal*, May 4, 1872, 3:3 and September 7, 1872, 3:2.
17. Myrick, *Railroads of Nevada and Eastern California, Vol. 1*, 157.
18. Wright, *History of the Big Bonanza*, 166.
19. *Reno Crescent*, October 26, 1872, 3:1; *Territorial Enterprise*, February 14, 1873, 2:2.
20. Wright, *History of the Big Bonanza*; Smith, *The History of the Comstock Lode*; James, *The Roar and the Silence*; Bancroft, *History of Nevada*, 136.
21. *Nevada State Journal*, April 30, 1873, 3:1.
22. *Nevada State Journal*, May 31, 1873, 3:1 and 3:2.
23. *Nevada State Journal*, May 14, 1873, 2:2.
24. *Nevada State Journal*, May 24, 1873, 3:2 and May 28, 1873, 3:1.
25. *Nevada State Journal*, May 28, 1873, 3:1; James, "Defining the Group."
26. *Nevada State Journal*, June 14, 1873, 3:2.
27. *Reno Crescent*, May 29, 1873, 3:2.
28. *Gold Hill News*, July 21, 1873, 3:2; emphasis from the newspaper article; James, "Defining the Group."
29. *Gold Hill News*, August 6, 1873, 3:3.
30. *Gold Hill News*, August 6, 1873, 3:3.
31. *Gold Hill News*, July 21, 1873, 3:2 and August 11, 1873, 3:2; *Nevada State Journal*, August 9, 1873, 3:2.
32. *Gold Hill News*, August 11, 1873, 3:2.
33. *Gold Hill News*, August 11, 1873, 3:2.
34. *Gold Hill News*, September 1, 1873, 3:2.
35. *Nevada State Journal*, September 24, 1873, 3:3.
36. *Carson Daily Appeal*, October 2, 1873, 3:2.
37. *Nevada State Journal*, December 20, 1873, 3:2.
38. *Gold Hill News*, April 27—October 8, 1874; advertisement; *Nevada State Journal*, April 23, 1874, 2:5.
39. *Nevada State Journal*, May 10, 1874, 3:2.
40. *Nevada State Journal*, May 10, 1874, 3:2 and May 8, 1874, 3:3.
41. *Nevada State Journal*, June 12, 1874, 3:2.
42. *Carson Daily Appeal*, June 14, 1874, 2:2.
43. *Carson Daily Appeal*, June 21, 1874, 3:2; *Gold Hill News*, June 3, 1874.

44. *Nevada State Journal*, June 23, 1874, 3:2; *Territorial Enterprise*, August 9, 1874, 3:2.
45. *1873–74 Nevada City Directory*, 382; *Nevada State Journal*, July 10, 1874, 3:2.
46. *Territorial Enterprise*, July 14, 1874, 3:2; *Carson Daily Appeal*, July 16, 1874, 2:2; James, "Defining the Group."
47. *Carson Daily Appeal*, July 16, 1874, 2:2.
48. Although undocumented, this observation has been attributed to a doctor who was asked to comment on the details as described by newspapers. Tradition at the mansion attributes this to an earlier curator.
49. *Carson Daily Appeal*, July 16, 1874, 2:2.
50. Letter to Alice Addenbrooke from Cora Cross Stoddard dated July 27, 1950. On file in the RWCC binder at Bowers Mansion. Also mentioned in *Nevada State Journal*, January 23, 1949, as told to by Cora before she wrote the letter.

Chapter 7: Seeress of Washoe

1. *Carson Daily Appeal*, August 6, 1874, 3:2.
2. *Territorial Enterprise*, August 9, 1874, 3:2.
3. *Nevada State Journal*, August 16, 1874, 3:2.
4. *Nevada State Journal*, August 15, 1874, 3:3.
5. *Territorial Enterprise*, September 25, 1874, 3:2.
6. Donald Tyson, *The Demonology of King James I* (Woodbury, MN: Llewellyn Publications, 2011); Christopher M. Moreman, ed., *Speaking with the Dead in American and around the World* (Santa Barbara, CA, 2013); Catherine L. Albanese, *A Republic of Mind and Spirit: A Cultural History of American Metaphysical Religion* (New Haven, CT: Yale University Press, 2007).
7. Lizanne Henderson, *Witchcraft and Folk Belief in the Age of Enlightenment Scotland, 1670–1740* (New York: Palgrave Macmillan, 2016); Alison Butler, *Victorian Occultism and the Making of Modern Magic: Invoking Tradition* (New York: Palgrave Macmillan, 2011).
8. Bernadette S. Franke, "Spiritualism and Fortunetellers on the Comstock," from James and Raymond, *Comstock Women*, 165–78; Korra Deaver, *Rock Crystal, the Magic Stone* (York Beach, ME: Samuel Weiser, Inc, 1992), 14, 20.
9. *Territorial Enterprise*, September 25, 1874, 3:2.
10. *Territorial Enterprise*, December 11, 1874, 3:2.
11. *Territorial Enterprise*, January 3, 1875, 3:2.
12. *Territorial Enterprise*, January 3, 1875, 3:2.
13. *Territorial Enterprise*, January 3, 1875, 3:2.
14. *Territorial Enterprise*, January 9, 1875, 2:4.
15. Circuit Court of Nevada Bowers vs. Mexican Gold and Silver Mining Company, March 13, 1875, District Court of the First Judicial District Records, Storey County, State of Nevada.

16. *Nevada State Journal*, January 15, 1875, 3:2, and May 27, 1875, 3:2. The newspaper described the addition of eighteen rooms, but the actual addition was only fourteen.
17. *Carson Daily Appeal*, June 26, 1875, 3:2; *Nevada State Journal*, January 15, 1875, 3:2; February 16, 1875; April 1, 1875, 3:2; June 9, 1875, 3:3; and August 4, 1875, 3:2.
18. *Carson Daily Appeal*, June 26, 1875, 3:2; *Gold Hill News*, June 28, 1875, 3:2.
19. *Nevada State Journal*, July 14, 1875 and July 16, 1875, 2:3; *Gold Hill News*, July 16, 1875, 2:4; Ratay, *Pioneers of the Ponderosa*, 230.
20. *Gold Hill News*, August 9, 1875, 3:4.
21. Smith, *History of the Comstock Lode*, 233–34.
22. *Territorial Enterprise*, August 19, 1875, 2:6.
23. *Nevada State Journal*, November 6, 1875, 3:2.
24. Angel, *History of Nevada*, 598–99; James, *The Roar and the Silence*.
25. *Nevada State Journal*, November 6, 1875, 3:2.
26. *Nevada State Journal*, December 21, 1875, 2:3.
27. *Nevada State Journal*, February 8, 1876, 3:2; *Nevada State Journal*, February 5, 1876, 3:4; *Territorial Enterprise*, February 5, 1876, 3:1 and March 15, 1881, 3:2.
28. *Nevada State Journal*, March 8, 1876, 3:2.
29. Timmer, *Reminiscences*, 35–36.
30. Timmer, *Reminiscences*, 36.
31. Ratay, *Pioneers*, 229.
32. Trimmer, *Reminiscences*, 363–64.
33. Storey County Criminal Files Book H, Storey County Court Office, 137.
34. *Nevada State Journal*, April 9, 1876, 3:2 and May 4, 1876, 3:1.
35. *Nevada State Journal*, August 6, 1876, 3:3.
36. Storey County District Court Records David B. Gates, et. al., execution, Sept 27, 1876, Storey County Court Office.
37. Ansari, *Mines and Mills of the Comstock Region*, 38–39.
38. *Territorial Enterprise*, April 1, 1877, 2:8 and April 29, 1877, 3:2; *Nevada State Journal*, June 30, 1877, 1:5 and September 8, 1877, 3:4.
39. *Territorial Enterprise*, June 6, 1877, 2:5.
40. *Territorial Enterprise*, August 12, 1877, 2:6; Ratay, *Pioneers*, 269.
41. James, *Monumental Lies*, 112–16.
42. *Nevada State Journal*, January 1, 1878, 8:2–5.
43. *Nevada State Journal*, January 1, 1878, 8:2–5.
44. *Nevada State Journal*, March 3, 1878, 3:3
45. Doten, *The Journals of Alfred Doten*, 883.
46. *Territorial Enterprise*, February 3, 1878, 3:3.
47. *1878–79 City Directory Virginia City*, 77, 105.

48. *Territorial Enterprise*, February 20, 1878, 3:3.
49. *Territorial Enterprise*, February 12, 1878, 3:2.
50. *Territorial Enterprise*, February 20, 1878, 3:3.
51. *Territorial Enterprise*, May 10, 1878, 3:2.
52. *Territorial Enterprise*, June 4, 1878, 3:3.
53. Waldorf, *A Kid on the Comstock*, 127; *Territorial Enterprise*, June 4, 1878, 2:7.
54. *Territorial Enterprise*, June 19, 1878, 3:2.
55. Wright, *History of the Big Bonanza*, 101.
56. *Gold Hill News*, October 6, 1878, 3:3.
57. *Territorial Enterprise*, October 6, 1878, 3:4.
58. As quoted in the *Territorial Enterprise*, March 26, 1878, 2:4.
59. *Territorial Enterprise*, February 20, 1878, 3:3.
60. Waldorf, *A Kid on the Comstock*, 181.
61. Margaret Marks, *An Interview with Margaret Marks* (Reno: University of Nevada, Reno Oral History Program, 1984) 14–15.
62. Warren Loose, *Bodie Bonanza* (Las Vegas: Nevada Publications, 1979) 56; James, *The Roar and the Silence.*
63. *Nevada State Journal*, May 12, 1878, 3:2 and May 23, 1878, 3:2; *Territorial Enterprise*, May 15, 1878, 3:4.
64. *Territorial Enterprise*, July 21, 1878, 3:3–5.
65. *Territorial Enterprise*, March 12, 1880, 2:8.
66. *Reno Evening Gazette*, February 9, 1881, 3:2.
67. *Reno Evening Gazette*, March 15, 1881, 3:2; February 10, 1881, 3:1; February 3, 1881, 3:2–3; and February 9, 1881, 3:2; *Carson Daily Appeal*, February 9, 1881, 3:3.
68. Angel, *History of Nevada*, 39.
69. Angel, *History of Nevada*, 39.
70. Angel, *History of Nevada*, 39.

Chapter 8: The Final Years

1. *Reno Evening Gazette*, February 7, 1881, 3:2.
2. Ratay, *Pioneers of the Ponderosa*, 85, 247; *Nevada State Journal*, September 13, 1884, 3:6 and September 13, 1884, 3:7.
3. *Reno Evening Gazette*, August 27, 1883, 3:4; Waldorf, *A Kid on the Comstock*, 184.
4. *Reno Evening Gazette*, August 30, 1883, 2:5.
5. Doten, *The Journals of Alfred Doten*, 1477.
6. *Nevada State Journal*, January 9, 1884, 3:2.
7. *Nevada State Journal*, February 16, 1884, 3:2
8. *Nevada State Journal*, March 14, 1884, 3:2.
9. *Nevada State Journal*, April 30, 1884, 3:2.

10. Doten, *The Journals of Alfred Doten*, 1514.
11. *Nevada State Journal*, June 14, 1884, 3:3.
12. *Nevada State Journal*, May 2, 1884, 2:2.
13. *Reno Evening Gazette*, June 20, 1884, 2:1.
14. *Reno Evening Gazette*, June 20, 1884, 3:3; Patty Cafferata, *Lake Mansion Home to Reno's Founding Families* (Eastern Slope Publications, Reno, 2006), 32–35. Washoe County Washoe County Deeds, Washoe County Recorder's Office, December 2, 1885, Book 11, page 320; *Carson Morning Appeal*, December 19, 1886, 3:3 and January 20, 1887, 2:1.
15. *Carson Morning Appeal*, December 19, 1886, 3:3 and January 20, 1887, 2:1.
16. *Carson Morning Appeal*, July 21, 1887, 3:4. This is also mentioned in a letter from Ella Worth to Alice Addenbrook dated October 19, 1945, on file in the Reno Women's Civics Club notes at Bowers Mansion.
17. *Reno Evening Gazette*, August 9, 1887, 3:5.
18. *Directories* (San Francisco) 1887, 1888, 1892, 1893, 1897–1901, California State Library (Sacramento).
19. *Reno Evening Gazette*, July 23, 1888, 3:5.
20. *Reno Evening Gazette*, July 23, 1888, 3:5 and July 18, 1942, 7:1–4.
21. Washoe County Deeds, Washoe County Recorder's Office, October 22, 1888, Book 23, 84.
22. Ratay, *Pioneers of the Ponderosa*, 308; *Reno Evening Gazette*, June 21, 1888, 2:2–3.
23. Wren, *A History of the State of Nevada Its Resources and People*, 479–81; Scrugham, *Nevada: Volume III Nevada Biographies*, 200–201; *Reno Evening Gazette*, November 29, 1953, 11:1–6.
24. *Reno Evening Gazette*, November 28, 1887, 3:2.
25. Ratay, *Pioneers of the Ponderosa*, 319, 248.
26. Ratay, *Pioneers of the Ponderosa*, 321, 248.
27. *Reno Evening Gazette*, March 23, 1892, 3:3; Washoe County Deeds, Washoe County Recorder's Office, October 22, 1888, Book 23, page 84.
28. *Reno Evening Gazette*, October 29, 1990, 2:1.
29. Washoe County Deeds, Washoe County Recorder's Office, July 10, 1893, Book 17, page 292; *Nevada State Journal*, July 19, 1893, 2:1.
30. *Midwinter Appeal and Journal of Forty-Nine* (San Francisco), February 17, 1894, 2:2.
31. *Harper's Weekly*, 1894, volume 38, 185.
32. *Territorial Enterprise*, January 12, 1894, 3:3.
33. *The Overland Monthly*, April 1894, 364–65.
34. Stewart Files (Reno: Nevada Historical Society).
35. Stewart Files (Reno: Nevada Historical Society), letter to Mrs. Clapp, March 2, 1900.

36. Stewart Files (Reno: Nevada Historical Society), letter to Stewart from W. M. Cary, February 27, 1900.
37. Stewart Files (Reno: Nevada Historical Society), letter to M. J. Henley from Senator Stewart, July 17, 1899.
38. Hunter Family History, Mary Frazee as told to Tamera Buzick by a family member, 1994.
39. *Nevada State Journal*, February 23, 1901, 3:2; the newspaper identified the friend as someone named Henry.
40. *Nevada State Journal*, July 19, 1901, 3:1.
41. *Nevada State Journal*, July 19, 1901, 3:1.
42. Stewart Files (Reno: Nevada Historical Society), Letter to Stewart from F. D. King, July 29, 1901.
43. Twain, *Roughing It*, Chapter 46.
44. *San Francisco Call Bulletin*, August 4, 1901, 11:1–7; *San Francisco Chronicle*, August 4, 1901, 35:2–7.
45. *Reno Evening Gazette*, July 26, 1901, 4:2 and August 20, 1901, 3:2.
46. *Reno Evening Gazette*, August 20, 1901, 3:2
47. *Nevada State Journal*, August 20, 1901, 1:7.
48. *Nevada State Journal*, August 20, 1901, 1:7.
49. Oakland Deaths, FHL Film #1577750 #11 in October 1902.
50. 1969 King's Daughters Home Flier on file at Bowers Mansion; *Oakland Tribune*, May 2, 1902, 4:1.

Chapter 9: A Resort for a New Century

1. *Carson City Appeal*, February 19, 1900, 4:1, *Reno Evening Gazette*, February 13, 1900, 1:4; Washoe County Deeds, Washoe County Recorder's Office, December 2, 1901, Book 24, page 217; *Nevada State Journal*, December 22, 1901, 1:7; previous to his death, the former attorney general signed ownership of Bowers Mansion over to his son, but after several months, the son gave it back, after which, the property shifted to Ida Clarke even before her husband's death.
2. *Reno Evening Gazette*, July 18, 1942, 7:2–4.
3. *Reno Evening Gazette*, October 7, 1943, 18:1–4.
4. Addenbrooke, *Mistress of the Mansion*, 35; *Reno Evening Gazette*, July 18, 1942; Washoe County Deeds, Washoe County Recorder's Office, April 3, 1903, Book 24, page 125.
5. Doten, *The Journals of Alfred Doten*, 2153, March 19, 1903.
6. Scrugham, *Nevada: Volume III Nevada Biographies*, 197–99; Wren, *A History of the State of Nevada: Its Resources and People*, 676–77; *Nevada State Journal*, September 2, 1949, 14:4–6 and May 28, 1902. 2:1–2. The maiden name of Barbara, Henry Riter's mother, was Hoff.

7. *Nevada State Journal*, February 24, 1903, 3:4; *Reno Evening Gazette*, May 26, 1903, 5:3.
8. *Reno Evening Gazette*, June 6, 1903, 1:2.
9. *Reno Evening Gazette*, June 13, 1903, 5:3–4.
10. *Nevada State Journal*, August 12, 1903, 1:1.
11. *Nevada State Journal*, September 1, 1903, 1:1.
12. *Nevada State Journal*, September 1, 1903, 1:1.
13. *Oakland Tribune*, April 28, 1902 (1:3–6); Oakland Deaths FHL Film #1577750 #11 in October 1903, deaths.
14. *Nevada State Journal*, November 10, 1903, 4:1; *Sacramento Union*, November 16, 1903, 5:3–4. See also Stewart Files (Reno: Nevada Historical Society), copy of letter from Eilley to Hannah Clapp, March 2, 1901.
15. *Nevada State Journal*, November 25, 1951, 5:1–4; Addenbrooke, *The Mistress of the Mansion*.
16. *Reno Evening Gazette*, November 16, 1903, 8:4.
17. *Sacramento Union*, November 16, 1903, 5:3–4.
18. *Reno Evening Gazette*, November 16, 1903, 8:4.
19. *Sacramento Union*, November 16, 1903, 5:3–4.
20. *Sacramento Union*, November 16, 1903, 5:3–4.
21. *Nevada State Journal*, April 7, 1905, 9:4; June 24, 1905, 1:3; and August 16, 1905, 3:3; *Reno Evening Gazette*, July 10, 1905, 5:4 and July 11, 1905, 4:2; New York, U.S., Arriving Passenger and Crew Lists (including Castle Garden and Ellis Island), 1820–1957, year *1905*; arrival, *New York*; Microfilm Serial: *T715, 1897–1957*; Page *88*, Line: *25*.
22. *Reno Evening Gazette*, October 19, 1905, 5:1.
23. *Nevada State Journal*, September 12, 1906, 2:7; *Reno Evening Gazette*, September 12, 1906, 7:2–3.
24. *Reno Evening Gazette*, October 7, 1909, 5:3; *Nevada State Journal*, October 14, 1910, 8:2 and July 9, 1911, 9:1–7.
25. *Nevada State Journal*, September 30, 1911, 3:1.
26. *Reno Evening Gazette*, July 22, 1912, 8:4–6.
27. *Reno Evening Gazette*, July 22, 1912, 8:4–6.
28. *Reno Evening Gazette*, May 12, 1915, 8:6–7; *Nevada State Journal*, April 16, 1915, 16:3.
29. *Nevada State Journal*, April 16, 1915, 8:7; Scrugham, *Nevada: Volume III Nevada Biographies*, 199
30. *Reno Evening Gazette*, September 1, 1949, 13:6 and April 16, 1915, 8:7.
31. Addenbrooke, *Mistress of the Mansion*, 36.
32. *Reno Evening Gazette*, February 7, 1921, 10:1–2; Opie Read, *The Jucklins* (Chicago: Laird and Lee, 1896).
33. *Reno Evening Gazette*, February 17, 1921, 13:1.

34. *Reno Evening Gazette*, May 11, 1922, 3:1; February 20, 1923, 6:6; and November 10, 1923, 8:6–7; *Nevada State Journal*, December 17, 1922, 9:2 and May 21, 1924, 8:5.
35. *Reno Evening Gazette*, December 13, 1919, 6:3 and March 16, 1920, 6:1–2.
36. Washoe County Deeds, Washoe County Recorder's Office, April 18, 1920, book 56, 1–3; University of Nevada, Reno Oral History Program, *Everett White Harris: My Years in Nevada: Life in Reno, A Career at the University of Nevada, Exploring the West*, 5; *Nevada State Journal*, September 15, 1922, 2:1 and December 16, 1924, 3.
37. Walter Van Tilburg Clark, *City of Trembling Leaves* (New York: Random House, 1945), 275.
38. *Reno Evening Gazette*, June 23, 1923, 7:7; *Nevada State Journal*, June 26, 1924, 8:1; State of Nevada Certificate of Appropriation of Water, Application number 6850, Certificate Record number 1055, Book 5, 1055; Application number 7900, Certificate Record number 1267, Book 5, 1267.
39. *Reno Evening Gazette*, June 1, 1929, 3:1.
40. *Reno Evening Gazette*, May 20, 1931, 2:4; *Nevada State Journal*, May 20, 1931, 8.
41. *Reno Evening Gazette*, August 1, 1932, 2:1; Bertha Raffetto, *How and Why "Home Means Nevada" Came to be Written* (Carson City: Nevada State Library, 1961).
42. *Reno Evening Gazette*, October 7, 1943, 18:1–3.
43. *Reno Evening Gazette*, October 7, 1943, 18:1–3.
44. *Reno Evening Gazette*, October 8, 1943, 4:1.
45. *Reno Evening Gazette*, October 8, 1943, 4:1.
46. Ethel Parker, "The Purchase of Bowers Mansion," April 20, 1953, 3, on file at Bowers Mansion.
47. Bowers Mansion committee of Reno Women's Civic Club minutes on file at Bowers Mansion, first meeting, January 26, 1946; Parker, "The Purchase of Bowers Mansion," 4.
48. Reno Women's Civic Club minutes, fourth meeting, February 11, 1946; Parker, "The Purchase of Bowers Mansion," 4–6; letter from the Carson City Orphans Home April 13, 1946, on file at Bowers Mansion.
49. Washoe County Board of Commissioners meeting minutes, February 20, 1946 and March 20, 1946; Reno Women's Civic Club minutes, fifth meeting, February 18, 1946; Reno Women's Civic Club minutes, eighth meeting, March 8, 1946.
50. Reno Women's Civic Club minutes, fifth meeting, February 18, 1946, and thirteenth meeting, March 26, 1946; Parker, "The Purchase of Bowers Mansion," 4.
51. Reno Women's Civic Club eighteenth meeting, Bowers Mansion Association meeting minutes, April 10, 1946; Reno Women's Civic Club seventeenth

meeting of the Bowers Mansion Association, April 5, 1946, Parker page 8; Washoe County Board of Commissioners minutes, April 20, 1946.

52. Washoe County Board of Commissioners minutes, May 6, 1946; *Reno Evening Gazette*, April 20, 1946, 14:4.
53. Minutes of Bowers Mansion Association meeting minutes, April 29, 1946, on file at Bowers Mansion.
54. Reno Women's Civic Club twenty-second meeting, April 29, 1946; *Nevada State Journal*, April 30, 1946, 12:1 and May 1, 1946, 14: 1.
55. Washoe County Board of Commissioners minutes, May 6, 1946; Reno Women's Civic Club twenty-fourth meeting, May 6, 1946, and twenty-ninth meeting, July 30, 1946; *Reno Evening Gazette*, May 16, 1946, 5: 6–7.
56. Washoe County Deeds, Washoe County Recorder's Office, May 10, 1946, Book 182, page 133; Washoe County Board of Commissioners meeting minutes, December 5, 1946; *Nevada State Journal*, September 2, 1949, 14:4–6.
57. *Nevada State Journal*, April 21, 1950, 11:2.
58. *Reno Evening Gazette*, June 17, 1950, 12:4.

Chapter 10: Restoration

1. *Reno Evening Gazette*, September 6, 1963, 2:3.
2. *Nevada State Journal*, January 19, 1964, 5:4.
3. *Reno Evening Gazette*, November 6, 1964, 10:4.
4. *Reno Evening Gazette*, February 12, 1964, 1:3.
5. *Nevada State Journal*, November 3, 1924, 8:4.
6. Ratay, *Pioneers of the Ponderosa*, 260.
7. *Nevada State Journal*, July 8, 1947, 2:7.
8. *Nevada State Journal*, May 6, 1948, 7:5 and May 21, 1948, 7:4; Ratay, *Pioneers of the Ponderosa*, 260; W. Wallace White, *Caring for the Environment* (University of Nevada Oral History Project, 1970), 62.
9. *Reno Evening Gazette*, February 12, 1964, 1:3 and April 14, 1964, 26:1; *Nevada State Journal*, April 16, 1964, 8:2.
10. *Nevada State Journal*, February 26, 1965, 12:5.
11. *Reno Evening Gazette*, November 26, 1964, 15:6. In 2022, the wading pool was turned into a splash pad.
12. Ratay, *Pioneers of the Ponderosa*, 252; Peterson, "Nonelectric Geothermal," 17; *Reno Evening Gazette*, October 7, 1909, 5:3, October 3, 1910, 6:6.
13. Peterson, "Nonelectric Geothermal," 17; Letter from Betty Hood to Richard Peterson of University of Hawaii. Based on "Survey for the Office of Washoe County Engineer re: Bowers Mansion Water Supply Investigation," September 30, 1972, on file at Bowers Mansion.
14. *Nevada State Journal*, June 18, 1965, 30:4 and August 7, 1965, 6:3; *Reno Evening Gazette*, November 26, 1964, 15:6.

15. *Nevada State Journal*, May 23, 1963, 23:5 and October 16, 1965.
16. *Reno Evening Gazette*, February 16, 1966, 36: 2–4.
17. *Reno Evening Gazette*, November 9, 1966, 12:8.
18. *Reno Evening Gazette*, February 17, 1967, 25:2; Linda Shapiro, *Edward S. Parsons, F.A.I.A: A Personal Reflection* (University of Nevada Special Collections, Oral History, 1983).
19. Shapiro, *Edward S. Parsons*, 4.
20. *Edward S. Parsons, Charrette: The Life of an Architect, An Oral History Conducted by Mary Ellen Glass* (University of Nevada Oral History Program, 1983), 41, 43, 58.
21. Parsons, *Charrette*, 58; Shapiro, *Edward S. Parsons*, 3, 4, 8; *Nevada State Journal*, May 25, 1966, 20:1.
22. *Nevada State Journal*, May 3, 1967, 15:5; personal communication with Patti McClelland, March 27, 2023.
23. Parsons, *Charrette*, 477.
24. Parsons, *Charrette*, 479–80.
25. Parsons, *Charrette*, 484–85.
26. Parsons, *Charrette*, 478–79.
27. *Nevada State Journal*, May 25, 1966, 20:1.
28. Parsons, *Charrette*, 480–81, 492.
29. Parsons, *Charrette*, 482–83; Shiela Lonie, Crissie Caughlin Pioneer (Reno: S. Lonie, 2004), 53–54.
30. Parsons, *Charrette*, 485.
31. Parsons, *Charrette*, 485, 490, 491, 492.
32. Cooke Family Papers, Thomas Cooke Speeches, 1968, UNR Special Collections.
33. Cooke Family Papers, Thomas Cooke Speeches, 1968, UNR Special Collections, 494; ellipses are in the original document, perhaps indicating pauses for the speaker.
34. Letter from Washoe County Manager C. B. Kinnison to the chair of Bowers Mansion Restoration Committee Frances Creek, August 28, 1968, on file at Bowers Mansion.
35. Letter from Gloria Mapes Walker to Doug Doolitle, director of Washoe County Parks Department, August 7, 2006, on file at Bowers Mansion.

An Architectural History

1. Virginia McAlester and Lee McAlester, *A Field Guide to American Houses: The Definitive Guide to Identifying and Understanding America's Domestic Architecture* (New York: Alfred A. Knopf, 1996), 139–67.
2. McAlester and McAlester, *A Field Guide to American Houses*, 211–14.
3. *Sacramento Daily Union*, September 2, 1872.

4. University of Washington, Pacific Coast Architectural Database, "Ruben S. Clark."
5. University of Washington, Pacific Coast Architectural Database "Henry Kenitzer"; Ronald M. James, *Temples of Justice: County Courthouses of Nevada* (Reno: University of Nevada Press, 1994).
6. A. J. Bicknell and Company, *Bicknell's Village Builder* (New York: Dover Publications, [1872] 1979).
7. John Riddell, *Architectural Designs for Model Country Residences* (Ventura, CA: Archival Reprint Company, 1994 [1861]) np.
8. Report of the Special Committee, The Journal of the Assembly of the State of Nevada, Sixth Session, 1873, Charles A.V. Putnam, State Printer, Carson City, Nevada.

A National Context

1. J. S. Holliday, *The World Rushed In: The California Gold Rush Experience* (New York: Simon and Schuster, 1981).
2. Malcolm J. Rohrbough, *Days of Gold: The California Gold Rush and the American Nation* (Berkeley, CA: University of California Press, 1977); Pierre Berton, *Klondike: The Last Great Gold Rush, 1896–1899* (Toronto: Anchor Canada, 2001); Sally Zanjani, *Goldfield: The Last Gold Rush on the Western Frontier* (Athens: Ohio University Press, 1992); Limerick, *The Legacy of Conquest.*
3. Young, *Western Mining*; Donald L. Hardesty, *Mining Archaeology in the American West: A View from the Silver State* (Lincoln: University of Nebraska Press, 2010).
4. Limerick, *The Legacy of Conquest*; James, *The Roar and the Silence.*
5. F. W. McQuiston, Jr., *Gold: The Saga of the Empire Mine, 1850–1956* (Grass Valley, CA: Empire Mine Park Association, 1986); Young, *Western Mining*; Susan Lee Johnson, *Roaring Camp: The Social World of the California Gold Rush* (New York: W. W. Norton and Company, 2000); James, *The Roar and the Silence.*
6. James and James, *A Short History of Virginia City*, 129–31. The so-called "Mackay Mansion" (1861) serviced the Gould and Curry Mine.
7. James and James, *A Short History of Virginia City*, 117–19.
8. Stanley, *Slipper Gulch*, 47; Makley, *The Infamous King of the Comstock.*
9. Angel, *History of Nevada*, facing and following page 48; Dorothy F. Regnery, *An Enduring Heritage: Historic Buildings of the San Francisco Peninsula* (Palo Alto, CA: Stanford University Press, 1976), 54–55.
10. Stanley, *Slipper Gulch*, 54; Smith, *The History of the Comstock Lode*, 128–35; Leonard Schlup, "Nevada's Doctrinaire Senator: John P. Jones and the Politics of Silver in the Gilded Age," *Nevada Historical Society Quarterly*, 36:4 (Winter 1993) 246–62.

11. Robert E. Stewart, Jr., and Mary Frances Stewart, *Adolph Sutro: A Biography* (Berkeley, CA: Howell-North, 1962).
12. Smith, *The History of the Comstock Lode*, 9, 17–18, 93, 134.
13. McQuiston, *Gold: The Saga of the Empire Mine*; Ferol Egan, *Last Bonanza Kings: The Bourns of San Francisco* (Reno: University of Nevada Press, 2009).
14. M. H. Staatz and R. C. Pearson, *The Republic Gold District, Ferry County, Washington* (Washington, DC: US Geological Survey Bulletin, 1990); Laura Arksey, "Ferry County—Thumbnail History," History Link: https://www.historylink.org/File/7787 (accessed February 20, 2023); Deborah Cuyle, *Ghosts and Legends of Spokane* (Charleston, SC: The History Press, 2021), 25–30.
15. Newell G. Bringhurst, "Thomas Kearns: Irish-American Builder of Modern Utah," *Journal of the West*, 31:2 (April 1992) 24–32, "Kearns, Thomas, Mansion and Carriage House," nomination for National Register of Historic Places, February 7, 1989.
16. Kristen Iverson, *Molly Brown: Unraveling the Myth* (Boulder, CO: Johnson Books, 1999).
17. Arthur M. Hill, *Coal Men of America* (Chicago: The Retail Coalman, 1918), 454–56.
18. Clark also built his infamous "Clark's Folly," costing $7 million with 121 rooms, in Manhattan, completed in 1911 and demolished in 1927. H. H. Langton, *James Douglas: A Memoir* (Toronto: University of Toronto Press, 1940); William Mangam, *The Clarks: An American Phenomenon* (New York: Silver Bow Press, 1941).
19. Laurence Beal, *The Carson Mansion: America's finest Victorian home and the man who built it* (Eureka, CA: Times Print, 1973).
20. David Nasaw, *The Chief: The Life of William Randolph Hearst* (Boston: Houghton Mifflin, 2000).
21. James and James, *Castle in the Sky*.

Selected Bibliography

Addenbrooke, Alice, *The Mistress of the Mansion* (Palo Alto, CA: Pacific Books, 1950).

Angel, Myron, *History of Nevada, 1881* (Berkeley, CA: Howell-North, 1958).

Ansari, Mary, *Mines and Mills of the Comstock Region* (Reno: Camp Nevada, 1989).

Atkin, Thomas, *Journal of Emigration* (Salt Lake City) available at Genealogical Society of Utah (FHL Film # 0182383).

Bancroft, Hubert Howe, *History of Nevada, 1540–1888* (Las Vegas: Nevada Publications, 1981).

Browne, J. Ross, *Mineral Resources of the Pacific States and Territories, 1868* (Washington, DC: Government Printing Office, 1868).

Carter, Kate B., *Heart Throbs of the West* (Salt Lake City: Daughters of Utah Pioneers, 1947), vol. 7.

Cowan, Viola, "History of Alexander Cowan" (Salt Lake City: Daughters of the Utah Pioneers files, May 1959).

Crowell, Max, *A technical review of early Comstock mining methods* (Reno: State Bureau of Mines, January 1941).

Doten, Alfred, *The Journals of Alfred Doten, 1849–1903* (Reno: University of Nevada Press, 1973).

Drury, Wells, *An Editor on the Comstock Lode* (Palo Alto, CA: Pacific Books, 1948).

Elliott, Russell R., *History of Nevada* (Lincoln: University of Nebraska Press, 1973).

Hutcheson, Austin E., editor, *Before the Comstock, 1857–1858: Memoirs of William Dolman* (Reno: University of Nevada, n.d.; reprinted from *New Mexico Historical Review*, July 22, 3 [1947]).

James, Ronald M., "Defining the Group: Nineteenth-Century Cornish on the Mining Frontier," *Cornish Studies 2*, ed. by Philip Payton (Exeter, UK: University of Exeter Press, 1994).

———, *The Roar and the Silence: The History of Virginia City and the Comstock Lode* (Reno: University of Nevada Press, 1998).

———, *Monumental Lies: Early Nevada Folklore of the Wild West* (Reno: University of Nevada Press, 2023).

James, Ronald M. and Buzick, Tamera with additional material from Donald L. Hardesty, "Bowers Mansion (Amendment)," National Register of Historic Places nomination (November 2012).

James, Ronald M. and James, Susan A., *Castle in the Sky: George Whittell Jr. and the Thunderbird Lodge* (Lake Tahoe, NV: Thunderbird Lodge Preservation Society, 2002; 2nd edition 2005).

———, *A Short History of Virginia City including a Walking Tour* (Reno: University of Nevada Press, 2014).

James, Ronald M. and Raymond, C. Elizabeth, editors, *Comstock Women: The Making of a Mining Community* (Reno: University of Nevada Press, 1998).

James, Ronald M. and Stewart, Robert E., editors, *The Gold Rush Letters of E. Allen Grosh and Hosea B. Grosh* (Reno: University of Nevada Press, 2012).

Kelly, J. Wells, *First Directory of Nevada Territory, 1862* (Los Gatos, CA: Talisman Press, 1962).

Limerick, Patricia Nelson, *The Legacy of Conquest: The Unbroken Past of the American West* (New York: W. W. Norton and Company, 1987).

Makley, Michael, *The Infamous King of the Comstock: William Sharon and the Gilded Age in the West* (Reno: University of Nevada Press, 2006).

———, *Imposing Order without Law: American Expansion to the Eastern Sierra, 1850–1865* (Reno: University of Nevada Press, 2022).

McAlester, Virginia and McAlester, Lee, *A Field Guide to American Houses: The Definitive Guide to Identifying and Understanding America's Domestic Architecture* (New York: Alfred A. Knopf, 1996).

Miller, Reuben, *The Journal of Reuben Miller, 1811–1882* (Salt Lake City: Salt Lake City Church Archives Historical Department).

Myrick, David F., *Railroads of Nevada and Eastern California, Vol. 1* (San Diego: Howell-North Books, 1962).

Page, Albert R., *Orson Hyde and the Carson Valley Mission* (Reno: thesis, University of Nevada, Reno, history department, 1970).

Paher, Stanley W., *Nevada Ghost Towns and Mining Camps* (Las Vegas: Nevada Publications, 1970).

Parker, Harry, Macpherson, Arthur, and Bowen, Frank, *Mail and Passenger Steamships of the Nineteenth Century: The Macpherson Collection with Iconographical and Historical Notes by Captain H. Parker and Frank C. Bowen* (London: S. Low, Marston, 1928).

Parsons, Edward S., *Charrette! The Life of an Architect, An Oral History Conducted by Mary Ellen Glass* (University of Nevada Oral History Program, 1983).

Peterson, Richard E., "Nonelectric Geothermal—A Versatile Resource," *Geothermal Energy Magazine*, 4:11 (November 1976) 8–21.

Pratt, David, *Life on Board a Mormon Emigrant Ship* (Salt Lake City: Corporation of the President of The Church of Jesus Christ of Latter-day Saints, ca. 1980).

Ratay, Myra Sauer, *Pioneers of the Ponderosa* (Sparks, NV: Western Printing and Publishing Company, 1973).

Scrugham, James G., *Nevada: A Narrative of the Conquest of a Frontier Land, Volume III, Nevada Biographies* (New York: The American Historical Society, 1935).

Shapiro, Linda, *Edward S. Parsons, F.A.I.A: A Personal Reflection* (University of Nevada Special Collections, Oral History, 1983).

Smith, Grant H. with new material by Joseph V. Tingley. *The History of the Comstock Lode, 1850–1997* (Reno: University of Nevada Press, 1998).

Stanley, Maitland, *Slippery Gulch: A Guide to Gold Hill, Nevada* (Virginia City, NV: Susy and Livy Publications, 2003).

Trimmer, Arnold R., *Reminiscences of the Number One Ranch in Carson Valley, Nevada* (Reno: University of Nevada Oral History Program, 1993).

Waldorf, John, *A Kid on the Comstock: Reminiscences of Virginia City Childhood* (Reno: University of Nevada Press, 1991).

Wren, Thomas, *A History of the State of Nevada: Its Resources and People* (New York: Lewis Publishing Company, 1904).

Wright, William [Dan De Quille]. *Snow-shoe Thompson* (Los Angeles: Glen Dawson, 1876; reprinted from *Overland Monthly*, October 1886).

———. *A History of the Comstock Silver Lode and Mines* (San Francisco: Pacific Press Publishing, 1889).

———. *History of the Big Bonanza* (Las Vegas: Nevada Publications, 1974).

Young, Otis E., Jr., with technical assistance of Robert Lenon, *Western Mining: An Informal Account of Precious-Metals Prospecting, Placering, Lode Mining, and Milling on the American Frontier from Spanish Times to 1893* (Norman: University of Oklahoma, 1970); Donald L. Hardesty, *Mining Archaeology in the American West: A View from the Silver State* (Lincoln: University of Nebraska Press, 2010).

Zanjani, Sally, *Devils Will Reign: How Nevada Began* (Reno: University of Nevada Press, 2006).

Index

Page numbers in italics indicate illustrations.

Addenbrooke, Alice: as Bowers Mansion Association officer, 115; correspondence, 70; and dealings with county commissioners, 117; item donations overseen by, xvi, 118; Mansion refurbishing overseen by, 119; photos, *116*; writings, xviii, 116
A. Dee Construction Company, 123
afterlife, interest in, 72
Alaska, gold rush in, 141
alcohol beverages, prohibition on, 111
Allen, D., 93
Allen, Dorothy, 115, *116*
Allen, Robert A., 114
Ambrose, Nicholas "Dutch Nick," 23–24, 25
American prosperity, promise of, 3
American Red Cross, 68
Angel, Myron, xvii, 30, 45–46, 56, 86–87
architectural plan books, 138, *139*
automobile transportation, 108–9

Babcock, W. F., 42
Baldwin horse, bet on, 77
ball to promote women's rights, 60–61
Bancroft, Hubert, xvii
"Bank Crowd," 57
bank loans, 53, 56
Bank of California, 57
Barbers of Reno, 71
Beatie, Hampton, 10
Beaupeurt, Frances, 115, *116*, 118
Becker, George F., *80*
bedroom set, 117, *117*
Behringer, William, 93, *94*, 103
Bennett, Jesse L., 30
Benny, J. B., 29
Bentley, Elizabeth, 17
Bentley, Frank Richard, 17
Bentley, Richard, 17, 18
Bewick, William, 56
Big Bonanza, 64, 67
Bishop, John, 24, 26
Bishop, Persia, 52
Bishop, Rowena, 52
Bishop, Simeon, 51–52, 107
blacksmith shops, 42
Bourn, William Bowers, 145
Bourn Cottage, 145
Bourn Mansion, 145
Bowers (L. S.) & Company, 29
Bowers, Eilley (née Alison Oram): biography, xv, xvii; birth and

childhood, 1–2, 86; in Carson County, 19; children, 33, 37, 39, 40, 48, *49*, 86, 92; death, 105–6, 112; descendants, xiv, xviii; and end of mining career, 78–79; final years, xiv, 89, 90–91, 92–93, 94, 96–101, 103, 106; financial challenges, 53, 60, 62, 64, 66, *67*, 68, 71, 73, 74, 78–79, 81, 87, 97, 98–99; near Franktown, 86, 91; friends, 14; in Genoa, NV, 15; in Gold Hill, 25; in Johntown, 21, 22, *22*, 23, 24; in King's Daughters Home, 100–101, 103, 106; lawsuits, 74; life and legacy, 106–7, 141; life summary, xiii–xiv; marriage, 1st, xiv, 2–3, 86; marriage, 2nd, 9, 10, 19–20, 29, 34, 86; marriage, 3rd, 29–30, 31, 86, 146–47; mental state, 77–78; mining claims bought by, *27*, 29, 106; mining transactions by, 52–53; as novel subject, 112; and opinion of Theodore Winters, 94; in poorhouse, 99; and role in mining camp exhibit, 96–97, *97*; in Salt Lake City, 8, 86; in San Francisco, xiv, 89, 92, 93, 100; separation and divorce, 1st, 7; separation and divorce, 2nd, 29, 34, 35, 45; stories of, 79, 81, 86–87, 97, 99–100; in Virginia City, 73, 81–82, 85; in Washoe Valley, 16; wealth, 33, 40, 43, 45, 49–50, 86, 97

Bowers, Eilley (née Alison Oram), and alleged spiritual powers: advice on gold searching, 28; crystal gazing, 24; disasters predicted by, 76; entertainment and publicity, 61; as fortune teller, xiv, 81–86, 89, 90–92, 93, *97*, 101; predictions, 98; as "Seeress of Washoe," 71–74, 76–77, 90–92, 99, 106; troubling visions, 83–84

Bowers, Eilley (née Alison Oram), in Bowers Mansion: bedroom set, 117, *117*; as boardinghouse keeper, xiii, 60, 61–62, 138; as events hostess, 60, 61, 64–65, 66, 68, 74, 76, 90, 99, 138; final days in mansion, 77–78; as guest, 93; home improvements, 67; inspiration for home design, 138; loss of mansion, *75*, 76, 78, 81, 112; mansion location, 148; moving in, 49–50; visualizing, 130–31

Bowers, Eilley (née Alison Oram), sources, xiv, xv, xvii, xviii–xix

Bowers, Eilley (née Alison Oram), travels: Europe, excursion to, 45–46, 47–48, *49*; Nevada, departure from, 1, 87, 100; Nevada, return to, 90–91, 99; Salt Lake City, arrival in, 7; Scotland, departure from, 1; Sierra, travel to base of, 13; United States, arrival in, xv, 3–5; westward journey, 5, *6*

Bowers, John Jasper, 37, 39

Bowers, Lemuel Sanford (Sandy): bedroom set owned by, 117, *117*; in Bowers Mansion, 49–50, 130–31, 148; Bowers Mansion plan and design, 138; business sense, 97; children, 33, 37, 39, 40, 48, *49*, 86, 92; death, 57–58, 59, 78, 81, 87, 90; and Eilley, other couples compared to, 146–47; Europe, excursion to, 45–46, 47–48, *49*; financial challenges, 53–54, 56; Gold Hill home, 30, *41*, 143; grave, 89–90, 92, 93; land sold by, 54; legacy, 90, 141; in local government, 28; marriage, 29–30, 86; mining claims and property, 26, *27*, 31, 33, 38, 46, 74, 145; mining interests, buying and selling of, 52; mining operations, 30–31, 35, 42; money management, 81; paintings, 58; property rights defended by, 35; Pyramid

Lake War (1860), financing of, 36, 98; recollections of, 106–7; Southern sympathies, 54; spirit, alleged contact with, 73; stories about, 99–100; wealth, 33, 40, 43, 45, 49–50, 58; will and estate, 57, 59

Bowers, Persia (Margaret Persia) (Eilley's daughter): birth, xiv, 48, 86; in Bowers Mansion, 49–50, 61, *69*, 128; education in Reno, 66; friends, 52, 128; grave, 92; illness and death, 69–70, 71; photos, *49*, *70*; stories about, 99; visit home, 68–69

Bowers, Theresa Fortunatus, 40

Bowers and Company, 43

Bowers and Plato Company, 53

Bowers and Plato Mine, 57, 59

Bowers empire, fall of, 56

Bowers Gold and Silver Mining Company, 53

Bowers home (Gold Hill), *41*, 60

Bowers Mansion (Mapes et al.), xviii

Bowers Mansion: additions and improvements, 74, *75*, 107, 108; architecture and design, xvii, 135–38, *139*; attractions, *109*; balcony, 113, 127, 128; as boardinghouse and resort, xvi, 61–62, 66–68, *72*, 79, 95, *96*, 104–5, 108, 127, 139; buildings nearby, 95; closing of, xv; coal oil, alleged near, 99; condition, 68, 93, 95–96, *101*, 103; construction of, 45, 47, 48, 94, 126, 137, 141; cupula, 127, 128, 129, *129*; curator, 131; as current destination, 132; dedication ceremony, 129–31; description, xiii, 49–50, 61, 104–5, 135–36; dismantling of, proposed, 92–93; electricity for, 111–12; as film location, 110; foundation, reinforcing, 126; fundraising for, 115–19; furnishings, xvii, 45, 47, 49–50, 61, 85, 118; as home, 110; image on flag, 121, *122*; as income source, 60; inventory, xvi; lawsuits, 48; leasing of, 68; location of, 45, 135, 145, 148–49; management, 75–76, 79, 85, 89, 104, 108; as museum, 118, 139; ownership, 92, 93–95, 103; paintings, 93, *94*, 103; park status, potential of, 113, 118; photos, *51*, *69*, *139*; porch, xvi, 127–28, *129*, 133, 136; preservation measures, xvi–xvii, 114–19; proprietorship, 85; railroad impact on, 59, 62, *63*, 85; refurbishing of, xvi–xvii; reopening of, xvi, 119; restoration, *96*, *101*, 104, 118, 124, 125–29, *129*, 130–31, 139; roof, 127, *128*, 135, 136, 139; sale, 76, 78, 113, *114*, 119, 139; sale, attempt at, 62, 64, 66, *67*, 79; sale, rumors of, 75; sources, xviii; special events held at, 60–61, 64–66, 69, 71, 74, 75, 76, 85, 90, 93, 105, 112–13; stories and recollections of, xvi–xvii, xviii, 89–90, 93, 113, 121, 133; as symbol, 121; third story, 74, *75*, 127, 128, *128*, *130*, 138–39; tours, xvi–xvii; travel to and from, 51, 79, 108–9, 113; value of, 49, 86, 118. *See also* Bowers Mansion Park

Bowers Mansion Association: founding of, 115; fundraising by, 116, 118–19; photos, *116*

Bowers Mansion Game Reserve, 108

Bowers Mansion Park, 117, 124, 139

Bowers Mansion Park and Recreation Complex, 121

Bowers Mansion Refurbishing Committee, 119

Bowers Mansion Restoration Group, 124, 128–29, 131–32

Bowers Mine: attempt to save, 53–54, 57; challenges for, 38; enlargement

of, 42; establishment of, *27*; excavations from, *80*; labor at, 30, 43; operation of, 33, 42–43, 45, 54; sale, 57, 60, 62, 78; stock in, 53; subsuming of, 79; yields, 56, 59
Bowers Mining Company: employees, 52; establishment of, 30; Old Pioneer Mill, business with, 38–39; ore processed for, 40; sale, 62; Savage Mine, dispute with, 35
Bowers Springs, 123
Bowers Well, 123
Boyle, Emmet, 111
Bramwell, West Virginia, housing in, 147
Britain, economic conditions in, 1
British Columbia, mines in, 146
Brown, Grafton T., *37*
Brown, James Joseph "J. J.," 146
Brown, Margaret "Maggie," 146–47
Browne, J. Ross, 33
Buchanan, James, 19, 39
buried treasure, false prophesy concerning, 84–85
Butte, MT, 147
Butterfield, John, 21

Cain, William, 91, 92
California: Carson County, attempt to annex into, 16, 17; hidden treasures, 5; telegraph line to, 38
California Gold Rush, xv, 5, 137, 141–42
California Trail, *12*
Camp, H. B., 23
"Carlsbad of Nevada," 61–62
Carlson, William, 147
Carson Brass Band, 68
Carson City, railroad connection to and from, 60, 62, 85
Carson County: establishment of, 13; law and government, post-Mormon, 29; Mormon church's final chapter in, 20; population, 30, 39; state possession of, battle over, 16; territorial election, 1st, 15; western expanse of, 15
Carson Mansion, 147
Carson Orphans Home, 115
Carson Pass route, *12*
Carson Range, 93
Carson River, 13–14
Carson Valley, 16
Cary, J., 29
Cary, Mrs. W. M., 98
Cary, William M., 68
casino, Bowers Mansion as potential, 95
Casteel, F. D., 31
cattle, 15
cattle industry, 55–56
Central Pacific Railroad, 59
Champions of the Red Cross, 68
Child, John, store, 23
Chollar Mine, 143
Church of Jesus Christ of Latter-day Saints, xv, 3, 9, 20
Church of Scotland, 3
cities, mansions in, 148
City of Manchester (ship), 47
The City of Trembling Leaves (Clark), 111
Civil War: devastation of, 40; end of, 55; New York City during, 46; start of, 39; threat of, 21; toll in East, 54
Clackmannan, Scotland, 2
Clark, Martha, 7
Clark, Patrick "Patsy," 145–46
Clark, Reuben S., 137
Clark, Walter Van Tilburg, 111
Clark, William A., 147
Clarke, Ida, 103
Clarke, Robert, 95

Clayton, Lloydine, 115, *116*, *132*
Clayton, Martin, *132*
coal barons, residences of, 149
coal country, housing in, 147
Coeur d'Alene, ID, mines in, 146
Cohn, Felice, 113
Colcord, R. K., 95, 113
Comstock, Henry P., 25, 26, *27*, 28, 29
Comstock Lode: boom, 64; Bowers Mansion in days of, xvi; claims along, 79; description of, 26, 28; discovery of, xv, 142; earthquake predicted for, 76; economic stranglehold on, 57; exploration of, 28; Gold Hill's share of, *80*; location of, 148–49; ore body, locating in, 73–74; people attracted to, 28, 29; productivity of, 39; road leading from, 48
Comstock mines: investors in, 144; wealth enabled by, 141
Comstock Mining District: boom, fading, 53; Californians traveling to, 33; claims staked in, 30; depression, 54, 56, 85; employment in, 39; end to isolation, 40, 42; glory days of, 105; law and government, need for, 28–29; newspaper coverage of, 38; as symbol, 142
Comstock Range, *27*
Consolidated Imperial Mining Company, 79
Cooke, Thomas, xviii, 124, 125, 130–31
Copper, Paul W., 31
copper mines and mining, 146, 147, 149
corporate superintendents, offices and homes of, 143
corporatization of mining West, 142
Cosser, Walter, 14
Cowan, Alexander: background and origin, 9; Carson County organization, role in, 13; divorce, 29, 34, 45; in Genoa, NV, 15; marriage, 1st, 9, 19–20, 86; marriage, 2nd, 35; property bought by, 126; ranch, profit from, 35; relatives of, xviii–xix; return to Johntown, 23; return to Salt Lake City, *22*, 24, 34; return to Utah, 20, 21; separation and divorce, 29; travels, 9, 10; in Washoe Valley, 16, 19
Cowan, John and Agnes, 9
Cowan, William, 9
Cowan family, 9, 16, 18, 19–20
Cowan Ranch, 16, 34, 35
Crandall, J. B., 22
Crawford, Andrew, xviii
Creek, Frances, 131
Crocker, Charles, 59
Crocker Mansion, 99
Cross, Cora, 70
Crown Point Trestle, 60, 82, 83, *83*, 100
crystal gazing, 24, 71–72, 73, 76, 84

DaCosta, A. R., 122
Dall's bridge and road, 67, 79
Dall's grove, 85
Daly, Marcus, 146
Davis, Sam, 103
dead man's body, vision of, 83–84
Dee (A.) Construction Company, 123
De Groot, Henry, 25
Deidesheimer, Philip, 42
DeLongchamps, Frederic, 125
Denver, CO, housing in, 146
De Quille, Dan, 55
Dettenreider, Laura, 81
disabled miners, Bowers Mansion as potential home for, 95
divorce, 7, 29, 34, 110–11
Dolman, William Hickman, 25
Donnelly, Henry, 54
Donnelly, Thomas, murder of, 77

Doolittle, Doug, 131
Doten, Alfred, 55, 90, 91
Douglas Mansion, 147
Dover, Will, 23
Downing, A. J., 136
Drury, Ella Bishop, 49, 52, 158n21
Drury, Wells, 52
dugouts (housing), 30

Eason, Ruth, 131
Eastern Star, 100, 106
Eclipse Mine, 55, 57, 79
Eighteenth Amendment, 110
Eilley Orrum, Queen of the Comstock (Paine), 112
electricity, 111–12
Elite Brewery, 103, 104
Ellis, Laura, 14
Emmett Guard, 64–65
Empire Mine: cave-in, 55; company absorbing, 79; company incorporated into, 29; gold yield from, 145; land near, 149; structure, *34*; subsurface mining, 142
entrepreneurs, houses constructed by, 143
Episcopal Church picnic, 65
Eureka, CA, 147
European Renaissance, 136

Fair, James, 64, 144
Fife family, 131
Fillmore, Millard, 10
Filofi estate, 145, 147, 148
Finney, James "Old Virginny," 24, 26
flags, commemorative, 121, *122*
Flood, James, 64, 144
Flood Mansion, 144
Flowery Mining District, 43
Forfar, Scotland, 1, *2*
Fort Sumter, attack on, 39
fortune seekers, hopes and ambitions of, 149
fortune-telling, xiv, 71, 73
'49 Mining Camp exhibit, 96–97, *97*
forty-niners, 5
Fowler, Trudy, 115, *116*
Fox, Elvira, 115
Frances, J. B., 93
Franktown: establishment and naming of, 17; false rumors reaching, 19; farm near, *17*; flourishing of, *52*; mining industry impact on, 50; Mormons in, 18; orders to vacate, 19; railroad going past, 62; water stop at, 64
Franktown School, 18
Freemasons, 100
Frey, Anna, 77
furniture, memories conjured by, xvii

Gage, Mart M., 23
gambling, legalization of, 112
gaming industry, 112
Gavin, Joe, 78
Geiger Grade toll road, 48
Gelder, Harriet, 115, 116, 117
Genoa, NV: adoption of name, 15; California-bound immigrants near present-day, 10; maps, *12*; Placerville, reaching from, 24; telegraph line from, 38; travel to, 22. *See also* Mormon Station (*later* Genoa, NV)
geological surveys, *80*
Georgian period, 136
Gillophy, George, 106
Glen White, WV, 147
gold: production of, 40; profits from, 39; separating from rock, 38; surface mining, 142; yields, 56
Gold Canyon, *22*, 23, 24
Gold Canyon Switch (newspaper), 26

Golden Gate (steamship), 46
Goldfield, NV, gold rush to, 141–42
Gold Hill (town): digging and claims near, 28, 29; economic conditions, 149; establishment of, 25; growth of, 48; housing in, 30, *41*, 143, 144; mines below, 39; mining affairs in, 51; mining facilities in, *34*; mining land in, 26; photos, *41*; population, 37–38; railroad through, 62, 85; road between, and Virginia City, *34*; travel to and from, 51, 60
Gold Hill Front Lodes, *27*
Gold Hill share of Comstock Lode, *80*
gold rushes, xv, 5, 137, 141–42
Gottschalck, Ella, xviii, 115, *116*
Governor's Mansion (Salt Lake City, UT), 146
Grand Gift Entertainment raffle (for Bowers Mansion), 64, 65, 66, *67*
Gray, Orin, 23
Great Basin, *11*, *12*, 21, 36, 38
Great Depression, 112, 125
Great Salt Lake Valley, 3, 5, 7
Griswold, Morley, 113

Hall, Spafford, 14
Hammack, J. A., 26
hard rock mining, 148
Harris, E. B., 38
Harris, Everett White, 111
Havana Lottery, 82
Haywood, J. L., 13
Hearst, George, 147
Hearst, William Randolph, 147–48
Hearst Mansion, 147–48
Henderson, Alec, 26
Henderson, Elizabeth, 46–47
Henderson, James, 43, 46–47, 52
Henderson, Margaret (Alexander Cowan's sister), 9, 13
Henderson, Robert (Eilley's nephew): assault and departure from Nevada, 78; in Carson County, 19, 20; E. B.'s divorce witnessed by, 35; Eilley and Alexander joined by, 13; family matters handled by, 46–47; in Genoa, NV, 15; in Gold Hill, 25; in Johntown, 21, 23, 24; in mining, 29, 43, 52
Hickok, E. L., 82
highway robbers, 53
historic mining districts, 143. *See also* Comstock Mining District
historic preservation program, xix
History of Nevada, 1540–1888 (Bancroft), xvii
History of Nevada, 1881 (Angel), xvii, 86–87
Hogan, John W., 59
Holmes, Nat, 85
"Home Means Nevada" (song), 113
Home Owners Loan Corporation, 125
Hood, Betty, xiii, xv, 131, 132
horse race, prediction concerning, 77
Houseworth, V. A., 28
housing: in Carson County, 30; of mine owners, 143–44; photos, *41*. *See also* Bowers Mansion; mansions
Hunter, Eilley (née Alison Oram). *See* Bowers, Eilley (née Alison Oram)
Hunter, Martha, 7
Hunter, Mary Ellen, 7
Hunter, Stephen: arrival in United States, 4–5; conversion to Mormonism, 3; death, 99; marriage, 1st, xiv, 2–3, 86; relatives of, xviii–xix; in Salt Lake City, 7–8; separation and 2nd marriage, 7; as ship passenger, xv, 4
Hyde, Orson: and attempt to keep under Utah jurisdiction Carson County, 15, 16; departure from Carson County, 18; in Washoe

Valley, 17; Washoe Valley cursed by, 20; Willow Creek mission organized by, 10
Hymers, Lew, 117
Hymers family, *117*

Imperial and Empire Mine, 56, 57
Imperial Mine, *34*, 55, 79
Imperial Mining Company, 54
Improved Order of Red Men, 68
Indigenous people, 9, 15, 36–37, 39, 156n23
influenza pandemic, 110
injuries at special events, 71
Internal Revenue Service, 54
International Hotel (Mount Davidson), 37
International Hotel (Virginia City), 45–46, 144
irrigation system, 124
Italian Renaissance, 136

Jacobs, Harris, 23
James I, King (King James VI of Scotland), 71–72
Jennings, William, 17
Job's store, 23
Johnson, J. Neely, 47, 57, 137
Johntown (mining camp): departure from, 25; description of, 21; development and population, 22–23; location change with seasons, 14; photos, *22*
Jones, John P., 144
Jones, Lyman, 23, 24
Jones Mansion, 144
The Jucklins (silent film), 110

Kearns, Thomas, 146
Kearns Mansion, 146
Kelley, John, 78, 79
Kelley, Mabel Powers, 85
Kelly, Henderson, and Gilchrist (liquor firm), 75
Kelly, John F., 75
Kelly Canyon, 123
Kenitzer, Henry, 137–38
Ketsdever, J. P. and Anna, 109
A Kid on the Comstock (Waldorf), 82–83
King, F. D., 99
King's Daughters Home, Oakland, CA, 100–101, 103, 106
Kinnison, C. B., 123, 131
Kirby, Joseph, 25
Klondike Gold Rush, 141
Knight, William, 26, *27*, 29
Knights of Pythias, 105

Lake, Jane, 92, 93
Lake, Mary Ann McFarland, 92
Lake, Myron C.: Bowers Mansion, attempt to dispose of, 79, 89; as Bowers Mansion owner, 78, 90; death, 91, 92; land sold for railroad by, 59; stepson-in-law of, 64
Lake's Crossing, 59
Lake Tahoe, NV, 148
Lamberti, Harold V., 126
Layton, Christopher, 17
Leadville, CO, 146
Lee, Robert E., 55
Lincoln, Abraham, 39, 54, 55
Lincoln Highway, 111
Linden Towers, 144
Lindsay, George, 104, 107
Lindsay, Nellie, 107
Little Gold Hill Mines: cave-in, 55; combining of, 79; establishment of, 26; expansions and improvements, 45; maps, *27*; ore body, end of, 53; photos, *34*; prospering of, 29; richest mine, 40

Little Jonny Mine, 146
Little Valley Dam, breaking of, 86
Livingston, Harry, 105
Livingston, James, 56
Livingston, Jeanette, 105
Lodge, Dave H., 89
lost and stolen items, help finding, 82
lotteries, 82
Loveland, Chester, 18
lower-value deposits, mining endeavors in pursuit of, 147
L. S. Bowers & Company, 29
Lucas, William, 70
Luksza, Paul, xviii
lumber mills, 50
Luning, Nicholas, 53

Mack, Effie Mona, 125
Mackay, John (J. W.), 64, 97, 143–44, 145, 149
"Mackay Mansion," 144
Mackay Mine, 143
Maguire's Opera House, 48
mail service, 21
mansion (term), 143
mansions: description of, 146; location of, 145, 147, 148, 149
Mapes, Gladys, 129
Mapes, Gloria, xviii, 131
Marker and Bastian Road, 67
Masonic Hall, Gold Hill, 85
Mawer, J. M., 108
McBride, John, 23
McClellan, George B., 54
McClellan, Robert, 45
McClelland, Patti, 126
McClintock, T. H., 75, 78
McFarlan, J. L., 93
McGrath, Thomas, 81
McKenzie, J. C., 121
McLaughlin, Patrick, 28
McMarlin, James, 14
Menlo Park, 144
mental institution, Bowers Mansion as potential, 64, 89, 95, 138
Mexican Gold and Silver Mining Company, 74
Mexican War (1846–1848), 10
Mighels, Philip, 103
"Millionaire's Row" (Virginia City), 143
mills, enclosed, 42
Mills, J. H., 31, 38
Mills, Russell, 125
mine owner mansions, 143–46, 147–49
Miner's Union gatherings, 79, 121
Miner's Union of Silver City, 67, 68
Miner's Union Picnic, 65–66, 76
miners unions, 39, 156n25
mines, enclosed, 42
mine superintendents, houses designed for, 143
mining: boom, 52, 53–54, 64; claims, ownership of, 26, 28; depression, 54, 56, 59, 85; development, socio-economic implications of, xix, 142–43; near Johntown, 24–25; land, information concerning, 84; Mormon attitudes concerning, 15; opportunities and challenges, 28–29, 30–31, 42–43; prospecting aspect of, 38–39; in Washoe Valley, 16, 50; wealth from, 142–43, 147; winter hardships, 33
mining camp exhibits, 96–97
mining camps. *See* Johntown (mining camp)
mining districts, 55–56, 143, 148. *See also* Comstock Mining District
mining millionaires, 142, 143
Miramar mansion, 144
Mistress of the Mansion (Addenbrooke), xviii

Mitchell, Jane, 35
Montgomery Guard, 69
Mormon militias, 19, 20
Mormon mission, 19, 21
Mormon/non-Mormon relations, 11, 13, 15, 16
Mormons: conversion, 3; in Franktown, 18; government, participation in, 15; in mining towns, 25–26; in Salt Lake, 5, 7; ships, 3–4; summoning of, 19, 86; in Utah, 10; in Washoe Valley, 16, 17, *17*; in Willow Creek, 9–10
Mormon Station (*later* Genoa, NV): arrival at, *14*; as Carson County seat, 15; establishment of, 10–11; name change, 15. *See also* Genoa, NV
Mormon temple, 9
motorized vehicles, 111
Mount Davidson: buildings in shadow of, 48; development of, 33, 37, 42

Napoleon, defeat of (1815), 1
National Guard Band, 66
National Guard Hall, 85
National Historic Landmark, xi
National Register of Historic Places, xi, xix
Native Americans, 9, 15, 36–37, 39, 156n23
Neuhausen, Carl M., 146
Nevada: anniversaries, 121; Civil War impact on, 39; connection of San Francisco to, 59; depression, 59; early years, 53; Eilley Bowers story connection to history of, xv, xvii; end to isolation, 42; statehood, xv, xix, 54, 121; territorial census, 39; as tourism destination, 112
Nevada Centennial Commission, 121
Nevada Federation of Women's Clubs, 124
Nevada residents, longtime, picnic in honor of, 112–13
Nevada veterans of World War II, 117
New Mexico, *11*
Nob Hill (San Francisco), 144, 145
Northern Paiutes, 36
North Star (steamer), 46
nouveau riche, 148
Numaga, Chief (Young Winnemucca), 36
Nye, James W., 54

O'Brien, William, 64
Odd Fellows Picnic, 64
Odett, Linda, 100
Old Chips (spirit), 73
Old Pioneer Mill, 38–39
Ophir (town): death of, 67; flourishing of, *52*; ore mill in, 50; railroad going past, 62; travel to Mansion from, 51
Ophir Company, 79
Ophir Grade, 51, 58, 67, 79
Ophir Mine, 28, 42, 73, 74
Ophir Mining Company, 50
Ophir Silver Mining Company, *52*
Oram, John (E. B.'s brother), 2
ore: locating, 73–74; processing and crushing, 38–39, 40; refining, 50; removal of, 42
orebody, 26, 42
ore mills, 50
O'Riley, Peter, 25, 28
Ormsby, Major's store, 23

Pacific Coast Pioneers, 68, 79, 85
Pacific Heights, 145
Pacific-Union Club, 144
Paine, Gustavus Swift, 112
Paiutes, 36, 37

Panama Canal, 103
panning, 24
Parker, Ethel, 115, *116*
parks, funding for, 124–25
Parsons, Ed (Edward Shier): Bowers Mansion restoration, role in, xviii, 125–29, *129*, 139; life and career, 125; recognition given to, 130
Peckham, James, 122
Peckham, Villa, 115, *116*
peepstone, 24, 72–73
Perrine, F. S., 108
Persia (ship), 46, 48
Piercy, Frederick Hawkins, *8*
Pioneers of the Ponderosa (Ratay), xviii
placer mining, 21, 23, 142
Placerville, 24
Placerville-to-Genoa stageline, 22
Plato, Joe, 26, *27*, 29, 31; widow of, 53
polygamy, 18, 19, 86
Pony Express, 38
pools and ponds, 121–24
Powers, Hannah, 85
precious metal miners, 147
precious metal mining barons, 149
precious metal mining districts, 148
precious metals, retrieval of, 142, 143
Presbyterians, 3
Price, J. C. C., 108
prospecting, 23, 26
Pyramid Lake War (1860), 36–37, 98

Quartz Mill, 40
quartz mining, 142

Raffeto, Bertha, 113
railroads: construction of, 55–56, 59, 60; plans for, 43; Washoe Valley, impact on, 62
Ratay, Myra Sauer, xviii, 77–78, 93
Ratz, Elizabeth, 35
Read, Opie, 110
Reese, John, 10, 11, 15
Reid, Harriett, 95
Reno: establishment of, 59; fire predicted for, 90–91; railroad connection to and from, 60, 62
Reno–Carson City Highway, 111
Reno Depot, 62
Reno Mineral Company, 123
Reno Mineral Water Company, 108
Reno Women's Civic Club: Bowers Mansion preservation, campaign for, xvi, xvii, xviii, 115, *116*, *132*; plaque recognizing, 131
resources, low-profit extraction of, 147
Riddell, John, 138, *139*
Riter, Edna: as Bowers Mansion owner, xvii, *96*, *101*, 109–10; as Bowers Mansion resident, 110; Mansion preservation funds donated by, 118; retirement and Bowers Mansion sale, *114*, 119
Riter, Henry: alcohol law violation, conviction for, 111; Eilley Bowers burial arranged by, 106; as Bowers Mansion owner, xvii, *96*, 103–4, 105, *109*, 127; as Bowers Mansion resident, 110; death, 119; gasoline sold by, 111; mansion improvements made by, 121–22; mansion preservation funds donated by, 118; painting purchased by, *94*; Reno, departure from, 109; Reno Women's Civic Club dealings with, 115; retirement and Bowers Mansion sale, 113, *114*, 119; trip to Germany, 107–8
Riter, Lila (Dixon), 104, 108
Riter Springs, 123
Robison, George, 109–10
Robison, Martha, 109–10
Roff family, 68

Rogers, James, 26, *27*, 29
Romanticism, 136
Roosevelt, Theodore, 103
Rose, Jacob, 18
Roughing It (Twain), 100
Route from Liverpool to Great Salt Lake Valley (Piercy), *8*
Royal Ginger Ale, 108

Salt Lake City: building of, 3; defense of, 18; description, 7; housing in, 146; maps, *12*; Mormons in, 5, 7; as seat of government, 17; sketches, *8*
San Francisco: housing in, 144, 145; Midwinter Fair (1894), 96–97; opulence of, 149; travel to, 22; western Nevada connection to, 59
San Francisco Gas Company, 145
San Simeon, CA, 148
Savage Mine, 35, 143
sawmills, 42
Scotland: clairvoyance/"second sight," belief in, 24, 71–72; industrial revolution in, 1–2
second-generation mansions, 147–48
"second sight" (term), 24, 72
settlers, protection of, 36
Seven Mile Canyon, 39
Sharon, William, 56, 57, 60, 79
Shelly, Carl, 118
Shoshone Mineral Water, 108, 123
Shoshone people, 9
Sierra Nevada: crossing of, 24; eastern base of, 10, *14*; eastern slope of, 10, 18, 106; timber from, 50; western slope of, 30, 149
silver: discovery of, 28, 142; finding, buying, selling, and trading, 33; production of, 40, 53; profits from, 39; separating from rock, 38; yields, 56
Silver City, population of, 37–38
Silver King Mine Company, 146
Silver Kings, 64
Simpson, James, *14*
Simpson, J. Cairn, 95
Six Mile Canyon, 23, 24, 28
Smith, Grant, xvii, 76
Smith, John, 100
Smith, Leonard, xviii, 126, 127, 130
South Carolina, secession by, 39
Spann, Harriett: as Bowers Mansion Association officer, 115; Mansion restoration and furnishing, suggestions for, 118; photos, *116*; Washoe County Commission, dealings with, 116, 117; writings, xviii
Spencer, Orson, 3
Spencer Company, 3–4, 5, 7
spiritualism, belief in, 81
Spiritualism movement, 72
spirit world, contacting people in, 72, 73, 74
Spokane, WA, mansion in, 146
Spring Valley Water Company, 145
spring water, natural, 126
Sproule, C. H., 79, 85
"square set" timbering, 42
Stafford, Dorothy, 121
stage lines, 21–22
stamp mills, 38–39, 40, 42, 50
stamps (mining) (defined), 38
Steamboat Springs, 16, 62, 85
Steinheimer Brothers, 108
Stewart, William M., 98
Stiles, George P., 13
Sullivan, Maurice J., 112
Sunday school picnics, 71
surface deposits, extraction from, 142
Sutro, Adolph, 144
Sutro Heights, 144

Sutro Tunnel, 144
Sutter's Creek, CA, gold strike at, 141
Swager, S. A., 23

Taylor, Maude, xviii
Teague, Fanny, 7
telegraph lines, 38, 40, 42
telephone, 108–9
thefts, resolving, 24
Thistle Mill, 40, *41*, 56, 57, 60, *83*
Thompson, John A. "Snowshoe," 24, 28
Thompson, William, 64, 66, *67*, 89, 92
Thunderbird Lodge, 148
Titanic (ship), sinking, rescue from, 146
trade centers, 21
trading posts, 10
transcontinental highway, 111
transcontinental railroad, 59, 60
transcontinental telegraph, 40, 42
transportation, improvements in, 21–22, 108–9, 111
Treadway's Ranch, 79, 85
Trimmer, Arnold, 77
Truckee Meadows, 48
Truckee River, 59, 62
Truckee Valley, 16
Twaddle, Alice, 78
Twaddle Ranch, 78
Twain, Mark, 55, 100

underground mining, 142
Union, tide shifting to, 54
Union Sunday School, 71
United States Judicial District, 3rd (Utah Territory), 13
United States maps, *6*
The Unsinkable Molly Brown (play), 146
Utah: divorces, 7; maps, *11*
Utah Territory: description of, 10; government, 13, 19, 20; transportation to and from, 22
Utah War, 20, 23

Vanderbilt, Cornelius, 46
V. C. Water Company, 43
Virginia, mines of, 60
Virginia City: bank, 1st in, 29; economic conditions, 62, 149; establishment of, 28, *52*; fire, 76, 138, 143; and Gold Hill, road between, *34*; growth of, 43, 48; housing in, 143–44; lithographs, *37*; mining decline in, 79; news into and out of, 38; outings away from, 121; population, 37–38; railroad impact on, 43, 85; rise of, 64; school construction, 138; timber supplied to, 50
Virginia Consolidated Mine, 64
Virginia Miners Union Picnic, 71
Virginia & Truckee (V&T) Railroad: Bowers Mansion round trip arranged by, 104; construction of, 60; extension, 62, 64; outings facilitated by, 85; photos, *83*; route, *63*; safe travel on, 82–83; station, 108
Volstead Act (1919), 111

Wadsworth, fire in, 91
Wagner, Sam, 82
wagon trains, 13, 21–22
Waldorf, John Taylor, 82–83, 84–85
Walker, Gloria Mapes, xviii, 131
Walker, John, 25–26
Washburn, Anna Belle, 115, *116*
Washington Guard, 65
Washington's Birthday dance, 61
Washoe, Rush to, 28
Washoe and Virginia Road, 51

Washoe Chamber of Commerce, 117
Washoe City, 62, 67, 93, 110
Washoe County, Bowers Mansion as symbol of, 121, *122*
Washoe County Commission, 116, 118, 124
Washoe County Commissioners, 100
Washoe County Department of Parks and Recreation, 131
Washoe County Parks Commission, 121
Washoe Indians, 10, 16
Washoe Lake, 67, 76, 108
Washoe Valley: governing of, 17; growth of, *52*; housing in, 94, 148; land purchased in, 93–94; mining industry impact on, 50; Mormon settlement of, 16, 17, *17*; oil, potential in, 98; as place of residence, 49, 158n21; railroad impact on, 62; travel to and from, 51; west side of, *17*
Waters, George, 56, 57, 60, 62
Weatherstone, Ruth, 110
Webb, Joseph (Joe), 24, 26, 31
Weil, Lal, 23
Wells Fargo Bank, 53
Wells Fargo & Company, 29
Wells Fargo mine, 73–74, 77
West: changes in, 21–22; post–Civil War, 55–56
western Great Basin, 36, 38
Western tycoons, children of, 149
Western Union, 40, 42
westward migration, 5, 148
westward routes, *6*
White, E. E., 147
White, W. Wallace, 122
Whitney, G. L., 82
Whittell, George, Jr., 53, 148, 158n35
William Fife family, 131
Williams, Edna, 108
Williams, Joyce, 115, *116*
Williams Station, 36
Willow Creek, 9–10
Winnemucca, Sarah, 23
Winters, Theodore, 93–94
Winters family, 144–45
witch craze, 71–72
women: in Johntown, 23; in mining, 14, 23, 146, 153n12; in Sierra Nevada, 106
women's rights, 60–61, 147
Woodside, CA, 148
World War I, 110
World War II, 125; veterans of, 117
Worth, Ella, *70*
Wright, James, 54
Young, Brigham: appointments, 13; better life offered by, 3; correspondence, 15; governing challenges, 11, 13; invasion, concern about possible, 18; Mormons summoned by, 19, 86; stepping down, 20; as Utah governor, 10
Yount, Jack, 26
Yukon Territory, gold rush to, 141

Zetland (ship), xv, 3–4

About the Authors

TAMERA J. BUZICK is the Bowers Mansion curator. While teaching at Hug High School, she worked closely with Betty Hood as the historical researcher and traveled extensively in search of new information about the Bowers family. She is a graduate of the University of Nevada, Reno.

RONALD M. JAMES is a retired Nevada state historic preservation officer, a former member of the National Park System advisory board, and one-time National Historic Landmarks Committee chair. He authored *The Roar and the Silence: A History of Virginia City and the Comstock Lode*, among other books, and was inducted into the Nevada Writers Hall of Fame.

MICHAEL A. "BERT" BEDEAU is a member of the Nevada State Board of Museums and History and a retired district administrator for the Comstock Historic District Commission. He has authored National Register of Historic Places nominations and secured a National Historic Landmark designation for McKeen Motor Car #70. Bedeau is a founding board member of Preserve Nevada, former president of the Society for Commercial Archaeology (SCA), and co-editor of its *SCA Journal.*